CW01424518

THE SMOKE THAT THUNDERS

A E Durrant

APG

AFRICAN PUBLISHING GROUP
PO Box BW 350, Harare
ZIMBABWE

Published to coincide with the centenary of the first
construction train to enter Bulawayo, 19 October 1897,
and official opening 4 November 1897.

© A. E. Durrant and published edition APG, 1997
ISBN: 1-77901-134-2
All photographs by the author unless otherwise credited
Design and Layout Paul Wade, Ink Spots, Harare
Origination by Crystal Graphics, Harare
Printed at Ajanta Offset, India

Dedication

This book is dedicated to the memory of the late F. C. (Chris) Butcher, who probably was the greatest steam enthusiast in former Rhodesia and present Zimbabwe. Arriving from England about 1950, he started as a junior clerk on the old Rhodesia Railways, rising to be a senior auditor in the National Railways of Zimbabwe. From the start he was active with his camera, producing first class results, although it is a tragedy that most of his earlier (and most interesting) negatives were destroyed as a result of marital strife. A few prints remain, and these together with some of his classic later work illustrate this volume. Chris was an excellent companion on a "bash", provided one came up to his high standards (he did not suffer fools gladly), and travelled widely through England, the continent of Europe, China, South America, and of course Africa. More of his photographic work will be found in the author's book on Angola.

List of Abbreviations

ACME	Assistant chief mechanical engineer
BCK	Bas Congo Katanga railway
B&MR	Beira & Mashonaland Railway
B&M&RR	Beira & Mashonaland & Rhodesia Railways
BP	Beyer Peacock & Co. Ltd.
BR	Beira Railway
CFB	Caminhos de Ferro de Benguela
CFK	Chemins der Fer de Katanga
CGR	Cape Government Railways
CFM	Caminhos de Ferro de Moçambique
CME	Chief mechanical engineer
CSAR	Central South African Railways
Dübs	Dübs & Co.
GM	General Manager
GVPM	Grootvlei Proprietory Mines Ltd.
GWR	Great Western Railway
HC	Hudswell Clarke & Co.
Huns.	Hunslet Engine Co.
IMR	Imperial Military Railway
K-M	Kitson-Meyer
lb.	pound
lb/yd.	pounds per yard
LMS	London Midland & Scottish Railway
MR	Mashonaland Railway
MRKB	Mashonaland Railway Kalomo-Broken Hill
MW	Manning, Wardle & Co.
NR	Neilson, Reid & Co.
NBL	North British Locomotive Co.
NRZ	National Railways of Zimbabwe
psi	pounds per square inch
REGM	Randfontein Estates Gold Mines
RISCO	Rhodesian Iron & Steel Corporation
RR	Rhodesia Railways
RKJR	Rhodesia Katanga Junction Railway
RS	Robert Stephenson & Co.
SANRASM	South African National Railways and Steam Museum
SAR	South African Railways
SCC	Societé Colonial de Constructions
Scr.	scrapped
sq. ft.	square feet
SR	Swaziland Railways
UK	United Kingdom
USA	United States of America
Wks	works
ZCCM	Zambian Consolidated Copper Mines
ZECO	Zimbabwe Engineering Co.
ZSR	Zambezi Sawmills Railway

Note: Titles and place names used throught out this book are relevant to the period concerned, thus "Rhodesia" before 1980 and "Zimbabwe" thereafter, etc.

Contents

A 20th class Garratt bellowing through "404 curve" with a southbound coal train superbly demonstrates this book's theme THE SMOKE THAT THUNDERS!

Introduction

In these days of jet aircraft and even interplanetary travel, it is difficult to realise that only one hundred years ago, central Africa, where mankind originated, was still very much "Darkest Africa". In the absence of navigable waterways, the only form of transport was on foot, or if one was fortunate, by animal power where the tsetse fly did not make this impossible. By then, Britain's railways covered the country in a dense network leaving few villages far from a railway station, whilst in North America, the coast-to-coast connection had been forged for thirty years.

Yet trade and commerce in central Africa had long been a fact of life, a trade mainly in gold, ivory, and human beings for the slave market. In the generally eastward and southward migrations of African peoples, mighty civilisations such as the Munhumutapa and the builders of Zimbabwe's ruins had thrived and declined, and there were legends of King Solomon and the Queen of Sheba, even today barely authenticated. Trade was mainly with the East coast, where Arabs and later Portuguese occupied the coastal areas, whilst inland were numerous tribes of diverse language and traditions living in often fearful coexistence with each other and with the magnificent wildlife, ranging from numerous antelope to provide meat, fierce large cats, especially lion and leopard who competed with humans for this protein supply, and the lordly elephant, the real king of the jungle, who literally bulldozed his way across the vast savannah then available.

In 1822, a remarkable event took place much further south, when Mzilikazi, a vassal chief of the Zulu King Chaka, defied his monarch and fled in a northwesterly direction, contra to the natural flow of African peoples, to settle eventually, after a long and bloody trek, in the western portion of what is now Zimbabwe, about 1837. In doing so he displaced the resident Mashona, who were despised as pastoralists, and set up kingdom in what is now known as Matabeleland, to use the European term. The Shona people remained in the Eastern areas, known as Mashonaland. North of the mighty Zambezi river were many tribes of which the Barotse were the most important, and as one travelled north and East, their languages shaded gently into the coastal Swahili, whose word for lion, *simba,* is internationally known today from tourism to East Africa, and is recognisable as *shumba* in siShona. siNdebele for lion is *isilwana,* differing fundamentally from the siZulu words for this cat, and the author has been unable to trace the real origin of this term. Readers of this discursion into African languages may wonder what it all has to do with steam locomotives, but we now come to the point in the book's title, *THE SMOKE THAT THUNDERS,* the term used for the Victoria Falls by the Makololo people, in their phrase *Mosi oa Tunya,* again with Swahili influence, *Mosi* meaning smoke, and familiar with East African travellers where *Gharri na moshi* (smoke carriage) is the term for a steam train!

Into this African maelstrom, during the nineteenth century, came the European invasion, missionaries like Livingstone, hunters such as Selous, various adventurers, the vanguard of the Dutch *boers* displaced from South Africa, and eventually Cecil John Rhodes with his dream of a British Africa linked by a railway, or series of railways, from Cape Town to Cairo. Rhodes has been variously described as a visionary, a money mad crook, or a British patriot, but whatever may be said for or against him, he was a ruthlessly powerful character in the real African tradition, (not unlike Chaka the Zulu!) who imposed his will and eventually had, for nearly a century, a country, Rhodesia, named after him. In those Victorian days, the current technology was steam, and the most efficient form of transport (which still prevails) was the railway. After a brief flirtation with more localised titles, Rhodesia Railways became the force which served the two territories, Northern and Southern Rhodesia, and for whom most of the locomotives described and illustrated in this book were ordered. There are always two sides to a coin, and on the positive it may be credibly claimed that the steam railway brought progress and affordable transportation to a wild, and untamed Africa, bringing to its people relief from famine, drought, and other problems from which they often failed to survive. On the negative side, the railway, together with its later derivative, the motor road, has destroyed the Real Africa, an increasingly elusive experience, although still available on a limited scale within more limited areas.

The ultimate compromise, as experienced with wonder by the author, has been to use the eventual destroyer, the motor car, to see and photograph the steam railway as it traverses the expanses of the Hwange wildlife reserve in northwest Zimbabwe. Here politics, a normally destructive phenomenon, led to a situation where the white Rhodesian government, pressed by international sanctions, had to reverse their rather ridiculous policy of replacing steam power (in a country with ample coal supplies and no oil) with diesels, leading to a superb situation where steam was refurbished and used to displace numerous "sanctions-busting" diesels of poor design which had become almost impossible to economically maintain.

Thus, from a base at the Baobab Hotel, Hwange, about twenty years of steam forays were made into the lovely bush country of the National Park, using a railway maintenance road barely traversable by ordinary motor cars, home only to the superb Garratts of the National Railways of Zimbabwe and the splendid species of wild life into whose habitats we roamed. The results from these trips contribute to this book.

A relaxing scene at Mbalabala as wives and children of the local gangers await preparation of the next meal while 16A Garratt 610 rolls past with a train from Mpopoma to Colleen Bawn, the last name being a curiously appropriate Irish phrase for "dark girl"!

Bechuanaland Railway, class 6th, 4-6-0

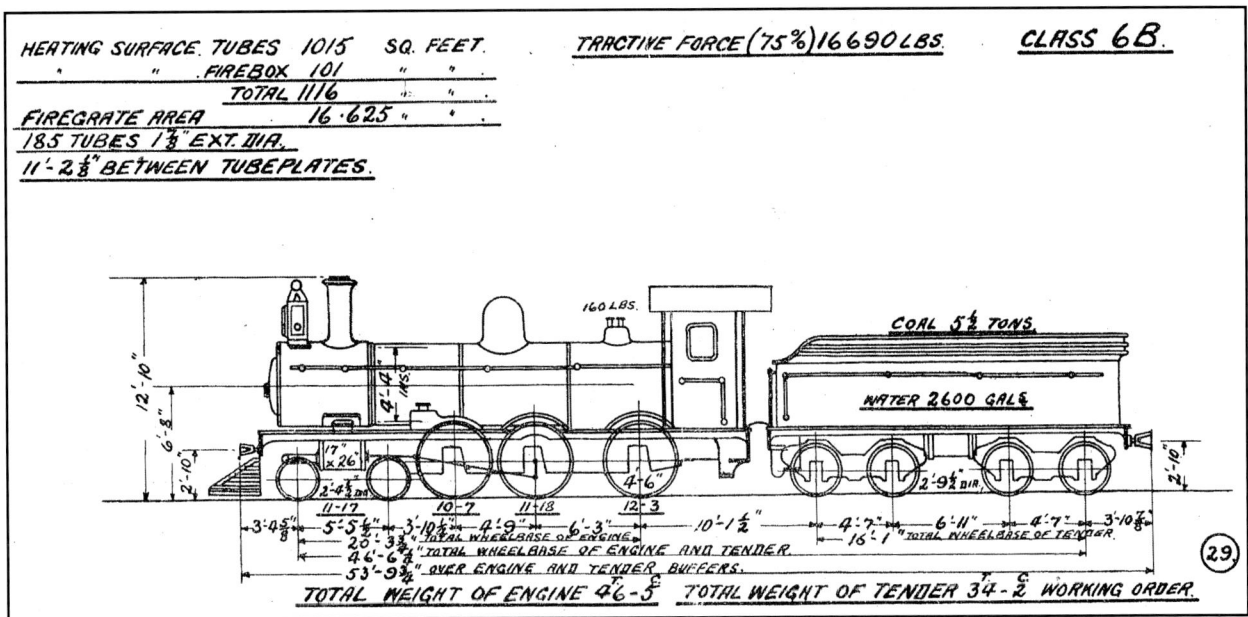

HEATING SURFACE. TUBES 1015   SQ. FEET.
" " FIREBOX 101 " "
TOTAL 1116 " "
FIREGRATE AREA 16.625 " " .
185 TUBES 1⅞" EXT. DIA.
11'-2⅝" BETWEEN TUBEPLATES.

TRACTIVE FORCE (75%) 16690 LBS.

CLASS 6B.

COAL 5½ TONS.
WATER 2600 GALS
160 LBS.

TOTAL WEIGHT OF ENGINE 46-5 TOTAL WEIGHT OF TENDER 34-2 WORKING ORDER.

Bechuanaland Railway Co. Ltd, 6th class 4-6-0 no 1 which ran as CGR 582 and later SAR 525. Neilson

The Bechuanaland Railway was the first section of the 3'6" gauge Rhodesia Railways system to have new locomotives ordered for it. Three 4-6-0 of the well tried Cape 6th class were ordered, plus four of the Cape 7th 4-8-0, but presumably due to cash flow problems these were sold upon arrival to the Cape Government Railways, who continued to hire locomotives and indeed to work all trains to Bulawayo under a suitable contract. It is possible that these engines in fact ran over their intended route when under lease from CGR, but no information to confirm or deny this seems available today. In due course they were taken over by the South African Railways, and two were fitted with larger, Belpaire, boilers. By 1930, the two Belpaire engines were stationed at Upington and Cape Town respectively, a long way from their intended operational sphere. Historical data are tabulated below:

Historical data

Bechuanaland Railway, class 6th, 4-6-0

Bechuanaland Railway nos.	CGR nos.	SAR nos.	Neilson & Co.	Built	In Service	Rebuilt Belpaire.	Withdrawn
1	582	525	5157	1897	1898	No	1956
2	583	526	5158	1897	1898	Yes	9/1957
3	584	527	5159	1897	1898	Yes	1/1951

Bechuanaland Railway, class 7th, 4-8-0

HEATING SURFACE TUBES 976 SQ. FEET.
" " FIREBOX 102 " "
TOTAL 1078 " "
FIREGRATE AREA 17·5 " "
185 TUBES 1 ⁷⁄₈" EXT. DIA,
10'-9" BETWEEN TUBE PLATES.

TRACTIVE FORCE (75%) 18880 LBS.

CLASS 7B.

Bechuanaland Railway 7th class no 6, which ran as CGR 349 and later SAR no 1016.

The four freight locomotives for Bechuanaland were again a standard Cape design, 7th class, and of a type which was later extensively used in Rhodesia. However like the 6th class, they were sold to the CGR upon arrival in Cape Town, and three of the four thereafter continued a career on the Cape and later South African Railways. One of four was sold by CGR to Paulings and used on construction of the Rhodesia Katanga Junction Railway, to whom it was sold in 1909. Mashonaland Railways purchased it, still with CGR number 348, in August 1927, accompanied by another ex-CGR locomotive, 398, which is convenient to deal with here. These two locomotives remained in Northern Rhodesia, generally with 348 at Livingstone and 398 at Broken Hill, although in 1929-30 both were at Livingstone. 348 was loaned to the Zambezi Sawmills Railway in 1931, and 398 hired to Paulings, its former owner, in 1930-31, for construction of the new branch lines in the copperbelt area. By January 1932, 348 had been stabled at Bulawayo, followed by 398 in October 1933, neither being used again before ultimate scrapping in March 1938. Meanwhile the three Bechuanaland engines which remained in South Africa were reboilered, lasting a quarter century later than their sisters in Northern Rhodesia. Historical data are tabulated next page.

Bechuanaland Railway, class 7th, 4-8-0

Bechuanaland Railway nos.	CGR nos.	SAR nos.	Neilson & Co.	Built	In Service	Reboilered SAR	Withdrawn
4	347	1015	5160	1897	1897	1929	5/1959
5	348	—	5161	1897	1897	—	3/1938
6	349	1016	5162	1897	1897	1924	1/1962
7	350	1017	5163	1897	1897	1924	7/1961
—	398	—	4925	1896	1896	—	3/1938

The three which became SAR property were classed 7B.

Bechuanaland Railways 7th class no 4, as Cape Government Railways no 347, on construction work in Bechuanaland.
Croxton collection

Bechuanaland Railways 7th class no 4, shown here in later years as SAR 1015.
Authors's collection

Bechuanaland Railways 7th class no 7, in later years as SAR 1017.
Authors's collection

11

Mashonaland Railway, class 1, 4-6-0

Mashonaland Railways 4-6-0 no 1 at the opening of the line from Umtali to Salisbury.

In 1880, long before any of the type were built for Britain itself, the 4-6-0 was being exported to British colonies and elsewhere. In that year, the Cape Government Railways introduced their 4th class, whilst in India the famous "L" class appeared on the North Western Railway. The Cape engines initially had side tanks as well as tenders, and were fitted with Joy's valve gear, sensibly outside and actuating valves above cylinders. Ninety-two of this class were built, with slightly varying wheel diameters, and most were rebuilt with inside Stephenson valve gear a seemingly retrograde step on a narrow gauge locomotive, whilst side tanks were removed. Only fifteen years after construction they were evidently expendable, being replaced by the larger but similar 5th class and several were made available for sale, with the Lourenço Marques taking three in 1895, followed by Paulings who purchased two in 1898 for construction work on the line from Umtali to Salisbury. After comple-

tion of this work, they were bought by the Mashonaland Railway, and were their first main line locomotives. It is interesting to note that when purchased the only way to Umtali for such heavy loads was over the two foot gauge Beira Railway, and the first six MR engines were conveyed over the narrow gauge until widening in 1900, when engines and rolling stock could be landed at Beira and conveyed upcountry on their own wheels. After arrival of the 7th class, these two engines were relegated to branch and minor duties, and Croxton relates that in 1906 No. 2 was allocated to Gwelo for the Selukwe branch. Both were written off in 1911, but evidently the hulks remained around the works yard, for their leading bogies were used in 1920 to rebuild two 7th class 4-8-0 into 4-8-4T engines, whilst the tenders became water tank wagons.

An engine of this type, owned by or hired to Paulings, hauled the first official train into Bulawayo, 4 November 1897.

Historical data

Mashonaland Railway, class 1, 4-6-0

Paulings 1898	Mashonaland Railway 1899	Cape Government Railways	Neilson & Co.	Date Built	Withdrawn
No 1	1	Western 71	2843	1882	1911
No 2	2	Western 59	2831	1882	1911

"Now we shant be long to Cairo", a jingoistic headboard on MR no 1 at the opening from Umtali to Salisbury. This early promise was never fulfilled! Archive photo

Mashonaland no 1 on a more typical goods train, photographed at the gravitation tank at mile 318, near Marandellas. A. Howat

Another shot of the Salisbury opening, showing the delightful coaching stock used in early days. Archive photo

▲ Preserved 12th Class heads out of Figtree Station with a Rail Safaris Train to Plumtree.

▼ Shortly before steam finished at Gweru, a refurbished 14A speeds past Lochart with the afternoon goods from Mpopoma, a regular steam turn.

▲ *Climbing through Bushtick with a limestone train from Colleen Bawn, 14As 518 with large tank leads 514 with small, as they struggle towards Bulawayo.*

▼ *After departing Balla Balla at 0700 in July 1975, a 14A plus 16A combination climbs up Mulungwane Bank with a limestone train from Colleen Bawn.*

▲ Blue Liveried 15A Garratt 414 hauls the Botswana Railway Blue Train between Plumtree and Bulawayo in 1992.

▼ Sunset on the Plumtree line throws a golden glint on 15A no 424 as it hurries towards Bulawayo.

Kenton Lloyd's painting of Kitson-Meyer no 51 hauling a southbound coal train along what is today the Sinamatella Road, between Entuba and Lukosi. Today's railway runs behind the distinctive koppie.

Kenton
24 Feb 96 Lloyd

▲ Lukosi dawn - the new day is heralded by a ruddy sky as a 15A rolls into Lukosi water stop.

▼ Belting through the bush near Lukosi 15A 414 speeds through a cold morning with southbound coal.

▲ Dawn reflection at Lukosi as a 15th Class speeds towards Thomson Junction with coal empties.

▼ Climbing Mulungwane Bank on a cold July 1975 morning, 16A 632 heads limestone for the factory at cement.

▲ A cold front is moving in as a refurbished 16A climbs out of Gwanda with limestone from Colleen Bawn.

▼ Heading Transnet's "Union Limited Zambesi" tour in 1992, 16A 612 in green roars round "404 curve" south of Hwange.

Mashonaland Railway, Class 3, 4-4-0

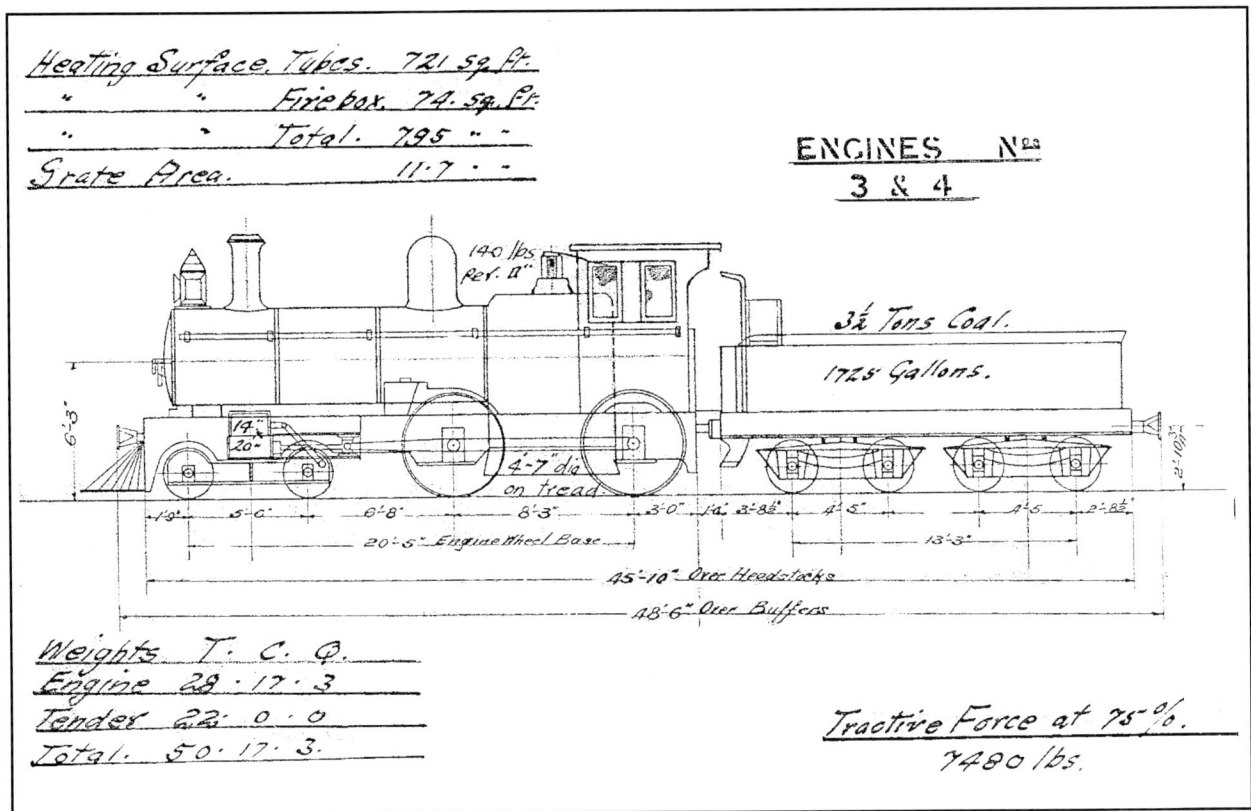

Heating Surface. Tubes. 721 sq. ft.
" " Firebox. 74 sq. ft.
" " Total. 795 " "
Grate Area. 11.7 " "

ENGINES N<u>os</u>
3 & 4

140 lbs.
per □"

3½ Tons Coal.

1725 Gallons.

6'-3"

4'-7" dia
on tread.

1'9" | 5'-0" | 6'-8" | 8'-3" | 3'-0" | 1'4" | 3'-8½" | 4'-5" | 4'-5" | 2'-8½"

20'-6" Engine Wheel Base

13'-3"

45'-10" Over Headstocks

48'-6" Over Buffers

Weights T. C. Q.
Engine 28 : 17 : 3
Tender 22 : 0 : 0
Total. 50 : 17 : 3

Tractive Force at 75 %.
7480 lbs.

Builder's portrait of MR 4-4-0 no 3, as shipped. Note tender cab and low coal space, also splasher over motion.

These two small engines were built by Nasmyth Wilson, of Patricroft, Manchester, for another customer whose identity is uncertain. As built they were of metre gauge, and were two-cylinder compounds, probably on the Worsdell-von Borries system, with 14 inch high and 20 inch low pressure cylinders. Driving wheel diameter was recorded as "4ft 7 1/8in." corresponding to 1400mm. Tony Croxton writes that the MR's first passenger coaches were obtained ex-stock from the Gloucester Carriage & Wagon Co., who had built them for the "San Paulo Railway, Brasil", and the two 4-4-0 could well have been destined for the same railway, as motive power. However, the São Paulo railway, to give it proper spelling, was a large and prosperous broad (5'3") gauge railway over which at the time the entire Brasilian coffee crop moved to Santos for export, and it is difficult to reconcile these narrow gauge locomotives and coaches with such a line. they did however, have a metre gauge branch line, worked by 1881 vintage Kitson 2-6-0, but it seems more likely that these engines and coaches were ordered for some other, stillborn, railway in the Brasilian state of São Paulo. As delivered to Mashonaland, the two engines were converted to simple expansion, and the wheel diameter was quoted at the more robustly accurate dimension of 4'7", a size, incidentally, neither equalled or exceeded in Rhodesia until the 15th class Garratts were introduced in 1940.

After a short spell on main line work, they were soon relegated to light passenger duties, and Croxton records them as being used on the services between Salisbury and Avondale, Gatooma and Eiffel Flats, Bulawayo - Matopos, and Livingstone - Victoria Falls. Perhaps because they were publicly visible as passenger engines, they seem to have received more photographic coverage than their contemporaries. An interesting detail is that as built there was a low splasher from valve covers to sandboxes, visible on the builder's portrait, apparently soon discarded, as few of the photographs in service include this feature. By January 1927, possibly earlier, both were in store, but were not written off until 1929.

Historical data

Mashonaland Railway, class 3, 4-4-0

Mashonaland Railway	Name	Nasmyth Wilson	Date Built	Date in Service	Last Used	Written Off
3	Salisbury	423	1891	1899 }	before 1927	December 1929
4	Umtali	424	1891	1899		

MR no 3 poses on Victoria Falls bridge whilst hauling the "Weekender" train from Livingstone. Croxton collection

An early service photo of MR no 4 with name UMTALI, at an unrecorded water tank. Splasher still over motion, but tender cab removed. Cape Archives

Photo of no 4, in final condition, probably shortly before scrapping. NRZ

MR no 4 arriving at Matopos in 1910. Croxton collection

Mashonaland Railway, class 5, 4-6-2T

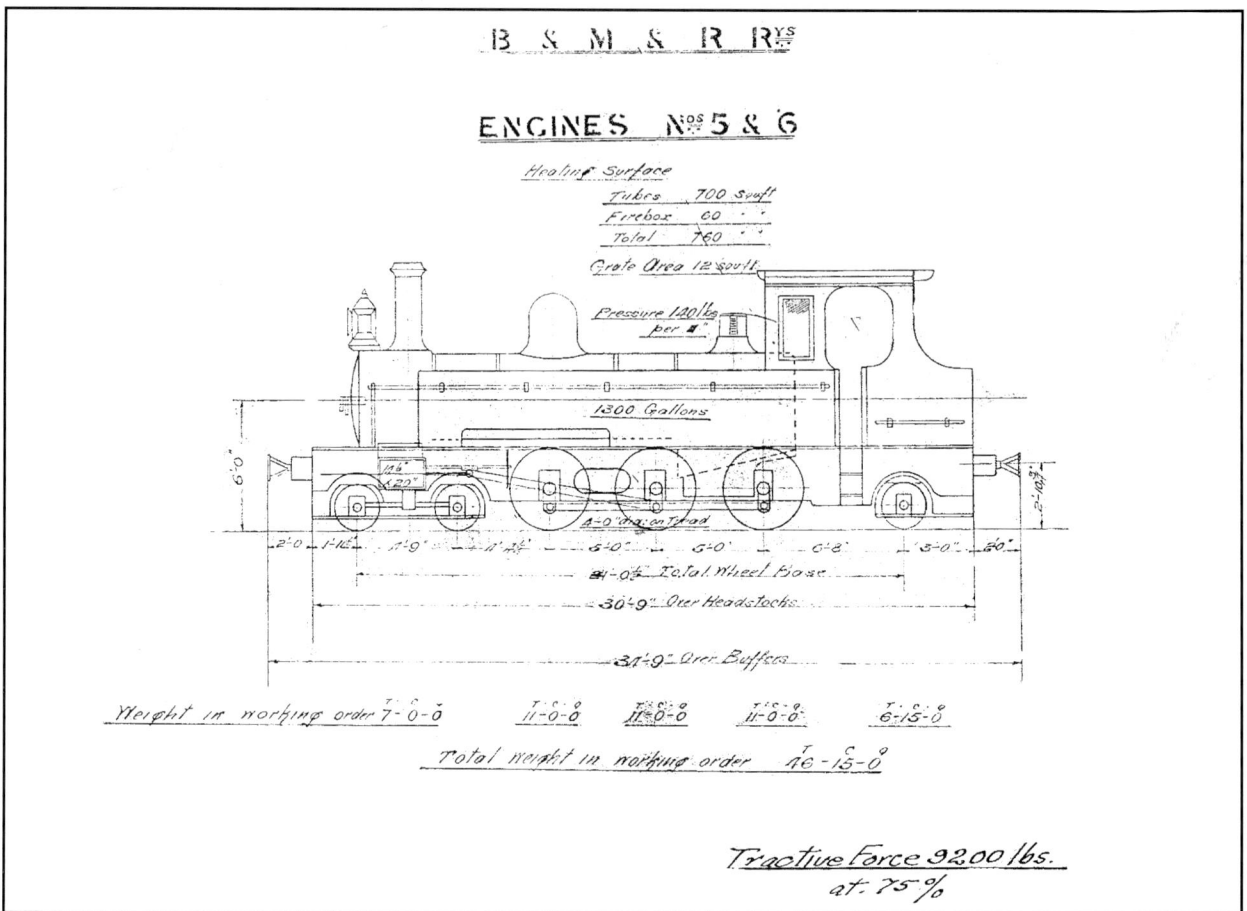

B & M & R Rys

ENGINES Nos 5 & 6

Heating Surface
Tubes   700 sqft
Firebox   60 "
Total   760 "

Grate Area 12 sqft

Pressure 120 lbs
per "

1300 Gallons

4-0" dia on Tread

Total Wheel Base

30'-9" Over Headstocks

31'-9" Over Buffers

Weight in working order 7-0-0   11-0-0   11-0-0   11-0-0   6-15-0

Total weight in working order 46-15-0

Tractive Force 9200 lbs.
at 75%

Builder's portrait of 4-6-2T GREENPOINT as delivered to the Metropolitan and Suburban Railway, Cape Town. This later became Mashonaland Railway no 6. Rural History Centre, Reading University

Like the previous four locomotives, these two engines were acquired second hand, at a time when locomotive builders enjoyed very full order books, with even several British railways having to order motive power from America and the continent. The Mashonaland Railway were thus very fortunate in being able to acquire a pair of locomotives which were not only the right rail gauge, but already on the right continent. These two engines were built for the Metropolitan and Suburban Railway, Cape Town, and as 4-6-2T were very advanced for their time being amongst the first suburban 4-6-2T in the world. They were, however, too rigid for the line's curves, and rapidly placed in store from whence they were thankfully purchased by the MR. As tank engines their range must have been fairly limited on their infrequent main line sorties, but were useful for shunting and short distance duties, being stationed at Salisbury and Umtali for that purpose. They were finally sold to a contractor in Elizabethville, Belgian Congo, in 1921 and 1924, and thereafter lost trace of.

Historical data

Mashonaland Railway, class 5, 4-6-2T

Met. & Sub Railway	John Fowler	Date Built	Mashonaland Railway	In Service	Date Sold
Sea Point	7450	1896	5 Inyanga	1900	1924
Green Point	7451	1896	6 Paulington	1900	1921

Like the earlier examples, these were railed over the narrow gauge from Beira before being erected at Umtali shops.

Mashonaland Railway 4-6-2T no 6 formerly named PAULINGTON. Transnet collection

Small class, 0-4-0ST, no. 5

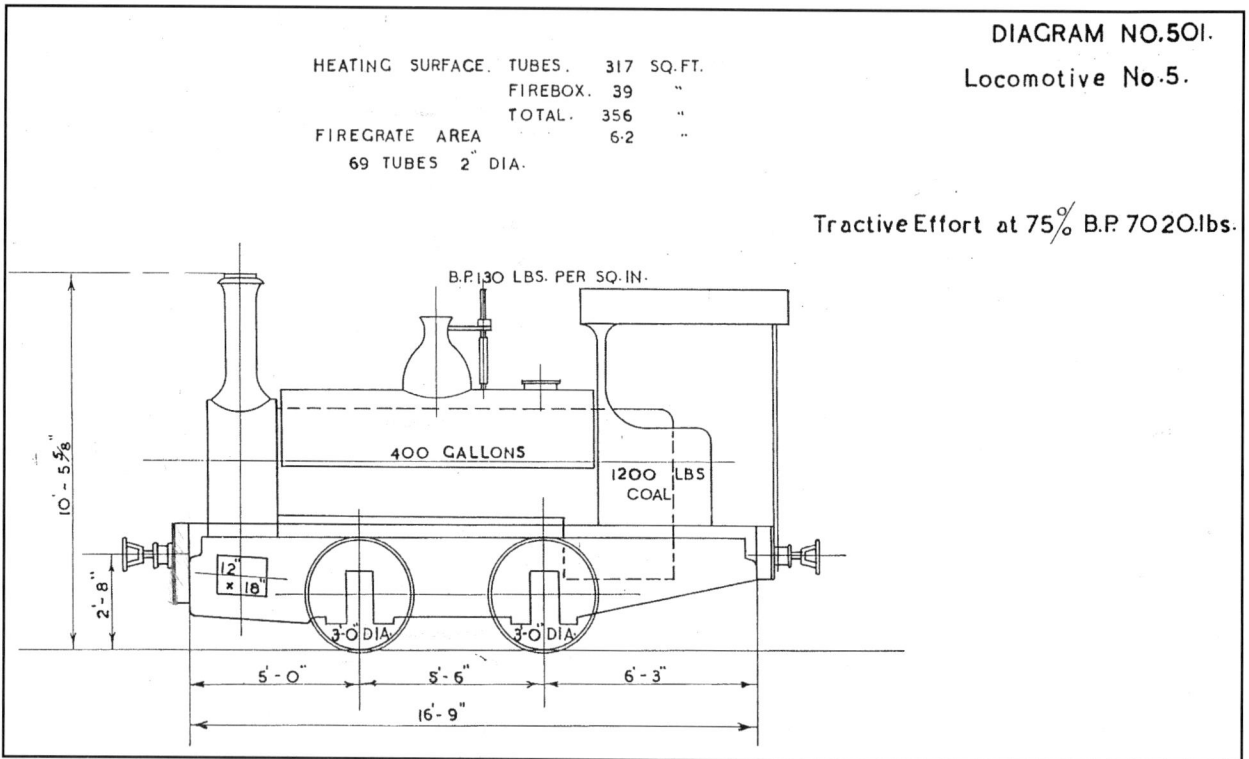

HEATING SURFACE. TUBES. 317 SQ.FT.
FIREBOX. 39 "
TOTAL. 356 "
FIREGRATE AREA 6·2 "
69 TUBES 2" DIA.

DIAGRAM NO.501.
Locomotive No·5.

Tractive Effort at 75% B.P. 7020.lbs.

B.P. 130 LBS. PER SQ·IN.

400 GALLONS

1200 LBS COAL

12" × 18"

3·0 DIA. 3·0 DIA.

10'- 5⅞"

2'- 8"

5'- 0" 5'- 6" 6'- 3"

16'- 9"

Port Elizabeth Harbour Board 0-4-0ST no 2, a sister engine to RR no 5. Author's collection

This little engine was not only the smallest engine ever owned by Rhodesia Railways, but also the only RR engine never to set wheels in Rhodesia! The South line from Vryburg (later from Mafeking) to Bulawayo was peculiar in that it was situated mainly in the Cape of Good Hope (later South Africa, Cape Province) and Bechuanaland (now Botswana) with its own locomotive stock maintained at a local works in Mafeking. It was also operated by CGR, later SAR, personnel and formed virtually a separate railway for accounting purposes. Until 1940, engines stationed at Mafeking were omitted from the monthly locomotive statistics, whilst certainly in the 1930s, there were two locomotive diagram books, with diagrams from 1 upwards referring to the main system and 501 up the South line! It must have been an accountant's idea of heaven! In 1929, for shunting at Mafeking works, this small saddle tank was obtained second-hand from South Africa, where it had originated on the Port Elizabeth Harbour board. After eleven years it was scrapped and replaced by more modern 0-6-0T no 1, and no photographs of it at work at Mafeking have so far emerged.

There seems some doubt as to the identity of this engine. Hamer quotes it as being built by Chapman & Furneaux of Leeds, works number 1208. This company was actually situated in Gateshead, south of Newcastle-on-Tyne, but was taken over by Hudswell Clarke of Leeds, so the engine may have been outshopped in Yorkshire.

Barrow's register shows this engine as being scrapped in September 1929, by then having become SAR no 01020 in the obsolete series. This register, from official SAR records show no 01021 as having been sold to Rhodesia in 1929, works number being given as Hudswell Clarke 1213. However, this was certainly a Chapman & Furneaux number, as HC 1213 was a standard gauge 0-6-0ST built for Britain in 1916. It seems unlikely now whether any evidence to uncover this enigma will ever become available. With both engines disappearing from the SAR lists the same year, there is always the possibility of clerical error, but assuming the SAR register is correct, the history of this engine is as follows:

Ordered by:	Port Elizabeth Harbour Board
Ordered from:	Chapman & Furneaux, Gateshead, Co. Durham
Completed by:	Hudswell Clarke, Leeds, Yorkshire
Works number:	1213
PEHB letter:	M
First SAR number	1021
Later SAR number	01021, sold 1929
RR number 5 scrapped	1940

Any further evidence of this interesting enigma will be greatly welcomed.

Small Class, 0-6-0ST, no. 7

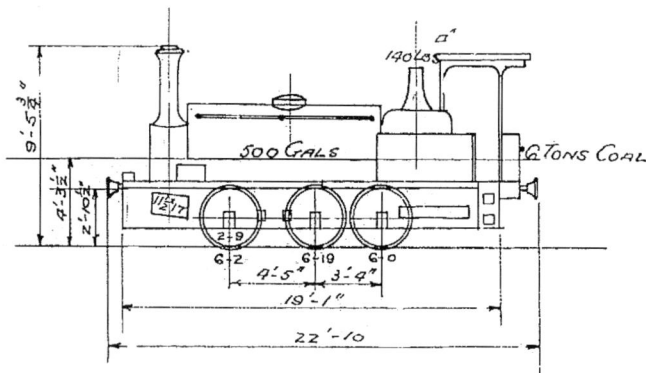

HEATING SURFACE TUBES 315 sq ft
" " FIREBOX 35 "
' " TOTAL 350 "
FIREGRATE AREA 5 '
56 TUBES 2" OUTSIDE DIA

Diag. No 13.

ENGINE No 7.
"JACK TAR"

TRACTIVE FORCE AT 75% = 7160 lbs

a'
140 lbs

9'-5½"

500 GALS

G TONS COAL

4'-3¾"
2'-0¾"

2-9
6-2   6-19   6-0

4'-5"   3'-4"

19'-1"

22'-10

TOTAL WEIGHT OF ENGINE 19 - 1

JACK TAR in earlier condition, with primitve cab and tank filler midway along tank. Rhodesia Railways

'JACK TAR', as it was known for most of its life, started off as a 3'0" gauge contractor's tank engine outshopped in November 1889 for J.P. Edwards of Chapel en le Frith, Derbyshire, who were widening the Midland Railway main line from Dore and Totley, across the Pennines, to Chinley. Typically of the builder, Manning Wardle & Co, Leeds, it had flat sided saddle tank and wheels with additional bosses opposite the crank pins. In 1896 he was purchased by Paulings for widening the Beira to Umtali line from 2 foot to 3'6" gauge, after which Jack became for many years the dock shunter at Beira, where he was the only engine allowed to cross the spindly bridge over the now silted up Chiveve creek. During the building of Victoria Falls bridge, Jack was carried over to the northern side by the "Blondin", a cable ropeway used to haul material from the southern side, and was the first locomotive to eventually cross the completed bridge, north to south, killing en route a leopard which had strayed onto the bridge but was too scared to turn round and return.

Eventually Jack returned to a normal life at Beira docks, until mid 1927 when it was transferred to Bulawayo where the rest of its life was spent, mainly in the workshops to whom it was nominally "sold" about 1935. About this time it was rebuilt with a new boiler, similar to the original, with raised top firebox, making a dome unnecessary. The rebuild has always been noted as having a domed boiler, but this is doubtful. The original tank filler was in the centre of the saddle, and the rebuild had a dome over the same spot. However, no alternative tank filler is discernable on the rebuild, and one is led to surmise that the splendid brass "dome" is in fact an elaborate cover for the tank filler!

Historical data:

Small Class, 0-6-0ST, No. 7

Manning Wardle Number	Date Built	Purchased Paulings	Purchased Mashonaland Railway	Withdrawn From Service	Disposal
1159	11/1889	1896	circa 1900	1942	Bulawayo Museum

JACK TAR as modified with improved cab and brass dome cover, the latter probably over tank filler. Rhodesia Railways

Small class, 0-6-0T nos 1 & 2

SMALL CLASS LOCOMOTIVE.

RHODESIA RAILWAYS. CLASS **SMALL**
3'-6" GAUGE. BATCH II.

WATER 700 GALLONS (2 SIDE TANKS)

180 lbs □"

TO" FEED.

9'-3¾" BETWEEN TUBEPLATES

COAL 1 TON.

8'-11⅛" ACROSS HANDRAILS

12'-1⅛"

5'-1⅛" / 11'-7⅝" / 7'-2¼" / 2'-0" (F.W.O.)

11-18-0   12-2-0   12-0-0

= (36 TONS. F.W.O.)

6'-4⅛"   5'-8"   6'-4"   6'-7⅞"

TOTAL WHEEL BASE 12'-0"

OVER COUPLERS 27'-9"

H.O. Creagh 4/6/49
C.M.E.

BATCH Nº	ORDER	NUMBERS.
II		1 & 2.

GENERAL PARTICULARS.

SATURATED.
TRACTIVE FORCE AT 75% B.W.P : 17785 LBS.
FACTOR OF ADHESION AT 75% B.W.P. & F.W.O : 4·534.
MAXIMUM COUPLED AXLE LOAD : 12 TONS. 2 CWTS.
WEIGHT ON ALL COUPLED WHEELS : 36 TONS.
TOTAL WEIGHT OF ENGINE:(EMPTY.): 31 TONS. 5 CWTS.
  " " " :(F.W.O.): 36 TONS.
WEIGHT PER FOOT RUN OVER BUFFERS : 1·297 TONS.
WATER CAPACITY : (BOTH SIDE TANKS.) : 700 GALLS.
COAL CAPACITY : 1 TON.
RIGID WHEEL BASE : 12 FT. 0 INS.

NUMBER OF ENGINES : BATCH II —— 2.   NOS : 1 & 2.

ENGINE

CYLINDERS : (2 OUTSIDE) : 16" DIA. x 22" STROKE.
COUPLED WHEELS : 3'-6¾" DIA.
AXLE JOURNALS : 8" x 7" DIA.
CONNECTING ROD CENTRES : 5'-8"
BRAKES : VACUUM.
BRAKE POWER : 23·817 TONS AT 66·11 %.
INJECTORS : Nº 9 GRESHAM'S.
VALVES : PISTON. 8" DIA. 4⅝" TRAVEL.
TYPE OF VALVE GEAR : WALSCHAERTS.

BOILER.

PRESSURE : 180 LBS. PER SQ. INCH.
SMALLEST OUTSIDE DIAMETER OF BARREL : 3'-8".
LENGTH BETWEEN TUBEPLATES : 9'-3¾".
GRATE INSIDE FOUNDATION RING : 3'-8" x 3'-8".
GRATE AREA : 13·5 SQ.FT.
HEATING SURFACES : BOILER TUBES : 557 SQ.FT.
  " " : FIRE BOX : 56 SQ.FT.
TOTAL EVAPORATION : 613 SQ.FT.

BATCH	SERVICE ENTRY.	COST PER ENGINE.
II	1929.	

Former Beira docks shunter no 1, RHODESIA, as currently preserved in the Bulawayo Railway museum.

These two shunting engines were ordered by the Beira Port authority in August 1928. After an unusually long period, they were shipped out in May 1929 (the next engine listed by Hudswell Clarke was ordered October 1928 and delivered December the same year), and presumably the long delivery period was due to either financial or technical problems, about which no details seem to survive today. By the time they were delivered, they had become RR engines, and were placed in service in July 1929, virtually immediately after delivery. In service, the wheelbase proved too long for the sharply curved dock sidings, leading to frequent derailments and one wonders whether wrangles as to design suitability led to delivery delays. In Britain, both the Great Western and LMS Railways built 0-6-0T dock engines around the same period, yet despite their broader rail gauge, both had shorter wheelbases than the Beira engines. It is interesting to tabulate brief details of the three types, as below:

Note that the Beira locos were on the same basis the most powerful, whilst they were the only engines with piston valves. Had they been designed to the same wheelbase as the LMS engines, derailment problems may have been averted, but the bugbear of excessive concentrated weight could have materialised. Locomotive design is always a compromise, and this time it evidently went wrong!

Historical data:

Railway	LMS	GWR	Beira
Gauge	4' 8 1/2"	4' 8 1/2"	3' 6"
Loco class	7160	1366	1
Loco weight, Tons	43.6	35.75	36.0
Tractive effort, lb.	18400 (85%)	16320 (85%)	17785 (75%), 20156 (85%)
Wheel diameter	3'11"	3'8"	3'6 3/4"
Wheel base	9'6"	11' 0"	12' 0"

Small Class, 0-6-0T, Nos. 1&2

Railway Number	Hudswell Clarke	Date Ordered	Date ex Works	Date in Service	Last used	Disposal
1	1627	8/1928	5/1929	7/1929	(a)	Bulawayo Museum
2	1628	8/1928	5/1929	7/1929	(b)	Umtali Museum

(a) Last recorded stationed at Mafeking 10/1958
(b) Last recorded stabled Bulawayo 11/1940. Thence Umtali shops.
Names: No. 1 named RHODESIA as built. No. 2 later named CHURCHILL, and later again WINSTON CHURCHILL

Former Beira docks shunter no 2, probably photographed at Mafeking, named WINSTON CHURCHILL. This engine is now preserved at Mutare city museum.
Rhodesia Railways

6th class, 4-8-2T

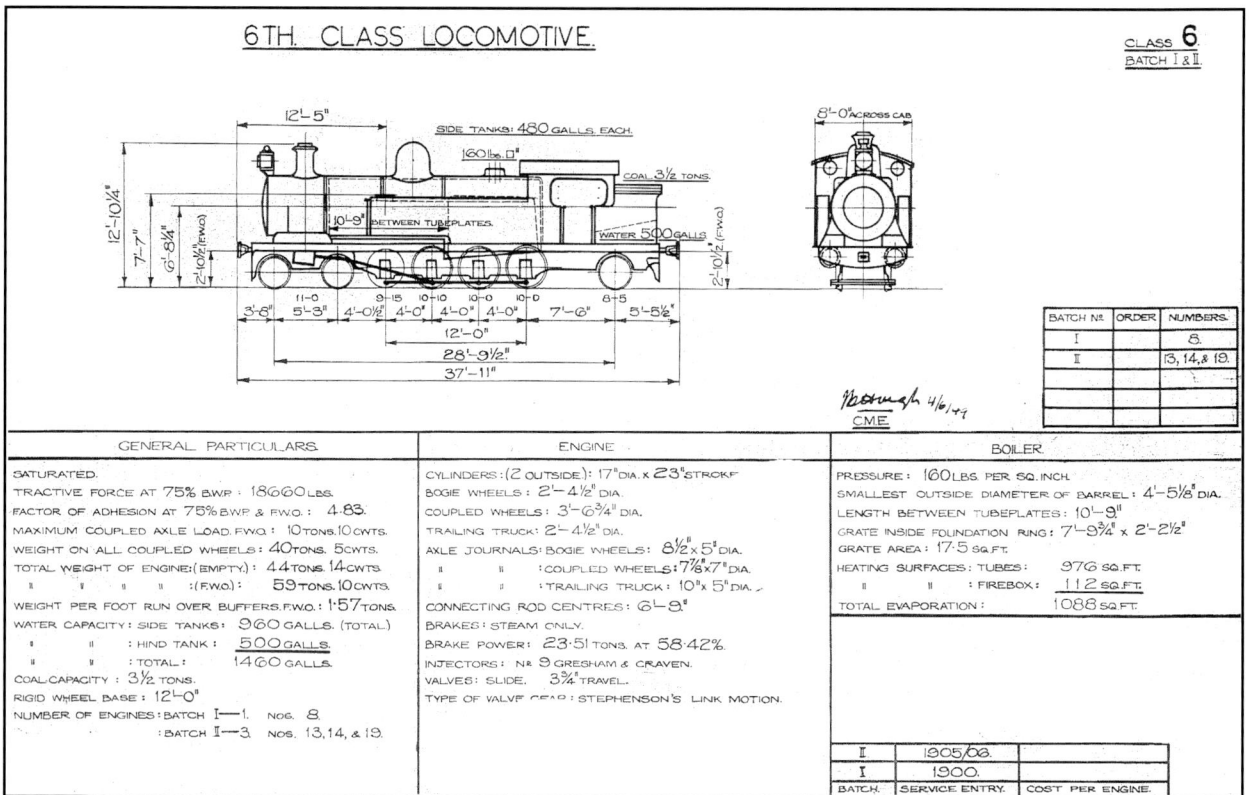

6TH. CLASS LOCOMOTIVE.

CLASS **6**
BATCH I & II.

SIDE TANKS: 480 GALLS. EACH.

160 lbs. □"

COAL 3½ TONS.

10'-9" BETWEEN TUBEPLATES.

WATER 500 GALLS.

8'-0" ACROSS CAB

12'-5"

12'-10¼"

7'-7"

6'-8¼"

2'-10½" (F.W.O.)

2'-10½" (F.W.O.)

3'-6" 11'-0" 9'-15 10'-10 10'-0 10'-0 7'-6" 8'-5"

5'-3" 4'-0½" 4'-0" 4'-0" 4'-0" 5'-5½"

12'-0"

28'-9½"

37'-11"

Harbrough 4/6/49
C.M.E.

BATCH Nº.	ORDER	NUMBERS.
I		8.
II		13, 14, & 19.

GENERAL PARTICULARS.	ENGINE.	BOILER.
SATURATED.	CYLINDERS: (2 OUTSIDE): 17" DIA. x 23" STROKE.	PRESSURE: 160 LBS. PER SQ. INCH.
TRACTIVE FORCE AT 75% B.W.P. : 18660 LBS.	BOGIE WHEELS : 2'-4½" DIA.	SMALLEST OUTSIDE DIAMETER OF BARREL : 4'-5⅛" DIA.
FACTOR OF ADHESION AT 75% B.W.P. & F.W.O. : 4·83.	COUPLED WHEELS : 3'-6¾" DIA.	LENGTH BETWEEN TUBEPLATES : 10'-9"
MAXIMUM COUPLED AXLE LOAD. F.W.O. : 10 TONS. 10 CWTS.	TRAILING TRUCK : 2'-4½" DIA.	GRATE INSIDE FOUNDATION RING : 7'-9¾" x 2'-2½"
WEIGHT ON ALL COUPLED WHEELS : 40 TONS. 5 CWTS.	AXLE JOURNALS: BOGIE WHEELS : 8½" x 5" DIA.	GRATE AREA : 17·5 SQ. FT.
TOTAL WEIGHT OF ENGINE: (EMPTY) : 44 TONS. 14 CWTS.	" " : COUPLED WHEELS : 7⅞" x 7" DIA.	HEATING SURFACES: TUBES : 976 SQ. FT.
" " " " : (F.W.O.) : 59 TONS. 10 CWTS.	" " : TRAILING TRUCK : 10" x 5" DIA.	" " : FIREBOX : 112 SQ. FT.
WEIGHT PER FOOT RUN OVER BUFFERS. F.W.O. : 1·57 TONS.	CONNECTING ROD CENTRES : 6'-8"	TOTAL EVAPORATION : 1088 SQ. FT.
WATER CAPACITY : SIDE TANKS : 960 GALLS. (TOTAL)	BRAKES: STEAM ONLY.	
" " : HIND TANK : 500 GALLS.	BRAKE POWER : 23·51 TONS. AT 58·42%.	
" " : TOTAL : 1460 GALLS.	INJECTORS : Nº 9 GRESHAM & CRAVEN.	
COAL CAPACITY : 3½ TONS.	VALVES: SLIDE. 3¾" TRAVEL.	
RIGID WHEEL BASE : 12'-0"	TYPE OF VALVE GEAR : STEPHENSON'S LINK MOTION.	
NUMBER OF ENGINES : BATCH I—1. NOS. 8.		
" " : BATCH II—3 NOS. 13, 14, & 19.		

BATCH.	SERVICE ENTRY.	COST PER ENGINE.
II	1905/06.	
I	1900.	

6th class 4-8-2T no 8 with Belpaire firebox. Lettered RR but with Mashonaland Railway number plate. At Bulawayo works. Rhodesia Railways

The Rhodesia Railways, with their constituents, (other than Beira docks) were remarkable in never having new steam locomotives built for shunting purposes. The invariable policy was to use downgraded main line locomotives for such purposes, but from 1914 to 1923, thirteen old 7th class 4-8-0 were converted to tank engines, in two classes, for shunting. Tank engines are clearly more compact and convenient for shunting than tender engines, whilst there is also in this case the advantage of slightly more adhesion, although the 7th class, with an adhesion factor of 4.5 were only slightly improved upon by the 6th class conversions whose adhesion factor was 4.8. On the other hand, braking was better with the tender engine, whose tender weight (full) almost equalled the adhesion, and braked,weight of the locomotive, which is possibly why the practice of using tank engines gradually declined. In later days, even Garratts were commonly used as shunting engines, but of course by then with much heavier shunting movements.

For the 6th class conversion, frames were extended in the rear to support the bunker, and tanks added beside the boiler, all main mechanical components remaining unaltered. The rear pony truck had outside bearings, rather surprisingly, probably to utilise the wheelsets with outside axleboxes from the discarded tenders.

Not unsurprisingly, the 6th class were used mainly at major centres having large marshalling yards, and were employed almost exclusively in Southern Rhodesia. The main users were Beira, Umtali, Salisbury and Bulawayo, although Wankie had a pair in the late 1920s while Livingstone, the only shed north of the Zambezi to have one, used it until the depression years. From time to time they were allocated to Gwelo, which in 1950 had three of the class, although one engine was the more usual complement at this shed. After the Beira line had been sold to Moçambique, a couple of 6ths were retained onhire until the new 0-8-2T shunters were available, and for a while no. 19, the last in service and the locomotive retained for the Bulawayo museum, was hired at Beira by the Trans Zambesia Railway where, judging by later practice, it was probably used for hauling transfer traffic between Dondo Junction (Entroncamento) and Beira yards. For some obscure accounting reason, separate locomotives were reserved for this operation.

Being rebuilt from 7th class tender engines, boilers and all mechanical components were interchangeable, and interchanged, with the parent class, with the result that at least two 6th class ran with Belpaire fireboxes during unknown periods, such being gleaned from available photographs. However, no attempt at finality of this aspect may now be found from available records.

Historical data:

6th class, 4-8-2T

Engine Number	As built, 7th class		Date Rebuilt	Last used	Withdrawn	Disposal
	Neilson Number	Date built				
8	5675	1899	10/1914	9/1956	10/1957	Scrapped
9	5676	1899	7/1914	8/1936	3/1938	Scrapped
10	5679	1899	1915	3/1946	7/1946	Scrapped
13	5793	1900	8/1915	12/1953	12/1953	Scrapped
14	5794	1900	5/1916	12/1955	12/1955	Scrapped
18	5798	1900	4/1921	3/1938	4/1940	Scrapped
19	5799	1900	1/1922	2/1955		Bulawayo Museum
21	5801	1900	4/1923	8/1936	2/1938	Scrapped
22	5802	1900	5/1923	8/1935	8/1937	Scrapped

6th class 4-8-2T no 13, lettered RRM. J. R. Lloyd

6th class 4-8-2T no 14, lettered RRM, at Bulawayo.
F. C. Butcher

6th class no 19, shortly before withdrawal.
Rhodesia Railways

6th class no 13 with Belpaire firebox at an unknown location which could be Kitwe, in which case it is before 1927.
J. Dele-Hoffman collection

6th class 19 as preserved in Bulawayo museum.

Class 6A, 4-8-4T

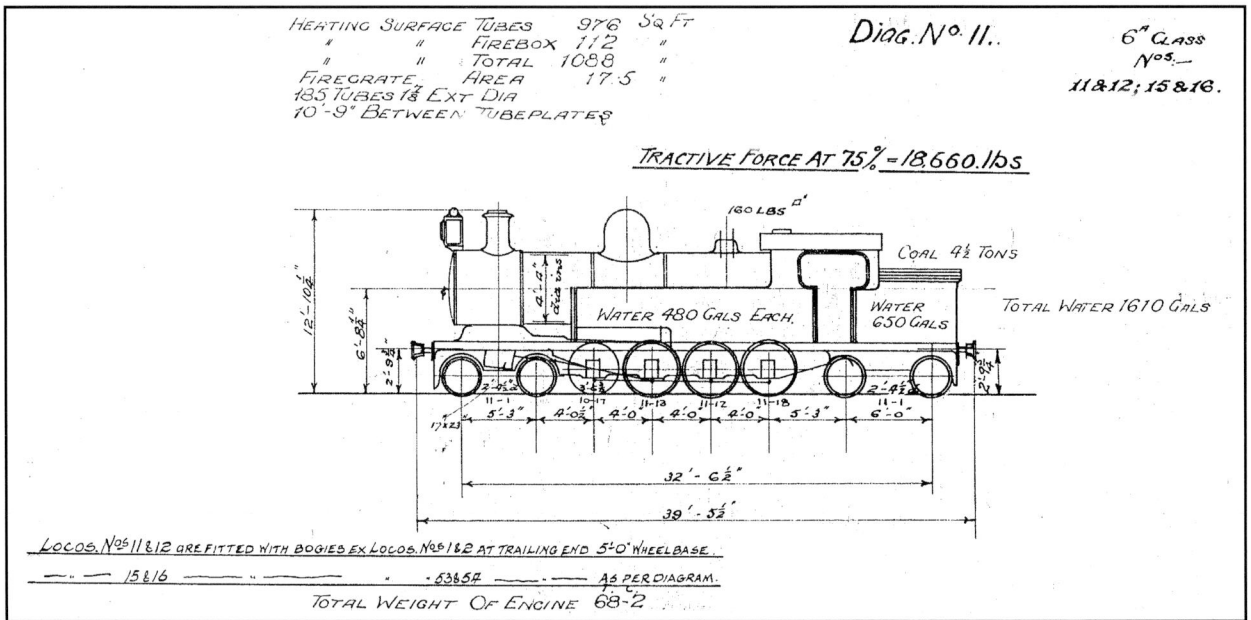

HEATING SURFACE TUBES 976 SQ FT
" " FIREBOX 112 "
" " TOTAL 1088 "
FIREGRATE AREA 17.5 "
185 TUBES 1⅞ EXT DIA
10'-9" BETWEEN TUBEPLATES

DIAG. Nº 11.

6" CLASS
Nºs:—
11&12; 15&16.

TRACTIVE FORCE AT 75% = 18,660 lbs

180 LBS

COAL 4½ TONS

WATER 480 GALS EACH.   WATER 650 GALS

TOTAL WATER 1610 GALS

LOCOS. Nºs 11&12 ARE FITTED WITH BOGIES EX LOCOS. Nºs 1&2 AT TRAILING END 5'-0" WHEELBASE.
— " — 15&16 — " — " — " — 53&54 — AS PER DIAGRAM.
TOTAL WEIGHT OF ENGINE 68-2

The official photograph of class 6A no 16, as later fitted with rear bogie from scrapped 8th class engine.
Rhodesia Railways

The 6A were also shunting engines converted from 7th class 4-8-0 tender engines, but instead of a trailing bissel truck, four-wheel bogies were supplied. These gave space for an extra ton of coal plus slightly augmented water supplies, but no advantage was taken of this as they were allocated randomly with the smaller 6th class. A minor mystery surrounds the bogies surrounded for two engines. Engines 15 and 16, converted in 1918 were shown in later diagrams as having trailing bogies six feet wheelbase taken from 8th class engines 53 and 54, which were not taken out of service until over ten years after the tanks were rebuilt. In fact, an older B & M & R R diagram book shows all four engines with six foot bogies, whilst 8th class 53 and 54 are shown still in stock. The second two engines were shown in later diagrams with five foot bogies taken from MR 4-6-0 numbers 1 and 2, withdrawn in 1911 and whose leading bogies could easily have been used, as was in fact indicated. The query thus stands as to which bogies engines 15 and 16 originally carried, the answer to which we will probably never know. As to boilers, like the 6th and

7th classes, Belpaire fireboxes may have been used from time to time as boilers interchanged, but these engines seemed camera-shy, and none of the very few photos available show anything other than round topped fireboxes.

Allocations were similar to the 6th class. Engine 11 was at Beira from 1927 to 1931, thence to Salisbury until 1936, and at Bulawayo until scrapped. No. 12 was Bulawayo to 1928, then Wankie until 1936, although stabled for its last two years there. It was then resuscitated and sent to Beira until withdrawal, after being stabled briefly at Umtali. No. 15 was a Beira engine until sent to Salisbury in 1931, going to Gwelo thence until withdrawal. Engine 16 was mainly at Bulawayo, but with spells at Gwelo in 1932 and from 1933 until withdrawal, being finally stabled back at Bulawayo. Thus none of these engines were stationed at outlandish places, making the lack of photographs inexplicable.

Historical data:

Class 6A, 4-8-4T

Engine Number	As built, 7th class		Date Rebuilt	Last used	Withdrawn	Disposal
	Neilson Number	Date built				
11	5680	1899	9/1920	3/1938	2/1940	Scrapped
12	5681	1899	9/1920	5/1939	4/1940	Scrapped
15	5795	1900	3/1918	1/1939	3/1940	Scrapped
16	5796	1900	1/1918	9/1936	2/1938	Scrapped

Enlarged from a locomotive line-up photograph, One of the 6A class with bogie from 8th class 4-8-0. Croxton collection

39

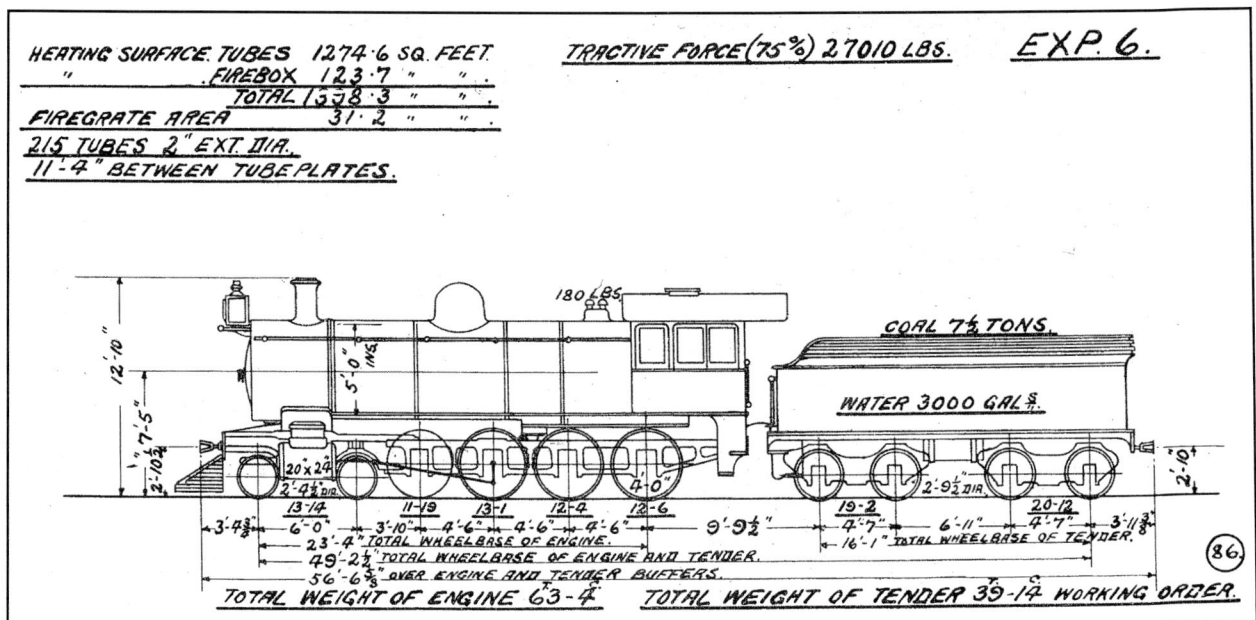

Diagram of Cape 10th class, later SAR Experimental 6.

Churchward dictum of long travel valves in straight ported cylinders was overlooked, and the 9th class had short travel valves in Z-ported cylinders.The amazing thing about the design was that the prototype was a Kitson engine but the production run from traditional suppliers North British. Hosgood must have obtained the Kitson drawings from Salt River and sent them to Glasgow with instructions to design "an engine like this but with superheater and piston valves"! Of course, the design office at Flemington Street, Springburn, were either ignorant or disinterested in those Sassenach developments down in Wiltshire, but despite the deficiencies in cylinder design, the 9th class was an immediate success. The wide firebox supplied the needed steam supply, and the superheater utilised it more efficiently, such that the second batch of 8th class, only two years older, were immediately outclassed.

So successful were the 9th class that a total of thirty were built, plus six of an Americanised version built by the American Locomotive Company during 1917, when World War I made new motive power imperative but cut off traditional suppliers, busy with munitions work, including war locomotives. In Angola, the Benguela Railway adopted the Rhodesia 9th class *in toto*, including the class designation, and had thirty built by North British. They also had a couple of American locos, by Baldwin and classed "9a classe B", but something went wrong with the specification, and these had narrow fireboxes and were technically more akin to the superheater rebuilds of South Africa's 8th classes. The amazing story resulting from all this was that the Cape 10th class, rejected for further construction,

led to a very successful type of locomotive amounting, with variations, to sixty-eight engines used on the Rhodesia and Benguela Railways.

Dealing more specifically with the Rhodesia examples, when new they represented the top main line power, and were first used between Vila Machado, Umtali and Salisbury, in the East, and on coal traffic between Bulawayo and Livingstone in the North. In mid 1927, the earliest date at which detailed records have been available to the author, all but no. 81 at Gwelo and 95 at Umtali were at Broken Hill, a situation which largely prevailed until mid 1930, when they started spreading more widely around both Southern and Northern Rhodesia, at most sheds except the Southern line at Mafeking, which only saw the class late in the day. Gwelo in particular, built up a large stud of these engines for the Selukwe, Fort Victoria and Shabani branches, as did Bulawayo for the West Nicholson line, all remaining until replaced by later Garratts. During the worst depression years all remained in service whilst later and more powerful engines, notably the 11th and 13th classes, were set aside due to lack of traffic. During the mid 1930s they had largely migrated south except for a batch which replaced 7th class at the new shed at Ndola, serving the copperbelt. By the end of 1940 the examples furthest north were at Wankie, and four had been transferred to the South Line at Mafeking, and a start was made to reboiler them as class 9B, which did not greatly alter their allocations nor duties. Only four remained unrebuilt, all of which were eventually sold to the Zambezi Sawmills Railway.

9th class, 4-8-0

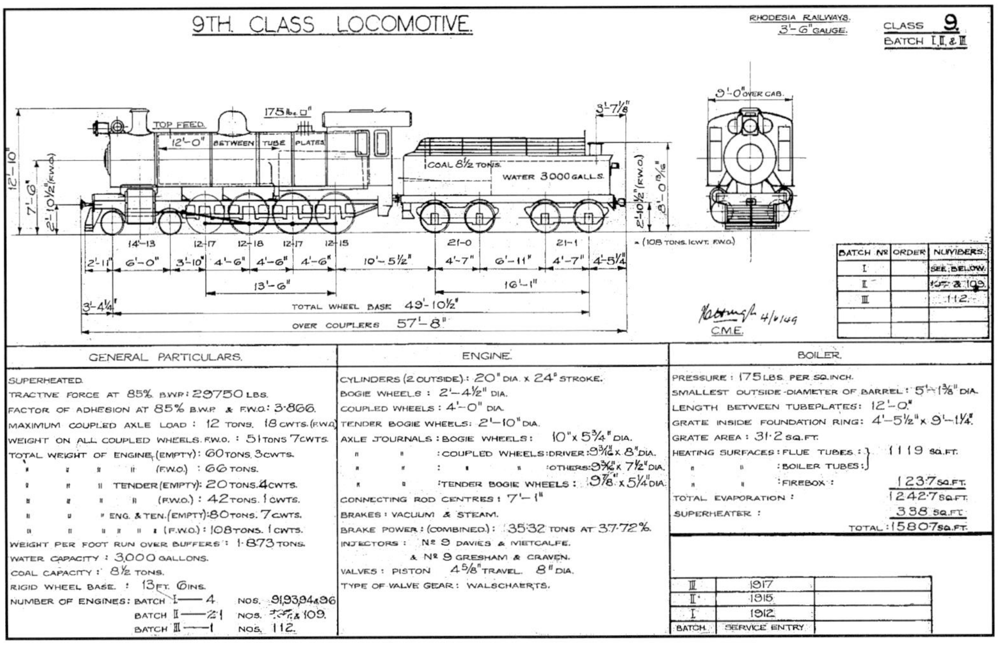

9TH. CLASS LOCOMOTIVE. — RHODESIA RAILWAYS, 3'-6" GAUGE — CLASS 9, BATCH I, II & III

Builder's photo of 9th class 113, carrying smokebox rondel lettered BRT, indicating finance by the Beit Railway Trust. *North British*

The Rhodesian 9th class typifies the extraordinary clannishness which RR had with the "mother" railway, the Cape government. When the inadequacy of the 8th class became apparent, greater steaming capacity was sought, and within the weight and other restrictions then applicable, it was decided that a wide firebox 4-8-0 would best fit the bill. Now the Natal Government railway already had a splendid example of this type, the Hendrie B class, of which fifty had been in service since 1904 with another twenty-one in 1910, but these were ignored, and Bulawayo went again to the Cape to find a design basis. It so happened that the CGR had a solitary engine of this type, their 10th class, built 1906, evidently not considered a complete success as it was not repeated, and by SAR

in 1910 was relegated to class "Experimental 6". This engine was built by Kitsons, of Leeds, yet its lack of success on its originating railway led to a widespread acceptance in both Rhodesia and Angola. For comparison with the RR 9th class diagram above, the CGR Kitson diagram is reproduced overleaf, and it will be seen how closely all major dimensions tallied.

With the 9th class, "Togo" Hosgood decided to apply superheaters and piston valves, these being the main difference from the Cape 10th, which was unsuperheated, with slide valves actuated by Stephenson valve gear. On the 9th class, piston valves actuated by Walschearts valve gear was adopted for the first time in Rhodesia, and although Hosgood came from South Wales, in the heart of Great Western territory, the

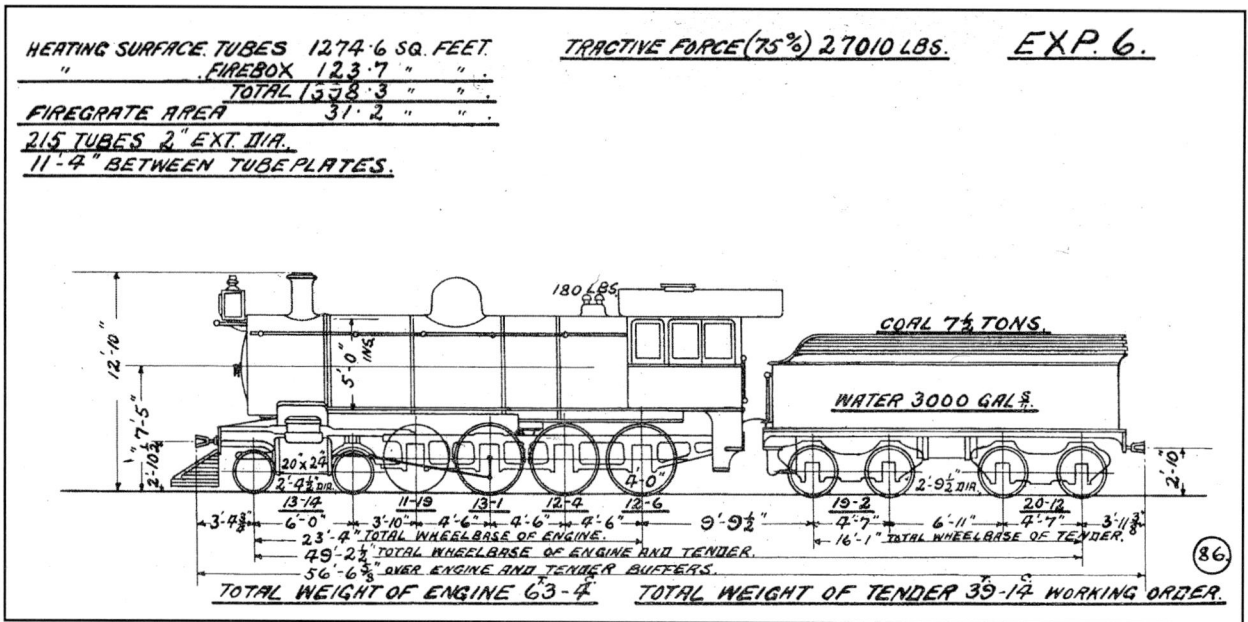

Diagram of Cape 10th class, later SAR Experimental 6.

Churchward dictum of long travel valves in straight ported cylinders was overlooked, and the 9th class had short travel valves in Z-ported cylinders. The amazing thing about the design was that the prototype was a Kitson engine but the production run from traditional suppliers North British. Hosgood must have obtained the Kitson drawings from Salt River and sent them to Glasgow with instructions to design "an engine like this but with superheater and piston valves"! Of course, the design office at Flemington Street, Springburn, were either ignorant or disinterested in those Sassenach developments down in Wiltshire, but despite the deficiencies in cylinder design, the 9th class was an immediate success. The wide firebox supplied the needed steam supply, and the superheater utilised it more efficiently, such that the second batch of 8th class, only two years older, were immediately outclassed.

So successful were the 9th class that a total of thirty were built, plus six of an Americanised version built by the American Locomotive Company during 1917, when World War I made new motive power imperative but cut off traditional suppliers, busy with munitions work, including war locomotives. In Angola, the Benguela Railway adopted the Rhodesia 9th class *in toto*, including the class designation, and had thirty built by North British. They also had a couple of American locos, by Baldwin and classed "9a classe B", but something went wrong with the specification, and these had narrow fireboxes and were technically more akin to the superheater rebuilds of South Africa's 8th classes. The amazing story resulting from all this was that the Cape 10th class, rejected for further construction,

led to a very successful type of locomotive amounting, with variations, to sixty-eight engines used on the Rhodesia and Benguela Railways.

Dealing more specifically with the Rhodesia examples, when new they represented the top main line power, and were first used between Vila Machado, Umtali and Salisbury, in the East, and on coal traffic between Bulawayo and Livingstone in the North. In mid 1927, the earliest date at which detailed records have been available to the author, all but no. 81 at Gwelo and 95 at Umtali were at Broken Hill, a situation which largely prevailed until mid 1930, when they started spreading more widely around both Southern and Northern Rhodesia, at most sheds except the Southern line at Mafeking, which only saw the class late in the day. Gwelo in particular, built up a large stud of these engines for the Selukwe, Fort Victoria and Shabani branches, as did Bulawayo for the West Nicholson line, all remaining until replaced by later Garratts. During the worst depression years all remained in service whilst later and more powerful engines, notably the 11th and 13th classes, were set aside due to lack of traffic. During the mid 1930s they had largely migrated south except for a batch which replaced 7th class at the new shed at Ndola, serving the copperbelt. By the end of 1940 the examples furthest north were at Wankie, and four had been transferred to the South Line at Mafeking, and a start was made to reboiler them as class 9B, which did not greatly alter their allocations nor duties. Only four remained unrebuilt, all of which were eventually sold to the Zambezi Sawmills Railway.

Historical data:

9th class 4-8-0

Engine Number	Builder	Works Number	Date Built	Date in Service	Rebuilt to 9B	Last Used	Disposal
80	NBL	19743	1912	6/1912	1/1940	6/1966*	Scr. 7/1980
81	NBL	19744	1912	6/1912	10/1945	5/1968	Scr. 1/1980
82	NBL	19745	1912	6/1912	11/1946	9/1972	Scr. 7/1980
83	NBL	19746	1912	7/1912	9/1945	2/1966	Scr. 4/1972
84	NBL	19747	1912	7/1912	9/1944	6/1967	Zambia
85	NBL	19748	1912	7/1912	10/1947	7/1948**	Scr. 9/1949
86	NBL	19749	1912	7/1912	3/1946	6/1965	Scr. 4/1972
87	NBL	19750	1912	7/1912	4/1945	5/1963	Scr. 4/1972
88	NBL	19751	1912	7/1912	8/1945	7/1967	Zambia
89	NBL	19752	1912	7/1912	10/1945	10/1969	Scr. 4/1972
90	NBL	19753	1912	7/1912	12/1939	12/1966	Scr. 4/1972
91	NBL	19754	1912	7/1912	Not	9/1960	ZSR 4/1964
92	NBL	19818	1912	8/1912	4/1947	1/1963	Scr. 9/1965
93	NBL	19819	1912	8/1912	4/1947	8/1962	Scr. 4/1972
94	NBL	19820	1912	8/1912	7/1956	10/1971	Scr. 7/1980
95	NBL	19821	1912	8/1912	5/1947	7/1970	Scr. 12/1964
96	NBL	19822	1912	9/1912	Not	1/1963	ZSR 9/1963
97	NBL	19823	1912	9/1912	2/1940	5/1962	Scr. 4/1972
105	BP	5914	1915	10/1915	3/1945	5/1963	Scr. 4/1972
106	BP	5915	1915	10/1915	2/1947	4/1961	Scr. 4/1972
107	BP	5916	1915	10/1915	2/1951	7/1972	Scr. 2/1976
108	BP	5917	1915	10/1915	5/1948	1/1963*	Scr. 12/1977
109	BP	5918	1915	10/1915	Not	2/1962	ZSR 4/1964
110	BP	5919	1915	10/1915	6/1945	6/1970	Scr. 4/1972
111	NBL	21474	1917	9/1917	1/1947	2/1963	Scr. 4/1972
112	NBL	21475	1917	9/1917	Not	1/1963	ZSR 7/1963
113	NBL	21476	1917	10/1917	12/1939	3/1967	Zambia
114	NBL	21477	1917	10/1917	12/1939	12/1962	Scr. 2/1965
115	NBL	21478	1917	11/1917	8/1948	Active	Bulawayo Mus
116	NBL	21479	1917	11/1917	10/1944	10/1966	Scr. 3/1965

Zambia

Of the three locomotives which went to Zambian Railways in 1967, no records seem available as to when they last operated. All three were listed in April 1985, stopped at Kabwe, "repairable, leaking tubes" and they may be still there today. Of those sold to Zambezi Sawmills Railway, 91 is semi-preserved as 96, 96 is derelict, and 109 is sectioned, all at Livingstone museum. 112 may be scrapped, or possibly at Mulobezi in derelict condition.

Beyer Peacock photo of 9th class no 107.

9th class 96, at Bulawayo, This loco is now at the Zambezi Sawmills museum at Livingstone. J. R. Lloyd

9th class no 90 with Mashonaland Railways number plate. J. Dele-Hoffman collection

9th class 116, on main line freight duty. NRZ

9th class no 91 also on a main line freight train. Author's collection

Class 9A, 4-8-0

AMERICAN LOCOMOTIVE SALES CORPORATION

EIGHT-COUPLED LOCOMOTIVE
BUILT FOR THE RHODESIA RAILWAYS LIMITED
CODE WORD "BEMCA"

The class 9A were a direct result of the first world war - with traffic demands rising, traditional locomotive suppliers were unable to provide, due to war work, and recourse had to be made for using non-British locomotives. These came in two batches, both from America. As a temporary measure, six 2-8-2 built by H.K. Porter for the Katanga railways were loaned "on the way up" whilst the six 4-8-0 class 9A were specifically purchased by RR from the American Locomotive Company. Both series were initially used between Vila Machado and Umtali over the Beira - Mashonaland line, and after the war the Katanga engines were released to their intended owners. The 9A class were dimensionally closely similar to the 9th class, but detailing was fully American and evidently little or no attempt was made, in these wartime circumstances, to insist upon mechanical compatibility with their British compatriots. After about a dozen years in main line service, they served a need for heavy shunting engines, more powerful than the 6th, 7th and 8th classes which previously tried to fulfill that role.

As such they were largely confined to the main centres of Salisbury and Bulawayo, with the whole class mainly at Salisbury in the late 1920s, gradually within a decade changing to a pattern of 117 and 120 at Salisbury, and the others at Bulawayo. Variations occurred from time to time, 121 was at Broken Hill in 1927, and 119 spent much time at Livingstone in 1931-34. 121-22 were at Wankie in 1931, but by the mid 1940s survivors were concentrated on Bulawayo,

engines 117, 119, 120 and 122, the others having been set aside. 122 was at Wankie in 1945, and right at the end of their lives, after all had been set aside in 1963, 122 was loaned to the Steelworks at Que Que in 1964, while 117 was sent to a training school at Broken Hill, and was to remain in Zambia. 122 after withdrawal was placed in the railway museum in Bulawayo, where it remains as a static exhibit. Those who remember them recall a very sharp, noisy, exhaust, in the full American tradition! Not surprising, when compared with the 9th class, having 8" valves with 4 5/8" travel, the noisy 9As boasted 11" valves with 5 1/2" travel, giving great freedom of exhaust.

Historical data:

Class 9A, 4-8-0

Engine Number	Alco Number	Date built	Date in Service	Last Used	Disposal
117	56724	1917	5/1917	11/1962	Training School, Broken Hill
118	56725	1917	5/1917	8/1941	Scrapped 4/1947
119	56726	1917	5/1917	8/1961	Scrapped 4/1972
120	56727	1917	5/1917	1/1963	Scrapped 4/1972
121	56728	1917	5/1917	10/1945	Scrapped 4/1947
122	56729	1917	5/1917	2/1963	Railway Museum, Bulawayo

9A class no 122 when still at work. This engine is now in the Bulawayo museum. RRM lettering and smokebox numberplate. RR

9A class no 119, evidently ex-works, shunting at Bulawayo. Plain smokebox door. J. R. Lloyd

9A class 117 at Bulawayo. Note modified smokebox door with centre dart fastener. F. C. Butcher

Class 9B, 4-8-0

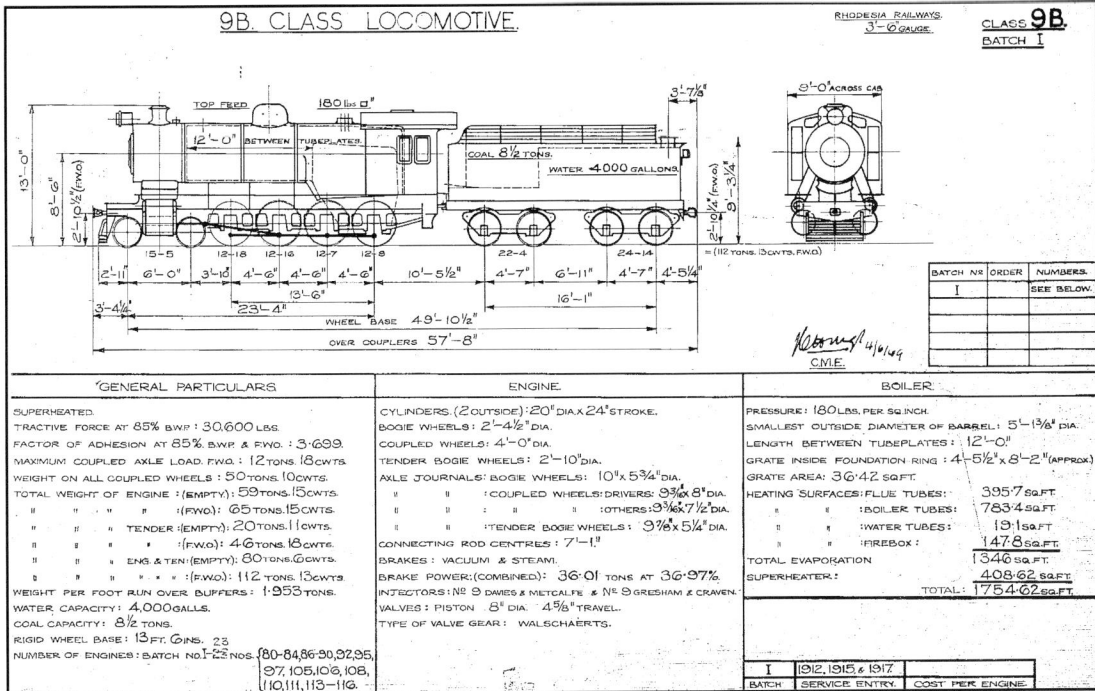

9B. CLASS LOCOMOTIVE.

RHODESIA RAILWAYS.
3'-6" GAUGE

CLASS 9B.
BATCH I

BATCH Nº	ORDER	NUMBERS.
I		SEE BELOW.

C.M.E.

GENERAL PARTICULARS

SUPERHEATED.
TRACTIVE FORCE AT 85% B.W.P. : 30,600 LBS.
FACTOR OF ADHESION AT 85% B.W.P. & F.W.O. : 3·699.
MAXIMUM COUPLED AXLE LOAD. F.W.O. : 12 TONS. 18 CWTS.
WEIGHT ON ALL COUPLED WHEELS : 50 TONS. 10 CWTS.
TOTAL WEIGHT OF ENGINE : (EMPTY) : 59 TONS. 15 CWTS.
"   "   "   " (F.W.O.) : 65 TONS. 15 CWTS.
"   "   " TENDER : (EMPTY) : 20 TONS. 11 CWTS.
"   "   "   " (F.W.O.) : 46 TONS. 18 CWTS.
"   "   " ENG. & TEN. (EMPTY) : 80 TONS. 6 CWTS.
"   "   "   "   " (F.W.O.) : 112 TONS. 13 CWTS.
WEIGHT PER FOOT RUN OVER BUFFERS : 1·953 TONS.
WATER CAPACITY : 4,000 GALLS.
COAL CAPACITY : 8½ TONS.
RIGID WHEEL BASE : 13 FT. 6 INS. 23
NUMBER OF ENGINES : BATCH NO 1-22 NOS. 80-84, 86-90, 92, 95, 97, 105, 106, 108, 110, 111, 113-116.

ENGINE

CYLINDERS. (2 OUTSIDE) : 20" DIA. X 24" STROKE.
BOGIE WHEELS : 2'-4½" DIA.
COUPLED WHEELS : 4'-0" DIA.
TENDER BOGIE WHEELS : 2'-10" DIA.
AXLE JOURNALS : BOGIE WHEELS : 10" X 5¾" DIA.
"   " : COUPLED WHEELS : DRIVERS : 9⅜" X 8" DIA.
"   "   "   " : OTHERS : 9⅜" X 7½" DIA.
"   " : TENDER BOGIE WHEELS : 9⅞" X 5¼" DIA.
CONNECTING ROD CENTRES : 7'-1".
BRAKES : VACUUM & STEAM.
BRAKE POWER : (COMBINED) : 36·01 TONS AT 36·97%.
INJECTORS : Nº 9 DAVIES & METCALFE & Nº 9 GRESHAM & CRAVEN.
VALVES : PISTON 8" DIA. 4⅝" TRAVEL.
TYPE OF VALVE GEAR : WALSCHAERTS.

BOILER

PRESSURE : 180 LBS. PER SQ. INCH.
SMALLEST OUTSIDE DIAMETER OF BARREL : 5'-1⅜" DIA.
LENGTH BETWEEN TUBEPLATES : 12'-0".
GRATE INSIDE FOUNDATION RING : 4'-5½" X 8'-2" (APPROX)
GRATE AREA : 36·42 SQ. FT.
HEATING SURFACES : FLUE TUBES : 395·7 SQ. FT.
"   " : BOILER TUBES : 783·4 SQ. FT.
"   " : WATER TUBES : 19·1 SQ. FT.
"   " : FIREBOX : 147·8 SQ. FT.
TOTAL EVAPORATION : 1346 SQ. FT.
SUPERHEATER : 408·62 SQ. FT.
TOTAL : 1754·62 SQ. FT.

I	1912, 1915 & 1917	
BATCH	SERVICE ENTRY.	COST PER ENGINE.

RR official photograph of 9B 4-8-0 as specially painted in green livery

The 9B were rebuilds from class 9th, using the same wheels, underframe, motion etc, but with a substantially modified boiler. The original 9th class boiler was low pitched, and the wide firebox had a Gaines combustion chamber in which the front two feet of the grate were bricked off, leaving a grate seven feet long out of an inside firebox length of 9'1 1/4". In the 9B, the same barrel was used but with a totally new firebox, pitched a foot higher, a longer grate and a sloping front tubeplate, all of which added up to 16,7 percent more grate and 19,5 percent more firebox heating surface, plus a substantial amount of extra combustion volume coupled with less cramped ashpan conditions. The net result was a boiler of substantially superior steaming capabilities within the same weight limitations - an excellent exercise in design. Slightly higher boiler pressure gave a proportionate increase in nominal tractive effort, and these very sturdy looking engines were an immense success, with 26 out of the original thirty locomotives so rebuilt from 1939 to 1956, mostly in the late 1940s. No. 85 was prematurely scrapped only a year after rebuilding, following a bad accident at Manga, on the outskirts of Beira, but typical allocations were, firstly in February 1949: Beira, 82, 83, 92, 111, 115 which were used on main line work from Beira to Vila Machado, from where Garratts took over. The remainder were used mainly on branch line work as follows: Umtali 89 and 110, Salisbury, 87, 88 and 112, Gwelo 80, 84, 86, 90, 106, 108, 113 and 116, Bulawayo 93, 95 and 107, Wankie 81, 97, 105, 114. After the Beira line was sold to Moçambique

they lost their main line duties and a typical allocation in July 1950 was Umtali 83, 89, Salisbury 82, 87, Gwelo 80, 90, 92, 95, 108, 110, 111, 114, Bulawayo 84, 86, 97, 106, 116, Wankie 88, 105, 113, 115, Livingstone 81. Especially after the 14A Garratts arrived in 1953, they were steadily reduced to shunting duties until finally withdrawn as detailed in the table given with the original 9th class.

An interesting technical detail is that although originally built with 8-inch piston valves, the diagram book shows these as later enlarged to the unusual size of 8 3/4", known only to the author on engines built for the old North Eastern Railway in England. It seems unlikely that a strange cleaving to Darlington practice should prevail, but probably this represented an attempt to improve steam flow within the limits of the existing cylinder castings.

9B no 115 whilst still in regular service. This engine is now an operable museum engine.
J. R. Lloyd

9B no 86, with capuchon on chimney.
Author's collection

The first 9th class, as rebuilt to 9B, no 80, lettered RRM. J. Dele-Hoffman collection

9B no 116. J. Dele-Hoffman collection

Broadside shot of 9B no 110. Author's collection

NRZ's active museum 9B no 115 is in great demand for railway enthusiast specials, and is here seen doubleheading with 14A no 515 roaring through Cement.

A pair of 9B, nos 94 and 115, leave Gwelo with a coal train for Gado. F. C. Butcher

An enthusiast special from Bulawayo to Plumtree and back is doubleheaded with 9B 115 and 19th class 330.

With an enthusiast special from Colleen Bawn, 9B no 115 climbs up Mulungwane bank, on a 1 in 40 gradient, banked by a 16A Garratt no 611. This was a Rail Safaris train for overseas visitors.

9B 115 leads a 14A Garratt near Heany Junction with a returning Transnet "Union Linited" train, heading home for Cape Town.

10th class, 4-8-2

Builder's portrait of RR 10th class no 102, the 20 000th locomotive produced by the North British Locomotive Company. NBL

Rhodesia's 10th class represented a last backward look at Cape Government Railway's practice, after which the umbilical cord to the mother railway was finally severed, although South African Railways was consulted from time to time as needed. In its quest for more powerful machines to cope with heavy passenger requirements over mountain routes, CGR had in 1906, a large passenger 2-8-2 built by Kitson's, and known as the 9th class. It was thirty years ahead of Britain's first and only passenger 2-8-2, the Gresley class P2, and with a boiler having a minimum inside diameter of 5'6 3/8", and 33 square feet of grate, the Cape 9th had greater steaming capacity than any British locomotive at that time. Not surprisingly, the two wheel leading truck, carrying only 6 1/2 tons, provided insufficient guiding capacity over the severely curved mountain route and after a few years in service the design was amended to include a four-wheeled leading bogie, carrying twice the "steering" weight. These 4-8-2, class 4, had unsuperheated boilers, slide valves actuated by Stephensons valve gear, and were thus rather outdated when they appeared in 1911.

Meanwhile, in Rhodesia, Hosgood was looking for something faster and more powerful for the principal passenger trains whilst in South Africa the "Cape Lobby", dismayed by development along Natal lines, as was natural by Hendrie, successfully pressed for an updated Cape design, with superheater, piston valves, and Walscheart's valve gear, the eventual 4A class. Thus North British Locomotive Company found themselves developing two similar designs for two adjacent railways in Africa, two superheated 4-8-2, a lighter and a heavier. A common feature with the original 4th class was a boiler with combustion chamber to both provide more combus-tion volume and keep tube length to reasonable proportions. Judging by the maker's works numbers, Rhodesia got in with the first order, followed soon after by SAR with their 4A class. However the initial scheming and pre-design must have kept going concurrently, and the three diagrams reproduced, the original class 4, the 4A, and the RR 10th, show how close these engines were in design, not only with the combustion chamber boilers (the only Rhodesian boilers so equipped) but in the rather peculiar wheel spacing of the frame. Weights were more restricted in Rhodesia, with their 60 lb/yd track, so the RR 10th class had a boiler six inches thinner, with smaller grate and smaller cylinders, keeping axle loading down to the permitted 13 tons.

In service, the SAR classes 4 and 4A were odd ones out compared with the numerous Hendrie class, but the 4A were rebuilt with standard boilers and classed 4AR, lasting until the 1970s. By comparison, the smaller RR 10th class was a total success, the largest engines on the system when built, with further batches in the 1920s and 1930 until a total of twenty were at work. Initially they were used on the main lines but soon found themselves drafted to the Southern section, based on Mafeking where, with South African crews they successfully hauled most traffic through Bechuanaland until replaced by the 12th class in 1959. Two were prematurely withdrawn after a head-on smash at Vakaranga, Bechuanaland, in 1938, but most were taken out of service in 1958, many years earlier than their SAR contemporaries. After this, a few were hired to Malawi, and some sold to the Zambezi Sawmills Railway in Northern Rhodesia, now Zambia. No. 156 of this latter batch has had an extraordinary late life. Presented by Kenneth Kaunda, then president of Zambia, to David

Shepherd, the famous wildlife and locomotive painter, in 1974, 156 got down as far as Bulawayo, where it was placed in the museum awaiting funds for transport to England. This never happened, so in 1983 it went back to Zambia and presented to the Livingstone museum, by David Shepherd on September 1st. In July 1994 it came south again, to ZECO's works in Bulawayo and was thoroughly overhauled and refurbished, even to the extent of fitting roller bearings to bogie and tender axleboxes, thereafter returning to Livingstone as an operable locomotive for tourist traffic, where it remains today. (See p. 206)

10th class no 157 at Bulawayo old loco shed. F. C. Butcher

Another Bechuanaland photograph, the line over which the 10th class did much of their work. No 158 at an unidentified station. Author's collection

Comparative diagrams, showing RR 10th class evolution

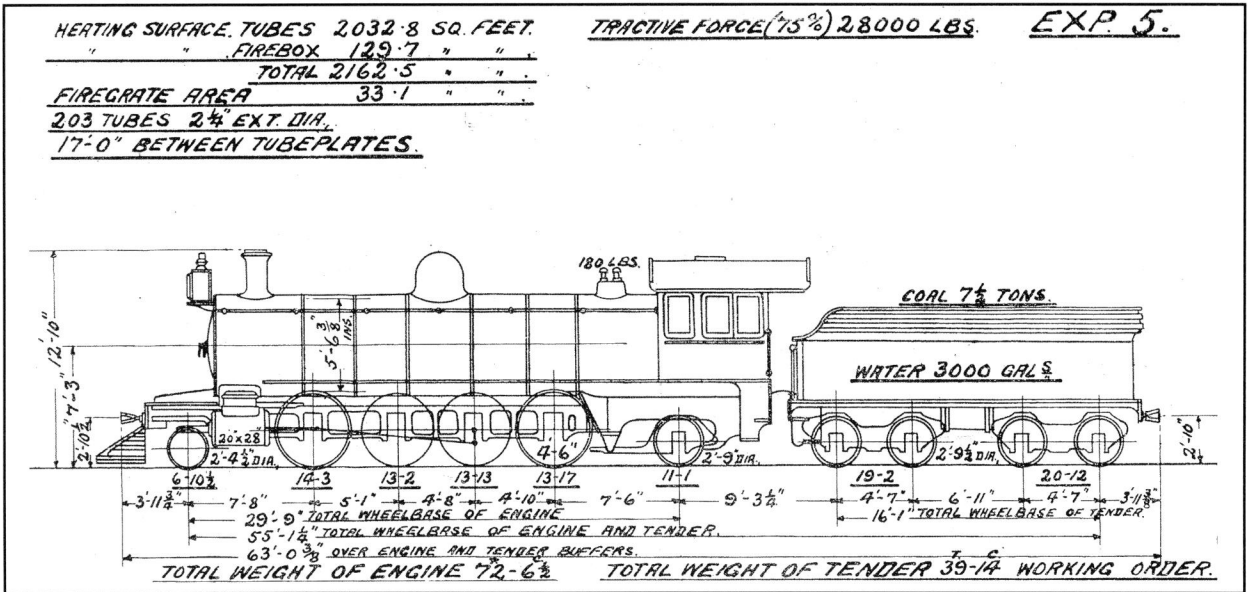

HEATING SURFACE. TUBES 2032·8 SQ. FEET.
" " FIREBOX 129·7 " "
TOTAL 2162·5 " "
FIREGRATE AREA 33·1 " "
203 TUBES 2¼" EXT. DIA.
17'-0" BETWEEN TUBEPLATES.

TRACTIVE FORCE (75%) 28000 LBS.   EXP. 5.

COAL 7½ TONS.
WATER 3000 GALS.

180 LBS.

TOTAL WEIGHT OF ENGINE 72-6½   TOTAL WEIGHT OF TENDER 39-14 WORKING ORDER.

Cape 9th class

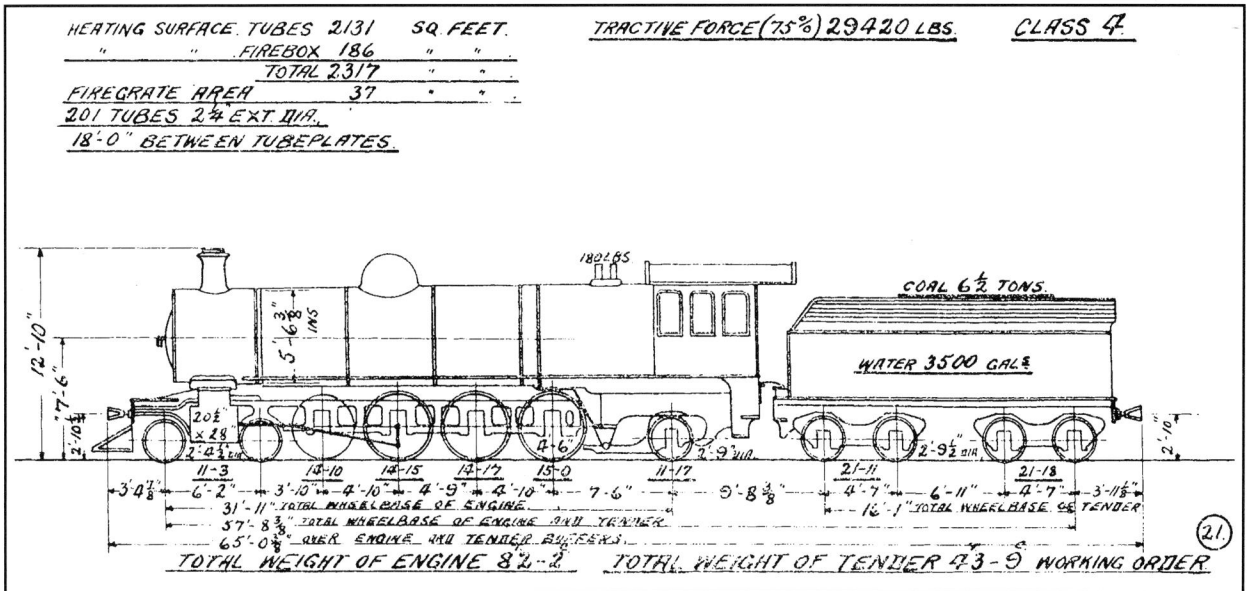

HEATING SURFACE. TUBES 2131 SQ. FEET.
" " FIREBOX 186 " "
TOTAL 2317 " "
FIREGRATE AREA 37 " "
201 TUBES 2¼" EXT. DIA.
18'-0" BETWEEN TUBEPLATES.

TRACTIVE FORCE (75%) 29420 LBS.   CLASS 4

COAL 6½ TONS.
WATER 3500 GALS.

180 LBS.

TOTAL WEIGHT OF ENGINE 82-2   TOTAL WEIGHT OF TENDER 43-9 WORKING ORDER.

(21.)

SAR class 4

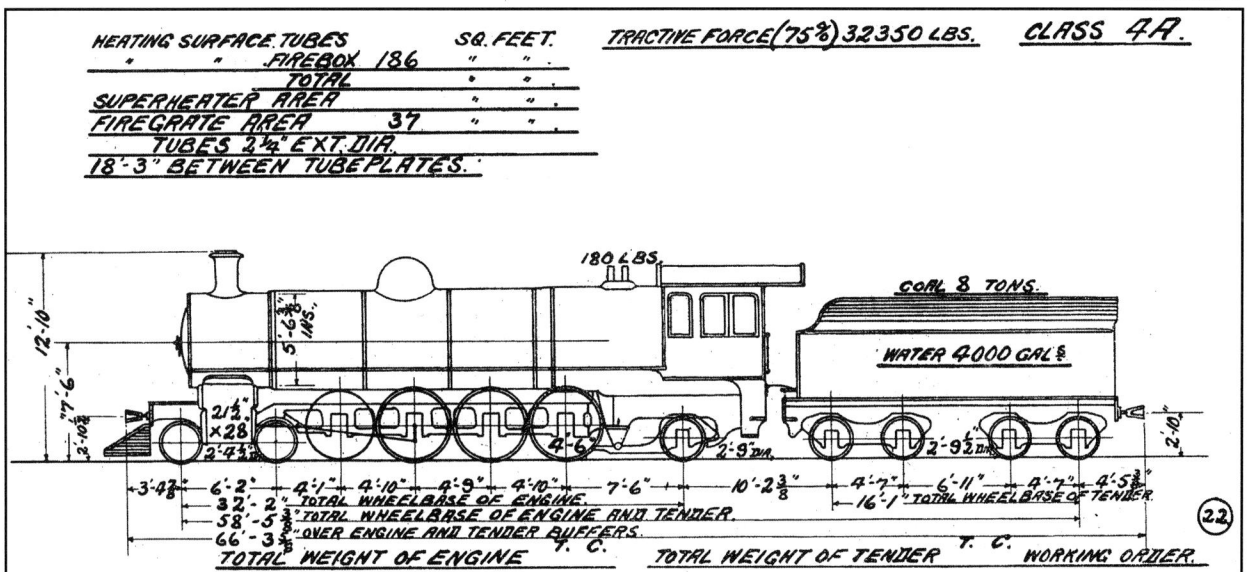

HEATING SURFACE. TUBES SQ. FEET.
" " FIREBOX 186 " "
TOTAL
SUPERHEATER AREA " "
FIREGRATE AREA 37 " "
TUBES 2¼" EXT. DIA.
18'-3" BETWEEN TUBEPLATES.

TRACTIVE FORCE (75%) 32350 LBS.   CLASS 4A.

COAL 8 TONS.
WATER 4000 GALS.

180 LBS.

TOTAL WEIGHT OF ENGINE T. C.   TOTAL WEIGHT OF TENDER T. C. WORKING ORDER.

(22)

SAR class 4A

69

RR 10th Class

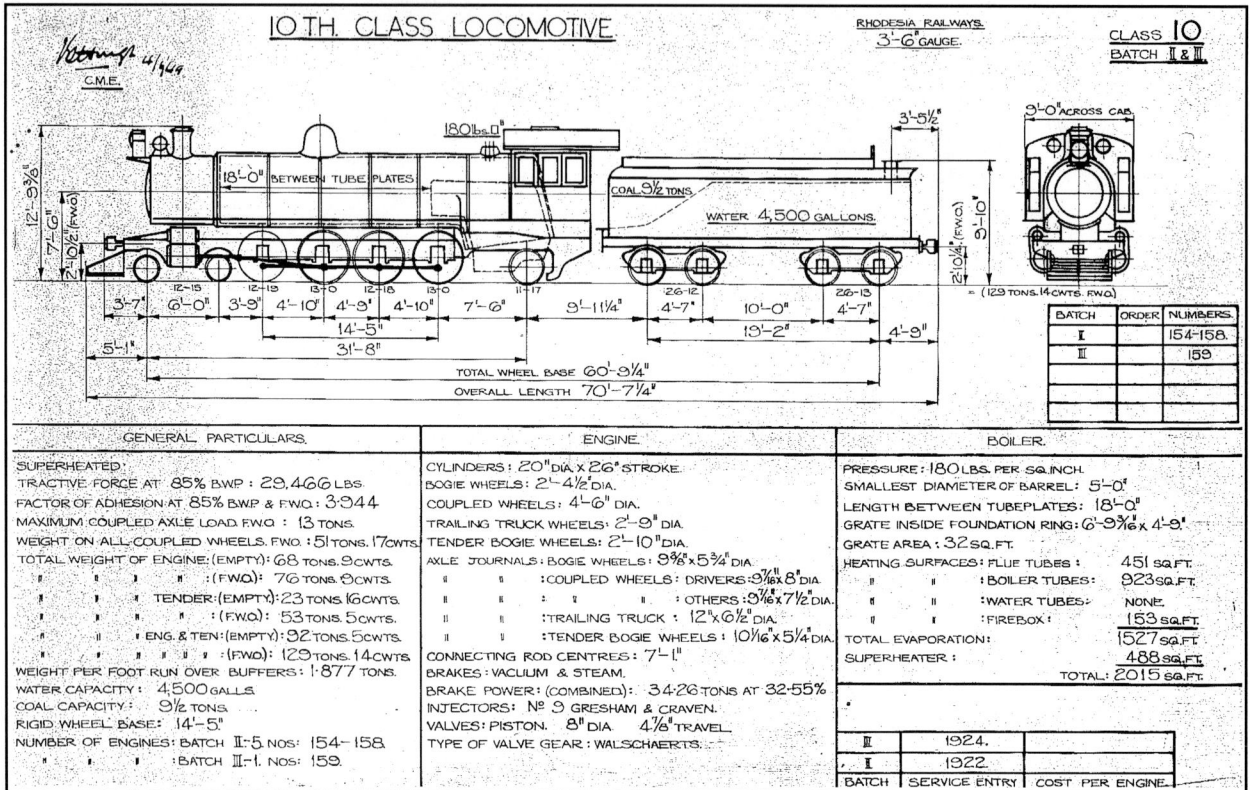

10TH. CLASS LOCOMOTIVE — RHODESIA RAILWAYS 3'-6" GAUGE. CLASS 10 BATCH II & III

Historical data:

10th Class 4-8-2

Engine Number	NBL Number	Date built	Date in Service	Last Used	Disposal
98	19996	1913	1913	7/1962	Bulawayo Museum 4/1963
99	19997	1913	1913	8/1958	Scrapped 1/1961
100	19998	1913	1913	9/1958	Scrapped 1/1961
101	19999	1913	1913	7/1958	Scrapped 1/1961
102	20000	1913	1913	12/1958	Scrapped 1/1961
103	20001	1913	1913	6/1958	Scrapped 1/1961
104	20002	1913	1913	6/1958	Scrapped 1/1961
153	22796	1922	4/1922	4/1938	Scrapped 1938**
154	22797	1922	4/1922	8/1958	ZSR 2/1959
155	22798	1922	5/1922	6/1958	ZSR 2/1959
156	22799	1922	6/1922	7/1958	Livingstone Museum***
157	22800	1922	7/1922	5/1958	Scrapped 1/1961
158	22801	1922	7/1922	10/1958	Scrapped 1/1961
159	23089	1924	8/1924	5/1958	ZSR 11/1958
241	23972	1930	5/1930	4/1938	Scrapped 1938**
242	23973	1930	6/1930	7/1958	Scrapped 4/1972
243	23974	1930	7/1930	12/1958	Scrapped 4/1972*
244	23975	1930	7/1930	9/1958	Scrapped 4/1972
245	23976	1930	7/1930	4/1958	Scrapped 4/1972*
246	23977	1930	7/1930	7/1958	Scrapped 4/1972*

* Hired to Nyasaland Railways: 98, 5/1960 - 8/1962; 243, 5-7/1960, 2/1962 - 4/1963; 245, 8/1960 - 9/1962; 246, 5/1960 - 8/1962
** Scrapped after head-on collision, Vakaranga, Bechuanaland, 4/4/1938
*** Sold from RR to ZSR 2/19/60

The pioneer 10th class, no 98 on a train probably in Bechuanaland, with water tank and caboose. A. L. Atwell

10th class no 246 heading train 105 down, arrives in Bulawayo via the original main line. The present locomotive shed is to the right of the picture. Author's collection

11th class, 4-8-2

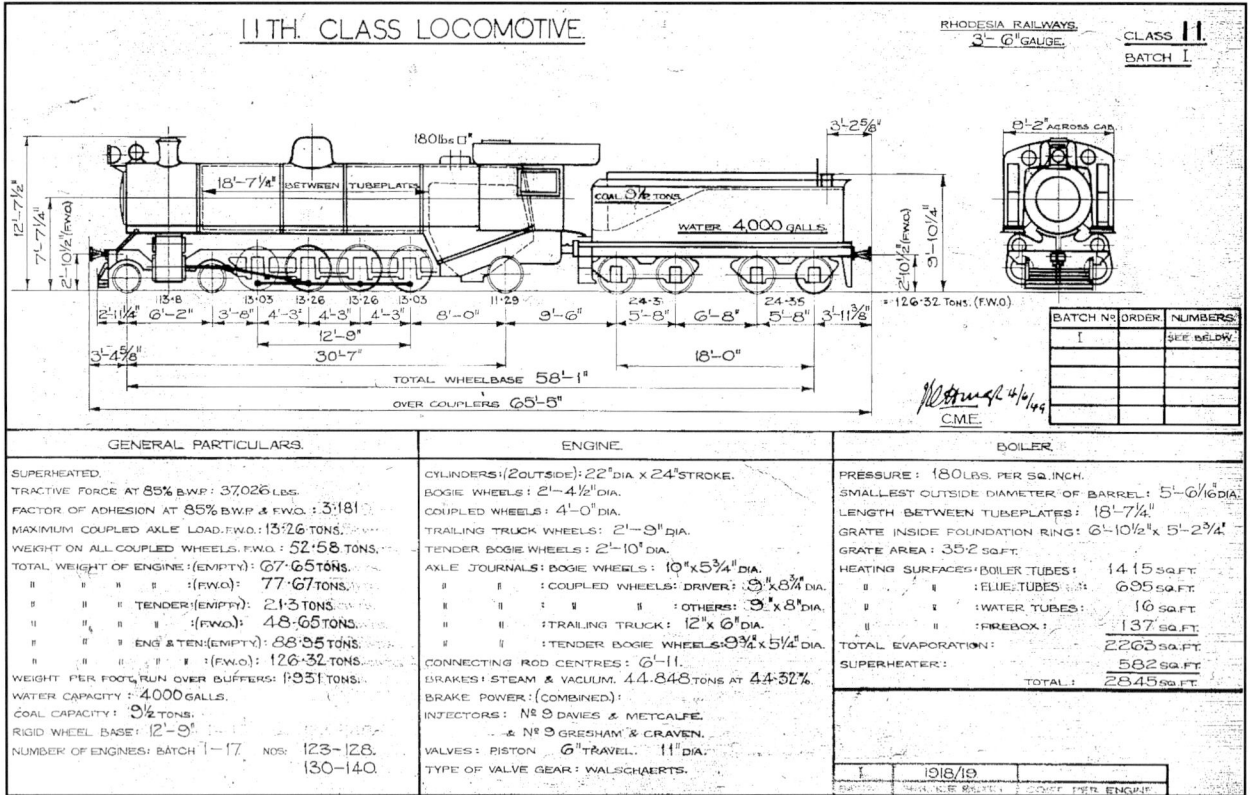

11TH. CLASS LOCOMOTIVE. — RHODESIA RAILWAYS. 3'-6" GAUGE. CLASS 11. BATCH I.

GENERAL PARTICULARS.

SUPERHEATED.
TRACTIVE FORCE AT 85% B.W.P.: 37,026 LBS.
FACTOR OF ADHESION AT 85% B.W.P. & F.W.O.: 3·181
MAXIMUM COUPLED AXLE LOAD. F.W.O.: 13·26 TONS.
WEIGHT ON ALL COUPLED WHEELS. F.W.O.: 52·58 TONS.
TOTAL WEIGHT OF ENGINE (EMPTY): 67·65 TONS.
" " " (F.W.O.): 77·67 TONS.
" " TENDER (EMPTY): 21·3 TONS.
" " " (F.W.O.): 48·65 TONS.
" " ENG & TEN (EMPTY): 88·95 TONS.
" " " (F.W.O.): 126·32 TONS.
WEIGHT PER FOOT RUN OVER BUFFERS: 1·951 TONS.
WATER CAPACITY: 4000 GALLS.
COAL CAPACITY: 9½ TONS.
RIGID WHEEL BASE: 12'-9".
NUMBER OF ENGINES: BATCH 1-17 NOS: 123-128. 130-140.

ENGINE.

CYLINDERS (2 OUTSIDE): 22" DIA x 24" STROKE.
BOGIE WHEELS: 2'-4½" DIA.
COUPLED WHEELS: 4'-0" DIA.
TRAILING TRUCK WHEELS: 2'-9" DIA.
TENDER BOGIE WHEELS: 2'-10" DIA.
AXLE JOURNALS: BOGIE WHEELS: 10" x 5¾" DIA.
" " : COUPLED WHEELS: DRIVER: 9" x 8¾" DIA.
" " : " " : OTHERS: 9" x 8" DIA.
" " : TRAILING TRUCK: 12" x 6" DIA.
" " : TENDER BOGIE WHEELS: 9¾" x 5¼" DIA.
CONNECTING ROD CENTRES: 6'-11.
BRAKES: STEAM & VACUUM. 44·848 TONS AT 44·32%.
BRAKE POWER (COMBINED):
INJECTORS: № 9 DAVIES & METCALFE. & № 9 GRESHAM & CRAVEN.
VALVES: PISTON 6" TRAVEL. 11" DIA.
TYPE OF VALVE GEAR: WALSCHAERTS.

BOILER.

PRESSURE: 180 LBS. PER SQ. INCH.
SMALLEST OUTSIDE DIAMETER OF BARREL: 5'-6 1/16" DIA.
LENGTH BETWEEN TUBEPLATES: 18'-7¼".
GRATE INSIDE FOUNDATION RING: 6'-10½" x 5'-2¾".
GRATE AREA: 35·2 SQ.FT.
HEATING SURFACES: BOILER TUBES: 1415 SQ.FT.
" " : FLUE TUBES: 695 SQ.FT.
" " : WATER TUBES: 16 SQ.FT.
" " : FIREBOX: 137 SQ.FT.
TOTAL EVAPORATION: 2263 SQ.FT.
SUPERHEATER: 582 SQ.FT.
TOTAL: 2845 SQ.FT.

BATCH No	ORDER	NUMBERS
I	1918/19	SEE BELOW

Diagram notes: 180 lbs □". 18'-7¼" BETWEEN TUBEPLATES. COAL 9½ TONS. WATER 4,000 GALLS. 3'-2⅝". 9'-2" ACROSS CAB. = 126·32 TONS. (F.W.O.) TOTAL WHEELBASE 58'-1". OVER COUPLERS 65'-5". 30'-7". 18'-0". 12'-8". C.M.E.

At the end of the first World war, Rhodesia, like South Africa and other colonial countries, experienced a need for motive power which traditional British firms were unable to satisfy, and rather than go to the USA, American practice was resorted to by using a Canadian builder which was still in British Empire! In a similar manner by which the RR 10th class were co-designed with the South African 4A, so the 11th class was similar to, and concurrent with, an SAR design. In South Africa, the need was for more Hendrie's 14 and 15A classes, 4-8-2 with 4 foot and 4'9" wheels respectively, and Canadian versions of each were supplied as classes 14C and 15B. Rhodesia's requirements could be met by a slightly lighter version of the 14C, and thirty of these were supplied in two batches. These were two and three tons heavier than the 10th class, yet considerably lighter than the SAR engines which were nearly 85 tons apiece. Frame design and wheels spacing were closely similar, and quite marginal reductions in boiler size were made, certainly insufficient to account for the seven and eight tons difference in weight between the RR and SAR locomotives, and probably frame thickness was also reduced, as certainly the RR locos had trouble later with frame cracking.

The close degree by which the Rhodesian 11th and SAR 14C locos were concurrently designed and built is shown by the following data. SAR seems to have placed its order first, maker's numbers 58637-56 being allocated to the initial batch, with Rhodesia's first batch following on with numbers 59115-23. Despite this, the RR were first off the mark in getting their engines into service, their first in service being July 1918, with SAR following in October the same year.

Compared to the 10th class, the RR 11th were nominally quite a lot more powerful, with a nominal tractive effort of 37026 lb versus the 10th class's 29466 lb. However, with only a quarter ton extra axle loading this was not effective in service, and the 11th class had a reputation for slipping under less than ideal track conditions. Cylinder diameter was later reduced slightly to alleviate this, and in this aspect it is interesting to note that the RR locomotives had a shorter piston stroke than their SAR counterparts.

The 11th class spent most of their working lives in Northern Rhodesia, and in October 1927 all were at Livingstone except for six locos at Bulawayo and three at Wankie. A year later all but two were at Livingstone but during the early 1930s they started migrating north to the developing copperbelt, and the beginning of 1932 saw most of the first batch at Broken Hill with the second batch at Livingstone and Wankie. They then started to migrate further to the copperbelt new sheds and branches, with the 1940-60 period seeing substantial allocations to the newer sheds at Ndola and Nkana. By the early 1960s most were set aside, but June 1963 saw 130/33/35 at Broken Hill and 142/48/49/52 at Nkana, whilst a month later 149 of Nkana was the last in normal service. However, a few years later several were reinstated for heavy shunting at Bulawayo, starting with 147/48 in December 1965 and ending with 137/42/47/48 withdrawn from Bulawayo January 1970. One has been preserved in the Raylton Museum, unfortunately inoperable, and six were sold to Moçambique where they shunted at Lourenço Marques until the early 1970s, the very last in service.

11th class no 130 at Victoria Falls station heading a mixed train to Livingstone. Author's collection

Historical data:

11th Class 4-8-2

Engine Number	Montreal Loco Co. Number	Date built	Date in Service	Last Used	Disposal
123	59115	1918	8/1918	5/1963	Scrapped 4/1972
124	59116	1918	7/1918	10/1962	Scrapped 4/1972
125	59117	1918	8/1918	10/1969	Scrapped 4/1972
126	59118	1918	7/1918	9/1962	Scrapped 4/1972
127	59119	1918	8/1918	10/1961	Museum
128	59120	1918	8/1918	9/1962	Scrapped 4/1972
129	59121	1918	8/1918	4/1937	Scrapped 12/1937*
130	59122	1918	12/1918	5/1963	Scrapped 4/1972
131	59123	1918	12/1918	6/1961	Scrapped 4/1972
132	59940	1918	3/1919	11/1962	Scrapped 4/1972
133	59941	1918	3/1919	6/1963	Scrapped 4/1972
134	59942	1918	3/1919	3/1961	Scrapped 4/1972
135	59943	1918	2/1919	6/1963	Scrapped 4/1972
136	59944	1918	2/1919	8/1962	Scrapped 4/1972
137	59945	1918	1/1919	3/1963	Scrapped 4/1972
138	59946	1918	2/1919	11/1962	Scrapped 4/1972
139	59947	1918	2/1919	3/1962	Scrapped 4/1972
140	59948	1918	2/1919	2/1960	Scrapped 4/1972
141	62273	1921	8/1921	10/1958	Scrapped 4/1972
142	62274	1921	8/1921	12/1969	Scrapped 4/1972
143	62275	1921	8/1921	6/1960	Scrapped 4/1972
144	62276	1921	8/1921	10/1958	Scrapped 4/1972
145	62277	1921	8/1921	5/1963	CFM No 441, 11/1964
146	62278	1921	8/1921	5/1963	CFM No 442, 9/1964
147	62279	1921	8/1921	1/1970	Scrapped 4/1972
148	62280	1921	7/1921	1/1970	Scrapped 4/1972
149	62281	1921	8/1921	8/1963	CFM No 443, 10/1964
150	62282	1921	8/1921	5/1963	CFM No 444, 11/1964
151	62283	1921	8/1921	5/1963	CFM No 445, 9/1964
152	62284	1921	7/1921	7/1963	CFM No 446, 11/1964

* Engine 129 prematurely scrapped due to collision at Katanino, Northern Rhodesia. It was then stationed at Broken Hill, and was ex-works from Bulawayo shops only a month before.

11th class 144, ex works, at Bulawayo. J. R. Lloyd

11th class no 127, as statically preserved in Bulawayo museum.

11 class no 144 about to depart from Shabani with the mixed train late 1956. At the time the class were barred from the branch due to weight! F. C. Butcher

11th class no 149 doubleheading with a 12th class, probably in Northern Rhodesia.
J. Dele-Hoffman collection

11A class, 4-8-2

11A CLASS LOCOMOTIVE.

RHODESIA RAILWAYS
3'-6" GAUGE.

CLASS 11A.
BATCH I.

TOP FEED. 200 lbs □
COAL 9½ TONS.
WATER 4500 GALLS.

9'-2" ACROSS CAB.

18'-7⅞" BETWEEN TUBEPLATES.

13'-0"
8'-0"
2'-10½" (F.W.O)

2'-10½" (F.W.O)

14.77 13.52 13.52 13.52 13.52 11.52 26·0. 25.75 = (132.72 Tons. F.W.O.)

3'-1½" 6'-6" 3'-8" 4'-3" 4'-3" 4'-3" 8'-0" 8'-11½" 5'-10" 8'-4" 5'-10" 4'-9½"

4'-3"
30'-11"
20'-0"

TOTAL WHEEL BASE 59'-10½"

OVER COUPLERS 68'-11"

BATCH Nº	ORDER.	NUMBERS.
I	89	304-315

C.M.E. 4/6/49

GENERAL PARTICULARS.

SUPERHEATED.
TRACTIVE FORCE AT 85% B.W.P. : 37,485 LBS.
FACTOR OF ADHESION AT 85% B.W.P. & F.W.O. : 3·232
MAXIMUM COUPLED AXLE LOAD : F.W.O. 13·52 TONS.
WEIGHT ON ALL COUPLED WHEELS. F.W.O. : 54·08 TONS.
TOTAL WEIGHT OF ENGINE (EMPTY) 71·86 TONS.
   "   "   " : (F.W.O.) 80·37 TONS.
   "   "   " TENDER (EMPTY) : 23·25 TONS.
   "   "   " : (F.W.O.) 52·35 TONS.
   "   "   " ENG. & TEN. (EMPTY) : 95·11TONS.
   "   "   " (F.W.O.) : 132·72 TONS.
WEIGHT PER FOOT RUN OVER BUFFERS : 1·926 TONS.
WATER CAPACITY : 4,500 GALLONS.
COAL CAPACITY : 9½ TONS.
RIGID WHEEL BASE : 12 FT. 9 INS.
NUMBER OF ENGINES : BATCH I — 12. NOS. 304-315

ENGINE.

CYLINDERS : (2 OUTSIDE) 21" DIA. x 24" STROKE.
BOGIE WHEELS : 2'-4½" DIA.
COUPLED WHEELS : 4'-0" DIA.
TRAILING TRUCK : 2'-9" DIA.
TENDER BOGIE WHEELS : 2'-10" DIA.
AXLE JOURNALS : BOGIE WHEELS : 9½" x 5¾" DIA.
   "   " : COUPLED WHEELS : DRIVER : 9" x 8½" DIA.
   "   " : OTHERS : 9" x 8" DIA.
   "   " : TRAILING TRUCK : 11¾" x 6" DIA.
   "   " : TENDER BOGIE WHEELS : 9¾" x 5½" DIA.
CONNECTING ROD CENTRES : 6'-11."
BRAKES : VACUUM & STEAM.
BRAKE POWER : (COMBINED) : 47·386 TONS AT 44·52%
INJECTORS : 10½MM. SELLERS.
VALVES : PISTON 10" DIA. 6" TRAVEL.
TYPE OF VALVE GEAR : WALSCHAERTS.

BOILER.

PRESSURE : 200 LBS. PER SQ. INCH.
SMALLEST OUTSIDE DIAMETER OF BARREL : 5'-6"
LENGTH BETWEEN TUBEPLATES : 18'-7⅛"
GRATE INSIDE FOUNDATION RING : 6'-10²⁷⁄₃₂" x 5'-3¾"
GRATE AREA : 36·38 SQ.FT.
THERMIC SYPHONS.
HEATING SURFACES : FLUE TUBES : 696 SQ.FT.
   "   " : BOILER TUBES : 1,414 SQ.FT.
   "   " : FIREBOX : 138 SQ.FT.
   "   " : SYPHONS : 48 SQ.FT.
TOTAL EVAPORATION : 2296 SQ.FT.
SUPERHEATER : 589 SQ.FT.
TOTAL : 2885 SQ.FT.

I	1948	
BATCH	SERVICE ENTRY.	COST PER ENGINE.

Class 11A no 315, probably ex-works. Croxton collection

The twelve members of this class were a stop-gap addition to Rhodesian motive power after the second World war, were based on the previous 11th class, and were from the same builders. For some reason, several cosmetic changes were made, in particular the running plate which was stepped down behind the valve gear, which did not improve appearance, whilst rather boxy looking tenders were fitted, slightly longer and with somewhat more water capacity. Compared with the original 11th class, cylinder bore was reduced but boiler pressure increased, although again due to frame cracking, the pressure was fairly soon reduced. Maximum axle loading was increased to 13.52 tons giving a marginally higher adhesion factor than the originals. Fireboxes were fitted with thermic syphons instead of the arch tubes of the 11th class, but these were eventually probably interchanged and also appeared on the 12A and 12B classes. With only thirteen years in Rhodesian service, they can hardly be called fully successful, and were happily sold to Moçambique at a time when many older locomotives remained in service. Three were damaged aboard ship en route from Canada to Beira, numbers 304/07/14, of which 304 was evidently the worst damaged and the last in service.

After erection, the engines spent an initial year stationed at Bulawayo, but by mid 1949 were mainly at Broken Hill. By 1955 Ndola housed most of the class but by mid 1958 they were back at Bulawayo where they remained until sold. They certainly spent more time working in Moçambique than in Rhodesia, and seven were initially used from Beira where they probably worked on the more level section to Vila Machado, the old Bamboo Creek of narrow gauge days. The remaining five went straight to Lourenço Marques and were eventually joined by the Beira engines, and used largely on the Swaziland line after opening in 1964, often being sub-shedded at Sidvokodvo, where they worked in pairs with each other, and with ex-Rhodesian colleagues of the 12A and 12B classes, which utilised the same boiler design. In Moçambique several were modified with a straight running plate, which considerably improved their appearance, whilst various front end modifications to smokebox fronts and doors, plus sometimes the addition of circular CFM style number plates were added, such that eventually few individual engines were alike. About the early 1970s, when the CFM 700 class replaced them in Swaziland, the entire class was shipped north to the Nampula division where they gradually fell out of use during the civil war then ravaging, being finally used about 1980.

Historical data:

11A Class 4-8-2

Engine Number	Montreal Loco Co. Number	Date built	Date in Service	Last Used	Moçambique Data Date Sold	CFM Number	Railed Via
304	75468	1947	9/1948	10/1961	10/1961	451	Malvernia
305	75469	1947	2/1948	10/1961	10/1961	452	Machipanda
306	75470	1947	4/1948	10/1961	10/1961	453	Malvernia
307	75471	1947	7/1948	10/1961	10/1961	454	Malvernia
308	75472	1947	3/1948	11/1961	11/1961	455	Malvernia
309	75473	1947	2/1948	10/1961	11/1961	456	Machipanda
310	75474	1947	2/1948	10/1961	10/1961	457	Machipanda
311	75475	1947	2/1948	9/1961	10/1961	458	Malvernia
312	75476	1947	2/1948	10/1961	10/1961	459	Machipanda
313	75477	1947	3/1948	11/1961	12/1961	460	Machipanda
314	75478	1947	5/1948	11/1961	12/1961	461	Machipanda
315	75479	1947	3/1948	10/1961	10/1961	462	Machipanda

NOTE: Malvernia is the border post on the Limpopo route between Rhodesia and Lourenço Marques. Machipanda is the border post near Umtali en route to Beira

Class 11A no 304.
J. R. Lloyd

Class 11A no 306, with 15th class Garratt 369.
J. R. Lloyd

Class 11A no 315, from left hand side.
J. R. Lloyd

12th class, 4-8-2

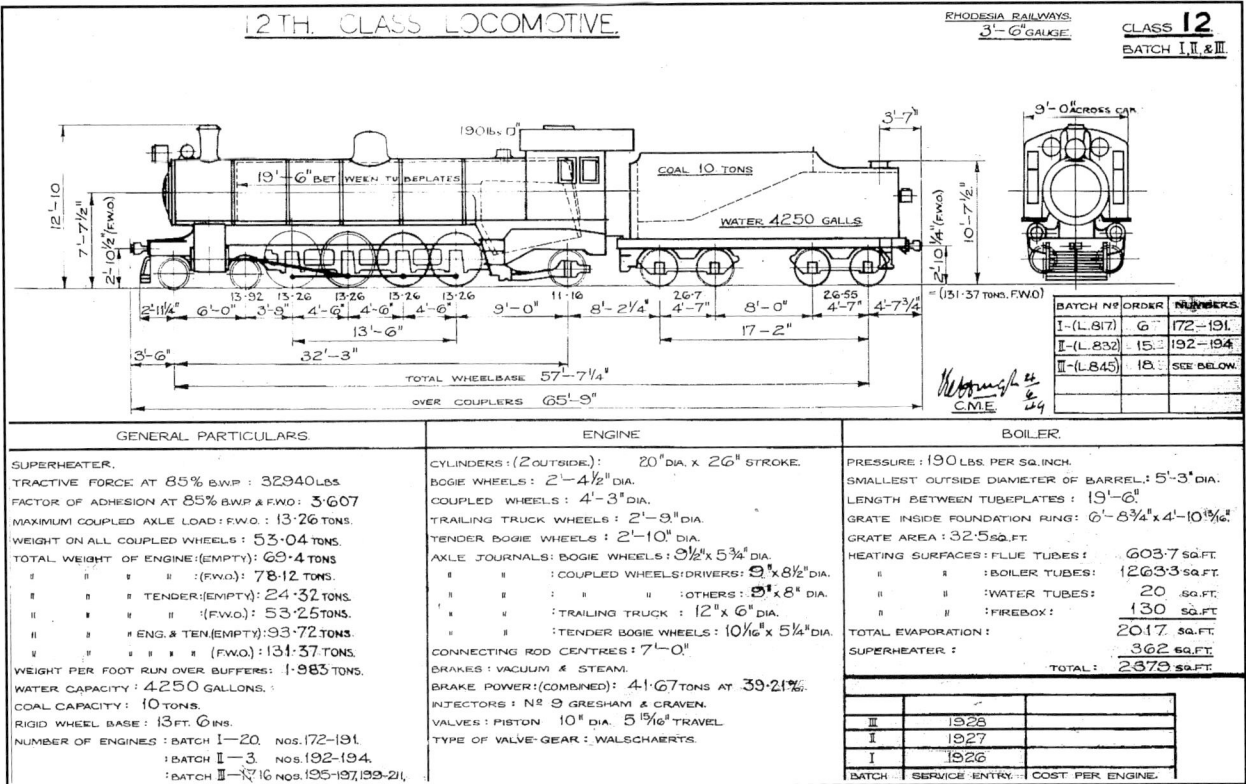

RHODESIA RAILWAYS. 3'-6" GAUGE.

CLASS 12 BATCH I, II, & III.

COAL 10 TONS
WATER 4250 GALLS.
19'-6" BETWEEN TUBEPLATES
190 lbs □"

BATCH Nº	ORDER	NUMBERS
I—(L.817)	6	172—191
II—(L.832)	15	192—194
III—(L.845)	18	SEE BELOW.

C.M.E.

TOTAL WHEELBASE 57'-7¼"
OVER COUPLERS 65'-9"

GENERAL PARTICULARS.

SUPERHEATER.
TRACTIVE FORCE AT 85% B.W.P. : 32940 LBS.
FACTOR OF ADHESION AT 85% B.W.P. & F.W.O. : 3·607
MAXIMUM COUPLED AXLE LOAD : F.W.O. : 13·26 TONS.
WEIGHT ON ALL COUPLED WHEELS : 53·04 TONS.
TOTAL WEIGHT OF ENGINE : (EMPTY) : 69·4 TONS.
" " " : (F.W.O.) : 78·12 TONS.
" " " TENDER : (EMPTY) : 24·32 TONS.
" " " " : (F.W.O.) : 53·25 TONS.
" " " ENG. & TEN. (EMPTY) : 93·72 TONS.
" " " " " (F.W.O.) : 131·37 TONS.
WEIGHT PER FOOT RUN OVER BUFFERS : 1·983 TONS.
WATER CAPACITY : 4250 GALLONS.
COAL CAPACITY : 10 TONS.
RIGID WHEEL BASE : 13 FT. 6 INS.
NUMBER OF ENGINES : BATCH I—20. NOS. 172—191.
: BATCH II—3. NOS. 192—194.
: BATCH III—16 NOS. 195—197, 198—211.

ENGINE.

CYLINDERS : (2 OUTSIDE.) : 20" DIA. x 26" STROKE.
BOGIE WHEELS : 2'—4½" DIA.
COUPLED WHEELS : 4'—3" DIA.
TRAILING TRUCK WHEELS : 2'—9" DIA.
TENDER BOGIE WHEELS : 2'—10." DIA.
AXLE JOURNALS: BOGIE WHEELS : 9½" x 5¾" DIA.
" " : COUPLED WHEELS: DRIVERS : 9" x 8½" DIA.
" " : " : OTHERS : 9" x 8" DIA.
" " : TRAILING TRUCK : 12" x 6" DIA.
" " : TENDER BOGIE WHEELS : 10⅟₁₆" x 5¼" DIA.
CONNECTING ROD CENTRES : 7'—0."
BRAKES : VACUUM & STEAM.
BRAKE POWER: (COMBINED) : 41·67 TONS AT 39·21%.
INJECTORS : Nº 9 GRESHAM & CRAVEN.
VALVES : PISTON 10" DIA. 5 ⅟₁₆" TRAVEL
TYPE OF VALVE-GEAR : WALSCHAERTS.

BOILER.

PRESSURE : 190 LBS. PER SQ. INCH.
SMALLEST OUTSIDE DIAMETER OF BARREL : 5'-3" DIA.
LENGTH BETWEEN TUBEPLATES : 19'-6".
GRATE INSIDE FOUNDATION RING : 6'-8¾" x 4'-10⅟₁₆".
GRATE AREA : 32·5 SQ. FT.
HEATING SURFACES : FLUE TUBES : 603·7 SQ. FT.
" " : BOILER TUBES : 1263·3 SQ. FT.
" " : WATER TUBES : 20 SQ. FT.
" " : FIREBOX : 130 SQ. FT.
TOTAL EVAPORATION : 2017 SQ. FT.
SUPERHEATER : 362 SQ. FT.
TOTAL : 2379 SQ. FT.

BATCH	SERVICE ENTRY.	COST PER ENGINE.
III	1928	
II	1927	
I	1926	

12th class in normal form, with piston valves, at the builder's Glasgow works. North British

Upon the retirement of "Togo" Hosgood in 1924, E.H. Gray was appointed Chief Mechanical Engineer as his successor. Gray had been Mechanical Engineer in charge of Pietermaritzburg workshops in South Africa, and had probably spent his earlier railway engineering years under Hendrie of the Natal Government Railways. With Colonel Collins appointed CME of the SAR in 1922 Gray was clearly at a dead end as regards promotion and the Rhodesian job was a heaven sent opportunity. As an ex-Natal man he will have had good experience with heavily graded railways, the 1 in 30 banks of the old Natal main line being even steeper than Rhodesia's formidable Beira line.

Rising traffic at the time of Gray's appointment showed a need for two new locomotive classes, a universal mixed traffic design to supercede the 9th, 10th and 11th classes, plus something much more powerful for the Beira line. Evidently the mixed traffic engine was first considered, as it became the 12th class, whilst the heavy gradient engine became the 13th class, although in the event the 13th preceded the 12th in service.

Gray was still restricted to light axle loads by the 60 lb/yd track in service, and had little room to manoeuvre in setting out his specifications. In service were the excellent 10th class 4-8-2 with 4'6" wheels for the South line via Mafeking, and the heavier 11th class with 4'0" wheels in

Northern Rhodesia. A cautious compromise was reached by using 4'3" wheels, coincidentally the same size as the South African 12th class although the two designs, apart from size and arrangement of wheels, had little else in common. The 12th class boiler indicated the cautious thoughts of a workshops-orientated man - it lacked the 10th class's combustion chamber and the 11th class Belpaire firebox. It had the longest tubes on the railway and but for the excellent engine front end, could have turned out a poor steamer. However, it was the front end which made the 12th class. Clearly Gray had no firm ideas of his own as to the design of cylinders and motion, for the ample sized valves, with moderately long travel, working in cylinders with well laid steam and exhaust passages, were absent in the contemporary 13th class. Had these been Gray's ideas, they would have been applied to both classes but evidently the superb front end of the 12th class was the brainchild of some unfortunately anonymous draughtsman at the North British Locomotive Company in Glasgow, to whom the detailing was entrusted.

At the time the 12th class was ordered, there was considerable early interest in poppet valves, of which several types were commercially available. In theory, the poppet valve with its independent actuation of steam and exhaust openings offers improved power and efficiency over normal valves and motion, albeit at some additional cost and complication plus more finicky maintenance requirements. As with so many refinements, poppet valves are subject to the law of diminishing returns - the better the original the smaller the degree of possible gain. In Italy, the Caprotti gear showed substantial improvement over what were excessively poor conventional front ends, but on the other hand, the experimental rotary cam gear used on a Churchward "29" on England's Great Western Railway showed no improvement over the standard front end. Nevertheless, Gray was sufficiently impressed to experiment with poppet valves on ten of his new 12th class, and a pair of 13th class Garratts. The apparatus used was of the Lentz oscillating cam type, actuated by ordinary Walscheart's valve gear. This had several advantages such as staff familiarity, and the ease by which further engines could be converted economically to poppet valves should they prove advantageous. In the event, the opposite prevailed, and the poppet valved locomotives were easily and economically converted to use ordinary piston valves! In fact, the operable museum 12th class, no. 190, is one of those originally fitted with poppet valves.

The 12th class were overall an excellent design, popular with crews, reliable, and light on fuel and maintenance. It is thus no surprise that they were multiplied, and in four years a total of 55 engines were built, the most numerous "straight" engine on RR, exceeded only later by the 15th/15A and 20th/20A Garratts. With so many engines, distribution was widespread, although not universal, as they were never used East of Umtali, on the Beira line, although Salisbury engines probably went as far as Umtali on occasions, this being generally Garratt territory in later years.

The first twenty engines were divided between Salisbury and Bulawayo, the ten piston valve examples were all at Salisbury, whilst Bulawayo had five poppet engines, the others being at Salisbury. Exact dates for conversion from poppet to piston valves seem unavailable, but it was possibly fairly early as the author has found no photographs of the poppet engines in service. Probably they were converted in the early 1930s as from then dispersal to other sheds started to occur. The second batch of twenty-three engines (officially divided into batches two and three) were also divided between Salisbury and Bulawayo other than two allocated to Wankie perhaps for passenger work. The final batch in 1930 were sent mainly to Livingstone, making the class available for main line duties all the way from Salisbury until well into Northern Rhodesia. Thereafter their use spread widely, and in fluctuating quantities, especially after the 15th class Garratts replaced them as principal main line mixed traffic duties, after which they gravitated to secondary main line, branch line, and shunting duties. Right to the end they enjoyed a little main line work, as those allocated to Thompson Junction for shunting still hauled trains from and to Bulawayo when returned to the main shed for periodic attention. In the table overleaf, detailing allocations at five-year intervals, the quantities do not add up to the class total due to now untraceable clerical errors in the official lists, but they give a good broad outline of the engine's distribution over the years. After Northern Rhodesia's independence as Zambia, available records simply state "Zambia".

Museum Locomotives

Four 12th class are preserved, three of which are operable. 190 is the Bulawayo, operable, locomotive, whilst the Zambian railway museum at Livingstone has 181 as a static exhibit with 197 and 204 operable. These operable locomotives in Zambia were overhauled at ZECO, Bulawayo, in 1993, and were totally refurbished with roller bearings on all axles. The bogie and coupled axles with bearings came from scrapped 20th class Garratt 737, while trailing bissel and tender bogie have wagon type package unit bearings.

Static exhibits

254 is preserved at Masvingo, and 256 at Gaberone, Botswana, although it is planned to move this to the new workshops at Palapye.

Fourteen are believed to be still dumped in Zambia, 176/83/84/86, 188/91/93/, 201/06/49/52.55, all at Livingstone except 184 at Kabwe.

Distribution

Mid Year	Salisbury	Gwelo	Bulawayo	Mafeking	Wankie	Livingstone	Kafue	Broken Hill	Nkana
1935	10	—	18	—	3	11	—	12	—
1940	5	—	20	4	3	10	—	11	—
1945	—	—	26	4	2	18	—	8	—
1950	—	—	9	10	3	24	—	6	—
1955	—	—	4	9	1	18	7	10	—
1960	—	—	32	3	6*	5	1	—	—
1965	2	10	11	2	2*	5	—	6	12
						———— Z a m b i a ————			
1970	6	5	12	—	4*	23			
1975	—	6**	3***	—	2*	23			

* Thomson Junction
** All set aside
*** Plus 7 set aside Bulawayo shed and 8 set aside Bulawayo works

NOTE: After the overhaul of ZR 197 an almost unbelievable event occured. On 27 October 1993 it ran it's trial trip on the local freight to Plumtree. By coincidence, this was the same day as the last run of the weekly Johannesburg to Bulawayo passenger train via Botswana. Due to late running, there was no diesel to take the train on from Pumtree, so 197 took over — a Zambian 12th class hauling South African coaches through Zimbabwe! *SA RAIL* for Nov/Dec 1993 details and illustrates this event.

Historical data:

12th Class 4-8-2

Engine Number	North British Number	Date built	Date in Service	Last Used	Disposal
172	23373	1926	8/1926	7/1973	Scrapped 2/1976
173	23374	1926	8/1926	2/1974	Scrapped 7/1980
174	23375	1926	8/1926	7/1976	Scrapped 7/1980
175	23376	1926	8/1926	8/1973	Scrapped 2/1976
176	23377	1926	8/1926	7/1967*	Zambia, derelict Livingstone
177	23378	1926	8/1926	9/1979	Scrapped 7/1980
178	23379	1926	8/1926	7/1967*	Zambia, Scrapped Kabwe 9/1978
179	23380	1926	8/1926	6/1967*	Zambia, Scrapped Kabwe 1/1979
180	23381	1926	8/1926	7/1976	Scrapped 2/1976
181	23382	1926	8/1926	4/1967*	Zambia
182	23383	1926	10/1926	9/1978	Scrapped 7/1980
183	23384	1926	10/1926	6/1967*	Zambia, derelict Livingstone
184	23385	1926	11/1926	6/1967*	Zambia, derelict Livingstone
185	23386	1926	12/1926	2/1975	Scrapped 7/1980
186	23387	1926	10/1926	6/1967*	Zambia, derelict Livingstone
187	23388	1926	10/1926	1/1979	Scrapped 7/1980
188	23389	1926	10/1926	6/1967*	Zambia, derelict Livingstone
189	23390	1926	10/1926	6/1967*	Zambia, scrapped 1980
190	23391	1926	10/1926	12/1980	Museum, Bulawayo, operable
191	23392	1926	12/1926	6/1967*	Zambia, derelict Livingstone

192	23592	1927	10/1927	6/1967*	Scrapped 7/1980
193	23593	1927	10/1927	6/1967*	Zambia, derelict Livingstone
194	23594	1927	10/1927	10/1974	Scrapped 2/1976
195	23724	1928	3/1928	6/1973	Scrapped 2/1976
196	23725	1928	3/1928	6/1967*	Zambia, Scrapped Kabwe 9/1978
197	23726	1928	4/1928	6/1967*	Zambia, museum, operable
198	23727	1928	4/1928		converted to 12A, 9/1943
199	23728	1928	4/1928	6/1967*	Zambia, Scrapped Kabwe 1/1979
200	23729	1928	4/1928	6/1967*	Zambia, Scrapped Kabwe 9/1978
201	23730	1928	4/1928	6/1967*	Zambia, derelict Livingstone
202	23731	1928	4/1928	6/1967*	Zambia
203	23732	1928	5/1928	3/1975	
204	23733	1928	5/1928	6/1967*	Zambia, museum, operable
205	23734	1928	5/1928	2/1980	Scrapped 7/1980
206	23735	1928	5/1928	6/1967*	Zambia, derelict Livingstone
207	23736	1928	5/1928	7/1973	Scrapped 2/1976
208	23737	1928	5/1928	6/1973	Scrapped 8/1981
209	23738	1928	5/1928	7/1973	
210	23739	1928	5/1928	6/1967	Zambia, Scrapped Kabwe 9/1978
211	23740	1928	5/1928	8/1972	Scrapped 2/1976
212	23741	1928	5/1928	8/1972	converted to 12A, 11/1944
213	23772	1928	8/1928	8/1972	converted to 12A, 11/1944
214	23773	1928	8/1928	8/1952	Scrapped 1/1953 (Igusi smash)
247	23996	1930	10/1930	5/1979	Scrapped 7/1980
248	23997	1930	9/1930	5/1973	Scrapped 7/1980
249	23998	1930	9/1930	6/1967*	Zambia, derelict Livingstone
250	23999	1930	9/1930	12/1973	Scrapped 7/1980
251	24000	1930	10/1930	5/1973	Scrapped 7/1980
252	24001	1930	10/1930	6/1967*	Zambia, derelict Livingstone
253	24002	1930	11/1930	4/1975	Scrapped 7/1980
254	24003	1930	11/1930	5/1974	Preserved Masvingo
255	24004	1930	11/1930	7/1967*	Zambia, derelict Livingstone
256	24005	1930	12/1930	8/1973	Preserved, Gaberone, Botswana
257	24006	1930	12/1930	9/1973	Scrapped 7/1980
258	24007	1930	12/1930	11/1974	Scrapped 2/1976

* Date marked thus are the last recorded in service before being taken over by Zambian Railways at independence. Actual last dates used in Zambia have not been ascertained.

A special train from Mbalabala, returning to Bulawayo, is doubleheaded by museum engines 12th class 190 plus 14th class 507.

12th class no 182, with poppet valves of the Lentz oscillating cam design. North British

No 190 as preserved operable today, heading a special train to Mbalabala.

No 190, as converted to normal piston valves. In regular service shunting at Thomson Junction in 1978.

The makings of a doubleheader, 12th class 176 backs onto a 15th class Garratt, probably in Northern Rhodesia.
J. R. LLoyd

12th class 177 at Thomson Junction, 1978.

A rare doubleheader, 12th class 172 leading 14th class Garratt 504 with a coal train near Gwelo, June 1962.
F. C. Butcher

12th class 211 arriving at Victoria Falls with the overnight mixed train from Bulawayo. F. C. Butcher

12th class no 182 standing in Victoria Falls with a passenger train. Transnet Heritage Collection

12th class 174 heading south through Wankie tunnel, the only one on the entire railway. E. Gibbons

12th class 248 in the immaculate condition maintained by its regular driver. J. Dele-Hoffman collection

A special passenger train returning from Balla Balla to Bulawayo behind a pair of 12th class, with no 190 leading.
F. C. Butcher

A heavy limestone train ascending Mulungwane bank doubleheaded by 12th class no 257 and an unidentified 16A class. F. C. Butcher

12th class 190, preserved operable, is a popular engine for enthusiast excursions. Here, wreathed in steam, it is seen at a photo runpast at Umganin.

12th class 190 at Coldridge with a special passenger train to Plumtree.

190 rounds "404 curve" with a mixed train laid on as part of a railway enthusiast Safari.

A grain train from South Africa to Zambia or Zaire is doubleheaded through Marula with 12th class 190 leading a 16A Garratt no 612, 1992.

12th class 252 on a special passenger train composed of SAR stock, at Victoria Falls station. J. Dele-Hoffman collection

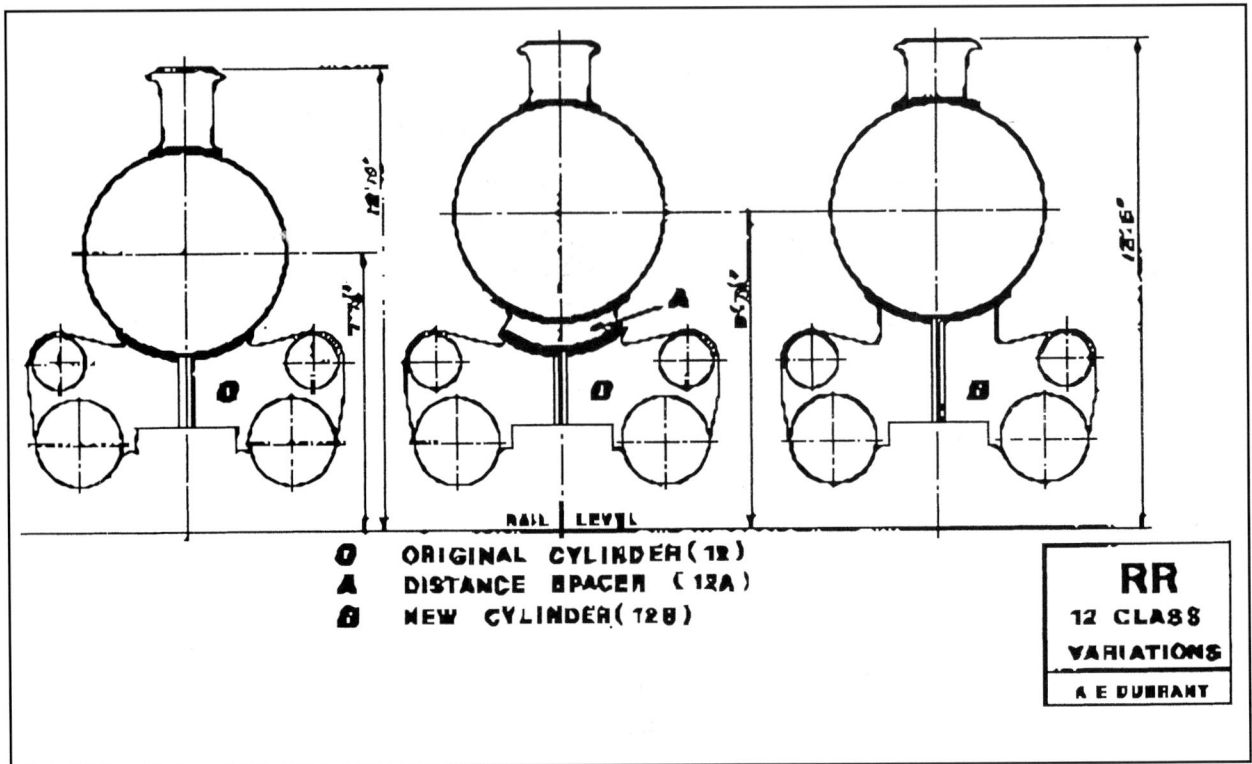

 O   ORIGINAL CYLINDER (12)
A   DISTANCE SPACER (12A)
B   NEW CYLINDER (12B)

RR
12 CLASS
VARIATIONS
A E DURRANT

12A class no 213, with rods removed, prior to railing at time of sale to Moçambique.   F. C. Butcher

12B class, 4-8-2

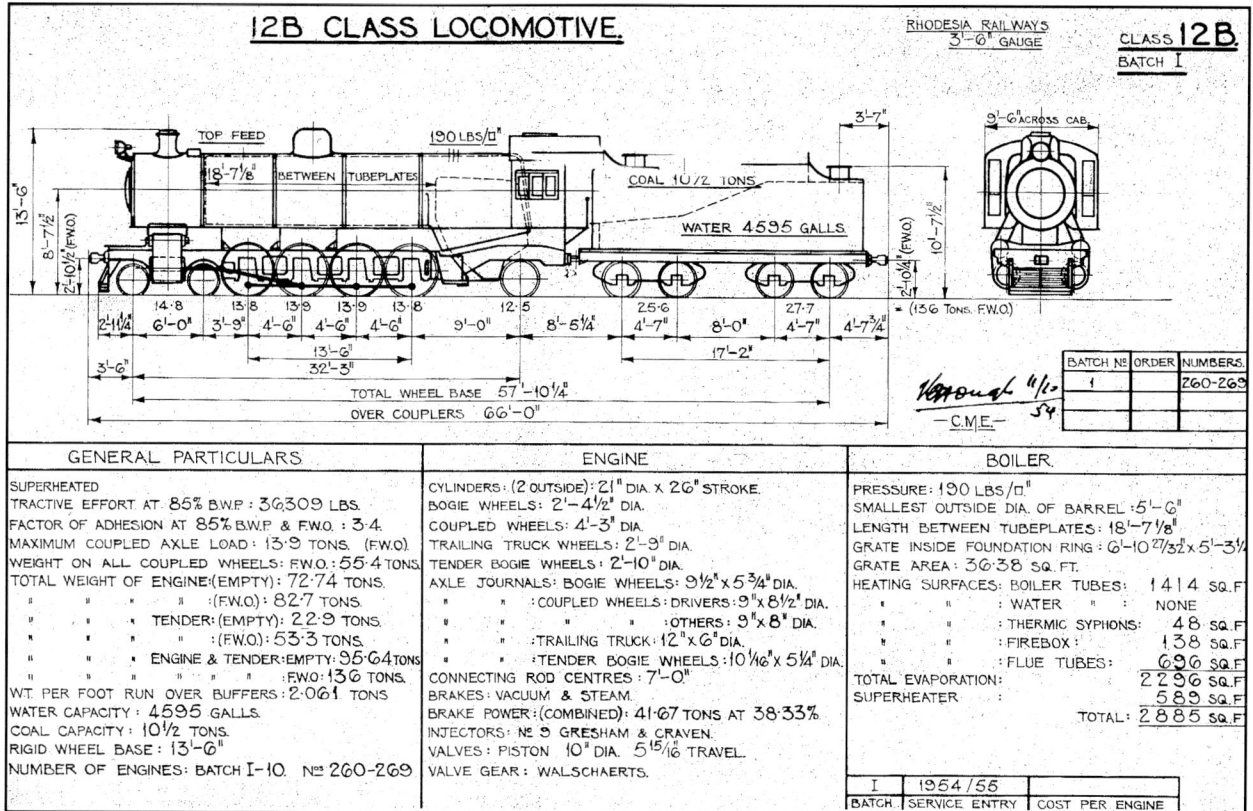

12B CLASS LOCOMOTIVE.

RHODESIA RAILWAYS
3'-6" GAUGE

CLASS **12B**
BATCH I

TOP FEED

190 LBS/□"

18'-7⅛" BETWEEN TUBEPLATES

COAL 10½ TONS

WATER 4595 GALLS.

3'-7"

9'-6" ACROSS CAB

= (136 TONS. F.W.O.)

BATCH №	ORDER NUMBERS
1	260-269

— C.M.E. —

	GENERAL PARTICULARS	ENGINE	BOILER

SUPERHEATED

TRACTIVE EFFORT AT 85% B.W.P. : 36,309 LBS.
FACTOR OF ADHESION AT 85% B.W.P. & F.W.O. : 3·4.
MAXIMUM COUPLED AXLE LOAD : 13·9 TONS. (F.W.O.)
WEIGHT ON ALL COUPLED WHEELS : F.W.O. : 55·4 TONS.
TOTAL WEIGHT OF ENGINE:(EMPTY): 72·74 TONS.
" " " " :(F.W.O.): 82·7 TONS.
" " " TENDER:(EMPTY): 22·9 TONS.
" " " " :(F.W.O.): 53·3 TONS.
" " " ENGINE & TENDER:EMPTY: 95·64 TONS
" " " " :F.W.O.: 136 TONS.
WT. PER FOOT RUN OVER BUFFERS : 2·061 TONS
WATER CAPACITY : 4595 GALLS.
COAL CAPACITY : 10½ TONS.
RIGID WHEEL BASE : 13'-6"
NUMBER OF ENGINES : BATCH I-10. Nº 260-269

CYLINDERS : (2 OUTSIDE) : 21" DIA. x 26" STROKE.
BOGIE WHEELS : 2'-4½" DIA.
COUPLED WHEELS : 4'-3" DIA.
TRAILING TRUCK WHEELS : 2'-9" DIA.
TENDER BOGIE WHEELS : 2'-10" DIA.
AXLE JOURNALS : BOGIE WHEELS : 9½" x 5¾" DIA.
" " : COUPLED WHEELS : DRIVERS : 9" x 8½" DIA.
" " : " : OTHERS : 9" x 8" DIA.
" " : TRAILING TRUCK : 12" x 6" DIA.
" " : TENDER BOGIE WHEELS : 10 1⁄16" x 5¼" DIA.
CONNECTING ROD CENTRES : 7'-0"
BRAKES : VACUUM & STEAM.
BRAKE POWER : (COMBINED) : 41·67 TONS AT 38·33%.
INJECTORS : Nº 9 GRESHAM & CRAVEN.
VALVES : PISTON 10" DIA. 5 15⁄16" TRAVEL.
VALVE GEAR : WALSCHAERTS.

PRESSURE : 190 LBS/□"
SMALLEST OUTSIDE DIA. OF BARREL : 5'-6"
LENGTH BETWEEN TUBEPLATES : 18'-7⅛"
GRATE INSIDE FOUNDATION RING : 6'-10 27⁄32" x 5'-3½"
GRATE AREA : 36·38 SQ. FT.
HEATING SURFACES : BOILER TUBES : 1414 SQ.F
" " : WATER " : NONE
" " : THERMIC SYPHONS : 48 SQ.F
" " : FIREBOX : 138 SQ.F
" " : FLUE TUBES : 696 SQ.F
TOTAL EVAPORATION : 2296 SQ.F
SUPERHEATER : 589 SQ.F
TOTAL : 2885 SQ.F

BATCH	SERVICE ENTRY	COST PER ENGINE
I	1954/55	

13'-6"
8'-7½" (F.W.O.)
2'-10½" (F.W.O.)
14·8 13·8 13·9 13·9 13·8
2'-11¼" 6'-0" 3'-9" 4'-6" 4'-6" 4'-6"
12·5 9'-0"
8'-5¼"
25·6 27·7
4'-7" 8'-0" 4'-7" 4'-7¾"
13'-6"
32'-3½"
TOTAL WHEEL BASE 57'-10¼"
OVER COUPLERS 66'-0"
3'-6"
17'-2"
10'-7⅝" (F.W.O.)
2'-10¼" (F.W.O.)

12B class no 260 PRECURSOR probably at Bulawayo. J. Dele-Hoffman collection

The 12B class originated with ten sets of 12th class frames, imported from North British to rebuild some 12th class whose frames were showing signs of fatigue, with cracks appearing. However, these faults were rectified without using the new frames, and as sufficient 11th/11A boilers were available (which might otherwise have gone to rebuilding further 12th class to 12A) it was decided to erect ten new locomotives in the Bulawayo workshops, using these available components. Other items such as cylinders and wheels were cast locally, and these became the first and only steam locomotives built in Rhodesia, although main line electric and shunting diesels for industrial use were later built in Zimbabwe. Instead of perpetuating the 12A arrangement using 12th class cylinders plus a spacer casting, new cylinders were cast with extended smokebox saddles, as shown in the accompanying sketch, this being the essential difference between the 12A and 12B classes.

The first 12B was erected almost entirely by apprentices, as a useful exercise, and was appropriately named PRECURSOR, presumably by somebody who had been trained at Crewe! The first engine was delivered immediately to Livingstone when new, and was soon followed by the remainder, which stayed there until 1957. Arrival of the 20th/20A Garratts made them redundant, and they found new homes further north especially at Ndola and Nkana. From late 1958 most were at Kafue until that shed closed late 1961, after which they were staged at Bulawayo pending sale to the CFM.

In Moçambique, all went straight to Lourenço Marques via Malvernia and after opening of the Swaziland Railway in 1964 they shared the heavy work on the upper section with ex-RR 11A and 12A classes from Sidvokodvo to the mine at Ka Dake, usually doubleheading in various combinations. After replacement by heavy 700 class CFM 4-8-2 about a decade later, the 11A went north to the Nampula division but the 12B remained at Sidvokodvo for shunting and working trains on the Matsapha industrial branch until CFM motive power collapsed and was replaced by SAR class 14R 4-8-2. The 12Bs then returned to what was then Maputo, and rotted away until scrapped in the 1980s.

Historical data:

12B Class 4-8-2

Engine Number	Date built	Last used	Sold to CFM	CFM Number
260	8/1954	12/1961	12/1961	470
261	9/1954	12/1961	12/1961	471
262	10/1954	12/1961	12/1961	472
263	10/1954	12/1961	12/1961	473
264	11/1954	12/1961	12/1961	474
265	11/1954	12/1961	12/1961	475
266	11/1954	12/1961	12/1961	476
267	12/1954	12/1961	12/1961	477
268	12/1955	12/1961	12/1961	478
269	1/1955	12/1961	12/1961	479

Note that CFM locomotives were usually numbered from a "1", thus these engines might have become 471-80, but presumably 470-79 was chosen to make renumbering more easy!

12B class 260 PRECURSOR hauling 7 down passenger train near Kafue. F. C. Butcher

13th class, 2-6-2 + 2-6-2 Garratt

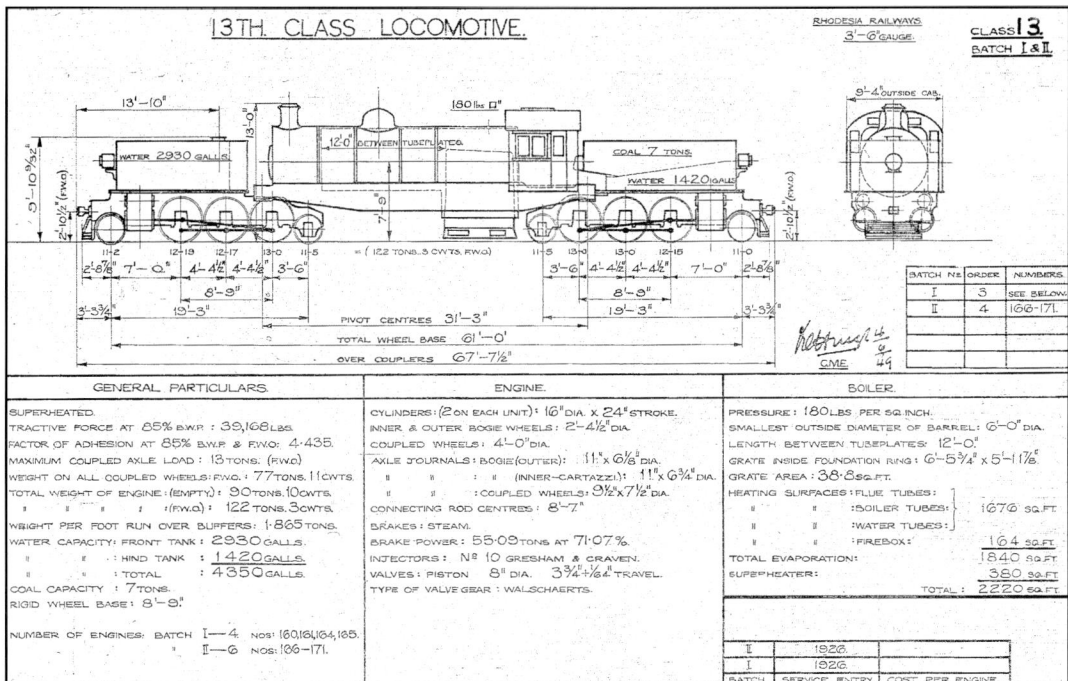

13TH. CLASS LOCOMOTIVE.

RHODESIA RAILWAYS 3'-6" GAUGE.

CLASS 13. BATCH I & II.

WATER 2930 GALLS.

12'-0" BETWEEN TUBEPLATES.

180 lbs ☐"

COAL 7 TONS.

WATER 1420 GALS.

9'-4" OUTSIDE CAB.

13'-10"

13'-0"

9'-10½" (F.W.O)

2'-10½" (F.W.O)

7'-9"

(122 TONS..3 CWTS. F.W.O)

2'-10½" (F.W.O)

1½2   12-13   12-17   13-0   11-5

2'-8⅜" 7'-0." 4'-4½" 4'-4½" 3'-6"

8'-9"

3'-3¾"

19'-3"

11-5   13-0   13-0   12-15   11-0

3'-6" 4'-4½" 4'-4½" 7'-0" 2'-8⅜"

8'-9"

19'-3"

3'-3¾"

PIVOT CENTRES 31'-3"

TOTAL WHEEL BASE 61'-0'

OVER COUPLERS 67'-7½"

CME 4/9/49

BATCH Nº	ORDER	NUMBERS
I	3	SEE BELOW.
II	4	166-171.

GENERAL PARTICULARS.

SUPERHEATED.

TRACTIVE FORCE AT 85% B.W.P. : 39,168 LBS.

FACTOR OF ADHESION AT 85% B.W.P. & F.W.O. : 4·435.

MAXIMUM COUPLED AXLE LOAD : 13 TONS. (F.W.O.)

WEIGHT ON ALL COUPLED WHEELS: F.W.O. : 77 TONS. 11 CWTS.

TOTAL WEIGHT OF ENGINE: (EMPTY.) : 90 TONS. 10 CWTS.

"   "   "   : (F.W.O.) : 122 TONS. 3 CWTS.

WEIGHT PER FOOT RUN OVER BUFFERS: 1·865 TONS.

WATER CAPACITY: FRONT TANK : 2930 GALLS.

"   "   : HIND TANK : 1420 GALLS.

"   "   : TOTAL : 4350 GALLS.

COAL CAPACITY : 7 TONS.

RIGID WHEEL BASE : 8'-9."

NUMBER OF ENGINES: BATCH I—4. NOS: 160,164,164, 165.

"   "   : II—6 NOS: 166-171.

ENGINE.

CYLINDERS: (2 ON EACH UNIT) : 16" DIA. X 24" STROKE.

INNER & OUTER BOGIE WHEELS: 2'-4½" DIA.

COUPLED WHEELS : 4'-0" DIA.

AXLE JOURNALS: BOGIE (OUTER) : 11" x 6⅛" DIA.

"   "   (INNER—CARTAZZI) : 11" x 6¾" DIA.

"   "   : COUPLED WHEELS : 9½" x 7½" DIA.

CONNECTING ROD CENTRES : 8'-7"

BRAKES : STEAM.

BRAKE POWER: 55·09 TONS AT 71·07 %.

INJECTORS : Nº 10 GRESHAM & CRAVEN.

VALVES : PISTON 8" DIA. 3¾"+1/32" TRAVEL.

TYPE OF VALVE GEAR : WALSCHAERTS.

BOILER.

PRESSURE : 180 LBS PER SQ. INCH.

SMALLEST OUTSIDE DIAMETER OF BARREL : 6'-0" DIA.

LENGTH BETWEEN TUBEPLATES : 12'-0.

GRATE INSIDE FOUNDATION RING : 6'-5¾" x 5'-11⅞."

GRATE AREA : 38·8 SQ.FT.

HEATING SURFACES: FLUE TUBES : }

"   "   : BOILER TUBES : } 1676 SQ.FT

"   "   : WATER TUBES : }

"   "   : FIREBOX : 164 SQ.FT

TOTAL EVAPORATION: 1840 SQ.FT

SUPERHEATER: 380 SQ.FT

TOTAL : 2220 SQ.FT

II	1926.	
I	1926.	
BATCH	SERVICE ENTRY.	COST PER ENGINE

Builder's photo of 13th class Garratt no 166. Beyer Peacock

By the early 1920s, of the various ports serving the lower East coast of Africa, the Beira and Mashonaland Railway was the least well off with motive power. Lower down, the Lourenço Marques railway, despite an easier route inland, had a pair of Mallets and fleet of 2-10-2 engines. The Natal Government Railways, with the heaviest route, was served by large numbers of heavy 4-8-0 and 4-10-2T engines, to which had been added several 2-6-6-0 compound Mallets and the first main line Garratt, whilst further Mallets were to be found elsewhere in South Africa.

It is surprising that Mallets had not been tried on the B & MR, and no doubt Alco's sales engineers, following their successes in Natal and elsewhere had visited Umtali to suggest this type for the severe line from Beira inland, but the Kitson-Meyer locomotives seem to have induced an awful fear of articulated motive power into the B & MR's executive, perhaps particularly to "Togo" Hosgood, the CME.

The 13th class Garratts have always been credited to Gray, the CME ruling at the time of their introduction, and he will certainly have been responsible for their entry into service. His earlier service as Mechanical Engineer, Pietermaritzburg, Natal will certainly have made him acutely aware of the motive power requirements over heavy gradients, plus the foibles inherent in the compound Mallet type of whose maintenance he will have been directly responsible. He will also have had some short experience and knowledge of the initial heavy Garratt, class GA, used in his area of the railway.

However, preliminary moves towards trying out the Garratt type were initiated before even Gray took office in Rhodesia. In a letter dated 11 October 1923, from G.F. Birney, General Manager of The Beira and Mashonaland and Rhodesia Railways, to the General Manager South African Railways, Johannesburg, cautious interest is expressed.

Protocol in those days demanded that all official correspondence from one railway to another passed via their respective general managers, and this was no exception. Referenced GM.6634, the letter read:

"Dear Sir,

We have under consideration the placing of a trial order for one or more locomotives of the Garratt type. Our experience with Articulated Locomotives has not been altogether satisfactory, but I understand that the Garratts which you have in service on your lines have given great satisfaction and have proved themselves superior to engines of the Mallet type.

I understand that on the 3'-6" gauge you have two types of Garratt now in service; one with an axle load of 7 1/2 tons and a tractive effort of 18290 lbs. (tender full) and the other with an axle load of something under 18 tons and a tractive effort of 47385 lbs. In addition I understand that there is now under order for the New Cape Central Railway a third type with an axle load of 10 1/2 tons and a tractive effort of 31250 lbs.

The designers and makers of these engines claim for them great advantages of steadiness in running, flexibility round curves, ample steaming and simplicity in design compared to other articulated engines.

The engine which we have in view would be one with a maximum axle load of 12 1/2 to 13 tons designed for running on steep gradients and on five chain curves.

Perhaps you could see your way to let me have your views as to the performance of these Garratt engines. Any information which you are able to give me would be very much appreciated.

Yours faithfully

G. F. Birney
GENERAL MANAGER"

The author has been unable to trace the reply to the above letter, but it must have been very positive for in the event the Rhodesia Railways placed an order for twelve engines, the largest single Garratt order to date. Doubtless Gray's close contacts with former colleagues in Natal will have made matters go especially smoothly, and his Garratt knowledge, however small, may have assisted in finalising his appointment as CME.

The letters also infers, however vaguely, to the possible consideration of Mallets for the Beira line, and by then these had already been built by North British in Glasgow, including even a pioneer simple expansion Mallet for South Africa, so Bulawayo will have been well aware of the type's possibilities.

The 13th class were designed and built concurrently with South Africa's class GD, with which they shared many features. Both were similar in size, and of the same wheel arrangement. The SAR locos were just ahead in Beyer Peacock's order book, with works numbers 6263-66, with the 13th class following hard on with numbers 6269-80, whilst 6281-90 were a further series of GDs. It appears that Gray had little to do with the design, for although Rhodesia had been a bar frame railway since the 8th class, the 13th class reverted to plate frames, which proved a mistake. Evidently Peacock's had simply been given a basic specification and left to get on with the detail design, following closely that of earlier SAR Garratts. Similarly, Gorton Foundry's drawing office were, like the Midland Railway in Derby, decidedly unenterprising in cylinder and valve design, and the 13th class had cylinders with tortuous Z-shaped ports served by piston valves having heads close together giving a very small steam chest volume. Maximum valve travel was quoted rather pedantically as "3 3/4" + 1/64", a far cry from the excellent cylinder and valve design of the contemporary 12th class. Nevertheless, despite their design deficiencies, the 13th class proved the worth of the Garratt to the Rhodesia authorities, and permanently cured their anti-articulated phobia! The last two engines of the order were included in the 12th class experiment with poppet valves, and were similarly fitted with Lentz oscillating cam valves actuated by Walscheart's valve gear. This probably showed up better against the poor conventional valve arrangements than was the case on the 12th class, but nevertheless it is believed that both locomotives reverted to piston valves in due course, although no definite reference to this conversion has been discovered, and no photographs of locos 170-71 with piston valves have been unearthed. The latest diagrams make no reference to poppet valves, so conversion at some times seems established. Allocation lists show both 170 and 171 in Umtali shops together from January to April 1929, an this was probably when they were converted from poppet valves, arrival of the 14th class enabling them to be released from duty.

From the time they were new, the 13th class were allocated to Umtali, where with typical incongruity, they worked mainly in another country, to wit Moçambique, operating the hard part of the line from Umtali to Vila Machado and back. As the 14th class were commissioned to replace them, they moved back to Salisbury which became their main home until withdrawal, being used on branch line trains and heavy shunting. During the depression years they were stabled, starting with 161/66 in May 1933, with the whole class stabled at both Umtali and Salisbury for much of 1934 and 1935. All were back in use at Salisbury by September 1936. From time to time one or two were allocated to Gwelo and Bulawayo, but nothing seems known about what they did at these depots. Various engines were hired, and eventually two sold, to Nkana copper mine, the only time they ventured north of Bulawayo, and one ended its life in spectacular manner when it collided with a lorry loaded with explosives, destroying both.

Historical data:

13th Class, 2-6-2 + 2-6-2 Garratt

Engine Number	Beyer Peacock	Date in Service	Last used	Disposal
160	6269	3/1926	3/1958	Scrapped 6/1958
161	6270	3/1926	7/1957	Scrapped 8/1957
162	6271	3/1926	10/1939	Sold to Rhokana Corporation, no 4
163	6272	3/1926	10/1939	Sold to Rhokana Corporation, no 5 Destroyed in explosive smash
164	6273	5/1926	7/1958	Scrapped 7/1958
165	6274	5/1926	7/1957	Scrapped 8/1957
166	6275	5/1926	4/1958	Scrapped 7/1958
167	6276	5/1926	3/1957	Scrapped 4/1957
168	6277	5/1926	10/1957	Scrapped 5/1958
169	6278	5/1926	11/1957	Scrapped 5/1958
170	6279	5/1926	7/1957	Scrapped 8/1957
171	6280	5/1926	5/1957	Scrapped 8/1957

Note that these locomotives were scrapped soon after withdrawal from service, unlike so many locomotives which lingered for long periods awaiting cutting up. This probably reflected both their unpopularity plus the practice of Umtali works.

As a brief postscript to these pioneer Garratts, the two Mallets built for the Lourenço Marques railway were transferred to the Beira line after purchase from Rhodesia, and an old copy of the "Rhodesia Railways Circle Newsletter" refers to a sighting of one of these Mallets at Umtali - long after the 13th class had disappeared from that

Close up of poppet valve motion, 13th class Garratt.
Beyer Peacock
Quarterly Review

13th class Garratt no 171 as built with oscillating cam poppet valve gear. Beyer Peacock Quarterly Review

13th class no 169. RR

13th class no 168. RR

13th class no 166, on shunt at Umtali. F. C. Butcher

Poppet valved 13th class Garratt no. 171 heads a passenger train at Umtali. Beyer Peacock Catalogue.

Rhodesian Railways 13th class Garratt evidently on a test train, judging by the staff car and personnel. Beyer Peacock Quarterly Review

After this they stayed in Northern Rhodesia, the two survivors going to Livingstone late 1953, and they alternated between there and Broken Hill for most of their lives, other than a period spent at Kafue from mid 1958 to late 1961.

Following their sale to CFM, the remaining two were, as far as is known, always stationed at Lourenco Marques from whence they were often sub-shedded at Sidvokodvo in Swaziland, for working the SR.

Historical data:

12A Class 4-8-2

Engine Number	Date Rebuilt	Last used	Disposal
198	9/1943	8/1952	Scrapped 1/1953, after Igusi crash
212	11/1944	7/1963	Sold to CFM 8/1964. number 491
213	11/1964	8/1963	Sold to CFM 8/1964. number 492

12th class no 212 heading a main line passenger train at an unknown location. This engine was later rebuilt to class 12A.
Author's collection

12A class no 212.
J. R. Lloyd

92

12A class, 4-8-2

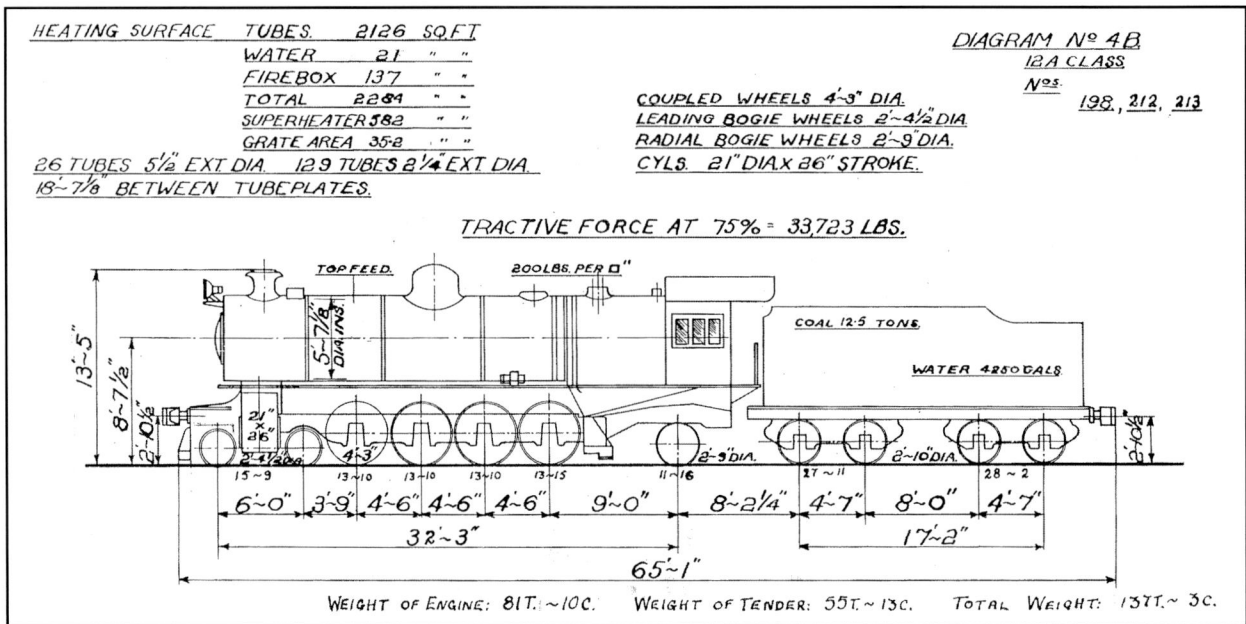

HEATING SURFACE TUBES.   2126 SQ.FT
WATER   21   "   "
FIREBOX 137   "   "
TOTAL   2284   "   "
SUPERHEATER 582   "   "
GRATE AREA 35.2 "   "
26 TUBES 5½ EXT DIA.   129 TUBES 2¼ EXT DIA.
18~7⅞ BETWEEN TUBEPLATES.

DIAGRAM N° 4B.
12A CLASS
N°s.   198, 212, 213

COUPLED WHEELS 4'~3" DIA.
LEADING BOGIE WHEELS 2'~4½ DIA.
RADIAL BOGIE WHEELS 2'~9"DIA.
CYLS. 21"DIA.x 26" STROKE.

TRACTIVE FORCE AT 75% = 33,723 LBS.

TOP FEED.   200 LBS. PER ☐"

COAL 12·5 TONS.
WATER 4250 GALS

WEIGHT OF ENGINE: 81T.~10C.   WEIGHT OF TENDER: 55T.~13C.   TOTAL WEIGHT: 137T.~3C.

12A class no 198, with experimental large diameter chimney. J. R. Lloyd

The 12A class were rebuilds of standard 12th class, using the larger diameter boilers from the 11th/11A classes. In order to accommodate these boilers, a cast distance piece was mounted on the cylinder castings, forming a higher saddle upon which was mounted the boiler. A sketch of this arrangement will be found on page 93. As with the 9B class, which had a similar arrangement, the boiler was pitched one foot higher, these being the first Rhodesian locomotives whose chimney tops were almost to the full height of the increased loading gauge. Only three locomotives were rebuilt in this manner, and they had fairly short lives in Rhodesia, one being written off after a head on smash with an unrebuilt sister at Igusi, whilst the other two were sold to Moçambique.

All three engines were originally allocated to Bulawayo, but in May 1950 they went to Wankie, they by early 1951 they were all at Broken Hill.

91

14th class, 2-6-2 + 2-6-2 Garratt

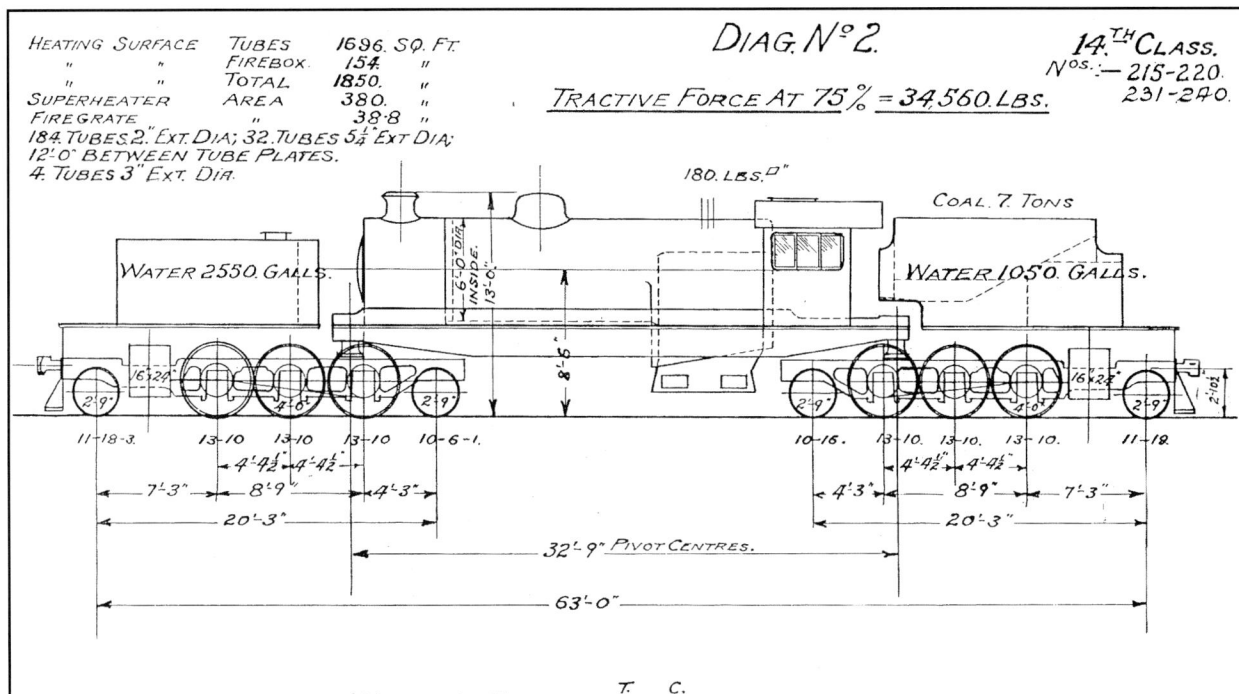

HEATING SURFACE TUBES 1696. SQ. FT.
" " FIREBOX 154 "
" " TOTAL 1850 "
SUPERHEATER AREA 380 "
FIRE GRATE " 38·8 "
184. TUBES 2" EXT. DIA; 32. TUBES 5¼ EXT DIA;
12'-0" BETWEEN TUBE PLATES.
4. TUBES 3" EXT. DIA.

DIAG. N°2.

TRACTIVE FORCE AT 75% = 34.560. LBS.

14.TH CLASS.
NOS.:— 215-220.
231-240.

180. LBS.□"

COAL. 7 TONS

WATER 2550. GALLS.

WATER 1050. GALLS.

32'-9" PIVOT CENTRES.

63'-0"

14th class Garratt no 220, later CFM no 906. RR

Whilst the 13th class successfully demonstrated the Garratt as being eminently suitable for the Beira line, some of its detailing proved inadequate for the severe conditions prevailing, and the 14th class although of similar basic dimensions and power output was far more sturdy and flexible. In place of plate frames with Cartazzi radial axleboxes for the inner wheels, the 14th class had bar frames with proper pony trucks each end, giving better strength and flexibility. Cylinder design was improved, with more direct steam ports, although the absurdly short valve travel was retained, and the boiler was pitched nine inches higher, giving better ashpan conditions whilst the firegrate was sloping instead of straight. Visually, the front tanks had rounded

top edges and the bunker was raised to give a better self trimming effect. Driving and leading pony truck bearings were increased in size, and the whole engine weighed two tons more, despite reduced water capacity.

When new the 14th class went straight to the Beira line after erection at Umtali, totally replacing the 13th class which then went to Salisbury for lighter duties. There were more than sufficient to work the Beira line, and the last two of the second batch, 239/40 went new to Salisbury where they were joined there later by 237/38. By 1938 traffic had evidently increased such that all were at Umtali, but the introduction of the second batch of 16th class caused a redisposition of motive power and five were at Bulawayo by end

1941, starting that shed's long association with the 14th class. Newer Garratts post war further changed allocations such that by early October 1949 215-32 were at Umtali, the engines which would eventually be sold to Moçambique. The remainder were distributed four each to Salisbury and Bulawayo. During October 1949, the Beira line was sold to Moçambique government, and all locomotives stationed at Umtali were transferred with it to what became designated CFM Estado, although why one line should be noted as *Estado* (State) on an otherwise national railway system remains obscure - probably some pedantic Portuguese accountant was trying to complicate accounting procedures to provide jobs for his colleagues.

In June 1951 the 14ths remaining in Rhodesia were renumbered 500-07. By April 1954, Salisbury was down to one 14th, three were on hire to Moçambique, and the rest at Bulawayo. Six months later Gwelo received 500/01, just returned from Moçambique, starting a long association of this class with that depot, ending only late 1962 when 14As arrived as replacements. For most of this period Gwelo had six of the eight 14th class, the other two being at either Salisbury or Bulawayo, but they remained in demand for heavy shunting, and a couple went back to Salisbury late 1965, which depot had six 14th by April 1968. In April 1973 there were two at Salisbury, three at Bulawayo, and again three on loan to Moçambique, where they joined their former sisters at the new shed at Gondola, built

after 1949 to replace Umtali as the main Garratt depot for the mountain sections. After their return, the whole class went to Bulawayo and with the dieselisation programme most were set aside and looked due for early scrapping. However, sanctions and the oil crisis came to their rescue and whilst Rhodesia's and later Zimbabwe's newer Garratts were being fully refurbished for further use, most of the 14th class were returned to shunting service at Bulawayo, lasting into the mid 1980s, by which time they were half a century old. Two survived until the 1990s, 505 which was used as stationary boiler at Bulawayo shed, and 507, last of class, which remains steamable as a museum engine and is in annual demand for enthusiast specials. In their long regular service, the 14th class never worked north or south of Bulawayo (other than on the West Nicholson branch) but in 1993 new ground was broken when 507 ran to Plumtree and back, doubleheaded with a 14A, both classes appearing on the pickup freight specially hauled by these engines for a large party of visiting overseas steam enthusiasts, the first visit of either class to the South line. Then in 1994, 507 again on a special for overseas enthusiasts, ran out of water near Cement, and was rescued by the 14A and 16A combination waiting at Heany to take the train on, thereby creating a triple-headed Garratt train to the delight of the participating enthusiasts, who quickly arranged a couple of photographic runpasts to record the event! *(See p. 118)*

Historical data:

14th Class, 2-6-2 + 2-6-2 Garratt

First Number	Second Number	Beyer Peacock	Date Built	Date in Service	Last Used	Disposal
215	(CFM) 901	6510	1929	4/1929	Sold to CFM 10/1949	Dere Gondola 1993
216	(CFM) 902	6511	1929	4/1929	Sold to CFM 10/1949	Scrapped
217	(CFM) 903	6512	1929	4/1929	Sold to CFM 10/1949	Scrapped
218	(CFM) 904	6513	1929	4/1929	Sold to CFM 10/1949	Scrapped
219	(CFM) 905	6514	1929	4/1929	Sold to CFM 10/1949	Scrapped
220	(CFM) 906	6515	1929	4/1929	Sold to CFM 10/1949	Scrapped
231	(CFM) 907	6616	1930	3/1930	Sold to CFM 10/1949	Scrapped
232	(CFM) 908	6617	1930	3/1930	Sold to CFM 10/1949	Scrapped
233	500	6618	1930	3/1930	4/1975	Preserved Kadoma
234	501	6619	1930	3/1930	1/1938	Derelict Bulawayo, '96
235	502	6620	1930	3/1930	12/1974	Scrapped 7/1980
236	503	6621	1930	3/1930	5/1973	Scrapped circa 1991
237	504	6622	1930	3/1930	11/1973	Scrapped 7/1980
238	505	6623	1930	3/1930	7/1983	Dumped, workshops
239	506	6624	1930	3/1930	10/1982	Cut up circa 4/1995
240	507	6625	1930	3/1930	4/1985	Preserved operable

14th class Garratt no 217, later CFM 903.
J. Dele-Hoffman collection

14th class Garratt no 237, at Bulawayo. Later renumbered 504. J.R. Lloyd

14th class Garratt no 238, ahead of a sister engine and an 18th class, probably at Umtali. Loco later 505.
W. H. C. Kelland

14th class Garratt no 239, later no 506.
W. H. C. Kelland

14th class no 500 at Shabani on the mixed train, late 1956.
F. C. Butcher

14th class no 500 as now preserved at Kadoma.

14th class 501 shunting behind Bulawayo on a rainy 1980 day.

14th class 501 on the passenger coach shunt at Bulawayo, in Zimbabwe days.

14th class 502 shunting at Salisbury in 1968.

14th class 505 shunting the goods yard in Bulawayo, 1970.

14th class 507 heads round the back sidings at Bulawayo, passing ZECO's works where a 15th class and a boiler are seen under the unfinished shop.

Business at Bulawayo. 14th class Garratt 507 eases on to empty stock whilst 20th class 743 backs onto a train of coal empties bound for Thomson Junction. In the background, an SAR class 14R is engaged on empty stock shunting, July 1982

Class 14A, 2-6-2 + 2-6-2 Garratt

14A. CLASS LOCOMOTIVE

RHODESIA RAILWAYS. 3'-6" GAUGE. CLASS 14A BATCH I.

BATCH Nº	ORDER	NUMBERS
1	112	508 - 525

GENERAL PARTICULARS.

SUPERHEATED.
TRACTIVE FORCE AT 85% B.W.P. : 39,168 LB.
FACTOR OF ADHESION AT 85% B.W.P. & F.W.O. : 4·639.
MAXIMUM COUPLED AXLE LOAD. F.W.O. : 13·57 TONS.
WEIGHT ON ALL COUPLED WHEELS. F.W.O. : 81·13 TONS.
TOTAL WEIGHT OF ENGINE : (EMPTY) : 102 TONS.
"   "   "   " : (F.W.O.) : 131·67 TONS.
WEIGHT PER FOOT RUN OVER BUFFERS : 1·817 TONS.
WATER CAPACITY : FRONT TANK : 2,460 GALLS.
"   "   " : HIND TANK : 1,140 GALLS.
"   "   " : TOTAL : 3,600 GALLS.
COAL CAPACITY : 7 TONS.
RIGID WHEEL BASE : 8'-9".
NUMBER OF ENGINES : BATCH 1-18. Nº 508-525.

ENGINE.

CYLINDERS : (2 ON EACH UNIT) : 16" DIA. x 24" STROKE.
BOGIE WHEELS : 2'-9" DIA.
COUPLED WHEELS : 4'-0" DIA.
ROLLER BEARINGS : BOGIE WHEELS & ECCENTRIC RODS.
AXLE JOURNALS : BOGIE WHEELS : 10⅝" x 6¼" DIA.
"   "   " : COUPLED WHEELS : 9½" x 8" DIA.
CONNECTING ROD CENTRES : 8'-3".
BRAKES : STEAM & VACUUM.
BRAKE POWER : 33·22 TONS AT 40·95 %.
INJECTORS : GRESHAM & CRAVEN Nº 10.
VALVES : PISTON 8" DIA. TRAVEL : 5 7/16".
TYPE OF VALVE GEAR : WALSCHAERTS.
PIVOT CENTRE : SELF-ADJUSTING.

BOILER.

PRESSURE : 180 LB : PER SQ. INCH.
SMALLEST OUTSIDE DIAMETER OF BARREL : 6'-0"
LENGTH BETWEEN TUBEPLATES : 12'-0⅝".
GRATE INSIDE FOUNDATION RING : 6'-5⅞" x 5'-1¾".
GRATE AREA : 38·6 SQ. FT.
HEATING SURFACES : FLUE TUBES :
"   "   " BOILER TUBES : } 1667 SQ.FT
"   "   " BRICK ARCH TUBES :
"   "   " FIRE BOX : } 174 SQ.FT
TOTAL EVAPORATION : 1841 SQ.F
SUPERHEATER : 374 SQ.F
TOTAL : 2215 SQ.F

BATCH Nº	SERVICE ENTRY.	COST PER ENGINE.
	1953/4	£41,010

Builder's photograph of 14A no 512 Beyer Peacock

The 14A was the last and best of Rhodesia's small Garratts, although the term "small" must be seen in the perspective of the other and successively larger machines. In terms of tractive effort, adhesion, and boiler capacity the 13th, 14th and 14A Garratts were the equivalent of British Railways' largest freight engines, the class 9F 2-10-0! The 14A was a thoroughly redesigned version of the 14th class, retaining the bar frames but including thoroughly modern cylinder design with straight ports and piston valve travel increased to 5 7/16", nearly half as much again as the older classes. As a result, they were very free-running engines, and are able to bowl along at 55-60 mph when given the opportunity. As built, roller bearings were fitted to the pony truck axles plus the valve gear return cranks, but during their refurbishment, driving and coupled axles were fitted with spherical roller bearings housed in cannon boxes with manganese steel liners, making them thoroughly modern units of motive power. The refurbishment specification, dated January 1978, included provision of new front tanks approximately 300 mm higher than the originals, whilst the bunker was also extended to increase both coal and water capacities. No new nor modified diagrams were prepared to officially record these new capacities, nor the increased locomotive axle and total weights resulting therefrom, and these can only be estimated. In the event, not all refurbished locomotives received new tanks and bunkers, units in good condition being retained for further service, such that certain locomotives left ZECO's shops in hybrid condition. A survey carried out by the author in 1988, and checked by the late F.C. Butcher, showed the following variations:

Old tank and bunker: 519. Also retained RR numberplates
Old tank, new bunker: 510
New tank, old bunker: 508/09/13/14/16/17/18
New tank, new bunker: 511/12/15/20/21/22/23/24/25

Several chimney variations were also noted at the time, 520 retained the original flared chimney, whilst 508/22 had short, 16A style chimneys. 520 was also the only known engine, in the short transitional period when the country was known as "Zimbabwe-Rhodesia", to sport numberplates carrying the inscription "ZRR", later replaced by the new NRZ standard number plates.

The operating history of the 14A class is quite simple, all having, like the 13th and 14th classes, having been confined to routes south of the Zambezi. When new 508-15 were allocated to Salisbury, and 516-25 at Bulawayo which, with minor variations continued for nearly ten years. By April 1962 Gwelo had acquired three from Salisbury, and from early 1963 Gwelo had half a dozen of the class until steam operation finished at this Midlands junction. Salisbury lost its last three in September 1963, after which the allocation was typically Gwelo six and Bulawayo twelve. Both depots used them for branch line work, with Gwelo's engines kept in immaculate condition, especially 508 and 525 usually to be found on the Fort Victoria mixed trains, with others on the Shabani and Selukwe lines. The Bulawayo allocation was mostly used on the West Nicholson branch, with its thrice weekly mixed train, plus several daily freights to and from Collen Bawn and Balla Balla. From December 1964 to June 1967, between one and three engines were allocated to Thomson Junction, where they were presumably used for shunting. Following refurbishment the class was based entirely at Bulawayo and used mainly for shunting with occasional trips down the West Nicholson branch. All were withdrawn unexpectedly in 1993 after a sudden drop in traffic, some immediately after overhaul. However, six have been retained for the railway museum, in working order, and others have been sold for continuing use, such that their lives are far from being over. Each year at least two are taken out of the museum for steam enthusiast specials, often being retained in service for shunting for longer than needed, as they are better shunting engines than the 15/A classes retained for that duty!

Additional weight

As built, the 14A class were designed to a 13 1/2 Ton axle load, the actual diagram weights being just over this, averaging 13.53T. After refurbishment, depending on which combination of tanks and bunkers were fitted, engines were about 6 to 7 tons heavier, with approximately 14 1/2 Ton axle load. The large front tanks held an extra 630 gallons (2.8 Tons, say 3 tons extra with plating), and rear bunkers held 396 gallons more (1.76 tons) plus 0.8 tons extra coal, again about 3 Tons with plating. In addition, there was the extra weight of the roller bearing cannon boxes, to make up the estimated total above. No diagram was issued to cover these modifications.

512 in normal service, on a freight train from Colleen Bawn, passing Eagle Vulture siding in 1968.

Historical data:

14A Class, 2-6-2 + 2-6-2 Garratt

Engine Number	Beyer Peacock No	Date Built	Date in Service	Date Refurbished	Last Used	Disposal
508	7581	1953	11/1953	9/1980	5/1993	Sold to Transnet, 1995
509	7582	1953	11/1953	8/1982	5/1993	Sold to Unicem, 1995
510	7583	1953	12/1953	8/1980	6/1993	Museum
511	7584	1953	1/1954	11/1979	5/1993	Sold to to Selebi-Phikwe, 1995 No L0811, in Service 1996
512	7585	1953	1/1954	7/1980	6/1993	Sold to Miss Bell, Harare, 1995
513	7586	1953	12/1953	5/1981	5/1992	Scrapped, 1/1993
514	7587	1953	1/1954	9/1979	1/1993	Museum
515	7588	1953	1/1954	12/1979	7/1993	Museum
516	7589	1953	2/1954	9/1982	5/1993	Sold to Miss Bell, Harare, 1995
517	7590	1953	2/1954	7/1980	5/1993	Museum
518	7591	1953	2/1954	4/1981	5/1993	Mothballed
519	7592	1953	2/1954	10/1979	6/1993	Museum
520	7599	1953	2/1954	1/1980	6/1993	Sold to to Selebi-Phikwe, 1995, No L0809
521	7600	1954	3/1954	10/1980	5/1993	Mothballed
522	7601	1954	3/1954	3/1980	6/1993	Mothballed
523	7602	1954	3/1954	5/1980	5/1993	Sold to to Selebi-Phikwe, 1995, No L0810
524	7603	1954	3/1954	8/1981	7/1993	Steam cleaning and shed pilot, Bulawayo
525	7604	1954	3/1954	6/1980	7/1993	Museum

508, sold to Transet, is for use on the George - Knysna line. Delivered via Beit Bridge 1/1997.
512 & 516, sold to Miss Bell, are for proposed tourist trains between Victoria Falls and Hwange Game reserve, no further details available.

14A 522 in 1980, ex works from ZECO, with enlarged tank and bunker, note the short, 16A style, chimney.

14A 520 shunting in Bulawayo, 1981. This carries temporary number plate lettered "ZRR", probably the only loco to do so.

Close up of ZRR number plate on 14A loco 520.

14A 516 as refurbished, with large tank but original bunker. In Bulawayo yards 1991.

14A 508 at Lalapansi with the mixed train from Fort Victoria, in 1968.

The mixed train from West Nicholson climbs through Kuduvale, south of Gwanda, in 1975, with 14A 512 in charge.

On a freezing winter's morning in 1981, refurbished 14A 522 heads out of Bulawayo with the last mixed train to West Nicholson.

A frequent occurrence in steam days was the doubleheaded crosstripper to and from Balla Balla. Here 14A 512 leads a 16A on the climb out of Bushtick siding, 1975

Two 14A, headed by 519, still in RR days, charge out of Balla Balla with the crosstripper to Mpopoma. F. C. Butcher

Two Chris Butcher classics. Colleen Bawn yard with a 16A under the Water column, left, whilst 14As 510 and 518 move towards the camera. F. C. Butcher

A rare shot of 518 climbing Mulungwane bank, as there was seldom a train when the light was right at the spot.
F. C. Butcher

The sturdy, speedy, 14A are popular for special workings along the West Nicholson line. Here 525 leads a 16A with a Union Limited train in 1992, blasting up Mulungwane bank.

Passing the Whaleback rocks near Mbalabala in 1992, 14As 517 and 525 head a Union Limited train to Gwanda .

Near the former Irisvale siding, the same tour train crosses the Nsesi river.

14A 517 leads 14th class 507 on 804 pickup goods train, organised for rail enthusiasts in 1994. Matebele girls carrying water pots, look on as the train leaves Coldridge siding.

In 1995 14th class 507 ran out of water near Cement. 14A 525 and a 16A, waiting to take over at Heany, backed down to rescue the train, creating a triple headed Garratt occasion!

118

The 15 series, 4-6-4 + 4-6-4 Garratts

The 15 series were the most numerous and least homogeneous of all Rhodesia's locomotives being built in five batches, each differing in detail, over a period of fourteen years. All were of basically the same configuration with similar major dimensions, and were divided into two separate classes, 15 with 180 psi boiler pressure, and 15A with 200psi. Despite the difference this made to their nominal tractive efforts, no variation was made in loads hauled, as boiler capacities were virtually identical. These boilers were interchangeable between the two classes, plus the 16 and 16A classes, and were in practice interchanged during overhaul such that 15 and 15A could not be assumed from the original classifications as built. The two classes were differentiated in the monthly stock returns, but these are too complicated to detail here. The various batches will be first commented on before continuing with more general matters.

Batch I Four engines originally numbered 271-74 and designed for the Bulawayo-Mafeking line. However, at the time this line needed strengthening and with wartime conditions this was not immediately possible, so they started life at Salisbury, working between there and Gwelo or Bulawayo, putting in some remarkable mileages for a line which by European standards was "narrow" gauge, heavily graded, and single track. For the first six years of their lives, the four engines averaged over 6 000 miles (10 000km) per month, with 250 000 miles (400 000km) between heavy overhauls. As built they had very rounded "streamlined" front tanks, and conventional rear bunkers, and with bunkers holding ten tons, weighed 179,5 imperial tons in working order. Later, bunkers were lengthened to hold 12 1/2 tons which with the extra plating should have made total weight something over 182 tons, but the official diagram showed only 181,23 tons, no doubt as some "Fiddle" making them acceptable to the civil engineer! Several similar cases may be worked out by comparing early and later RR diagrams, of which the 16th class Garratts as detailed were the most outrageous.

In January 1948 the four engines were renumbered 350-53, starting a block of possibly 150 numbers, 350-499, which may have been utilised had not the railway turned eventually to diesels. During the royal tour of 1947, these engines were painted blue to work the special train, 271-2 on the Bulawayo - Salisbury section, and 273-4 between Bulawayo and Livingstone. Each engine ended up in externally different condition. 350 had its bunker lengthened to 12 1/2 tons capacity, retaining the original tank, but being fitted with a multiple jet exhaust with large diameter chimney. 351 was similar, but it is uncertain whether it had the multiple jet exhaust. 352 was involved in a head on collision with new 361 at Gado, in August 1949, emerging December 1951 with a new front tank standard with the series III locomotives, plus a very boxy looking bunker similar to that used much later on the refurbished 16A locomotives. 353 was also involved in a collision and was fitted with both front tank and rear bunker of series III design, although it retained the narrower, straight-sided, cab, thus distinguishing itself from the series III proper which had wide cabs.

Two of the series I have been preserved, no 350 at Kadoma where it has been re-painted blue and given its original number 271 which is not authentic as it has the large bunker and multiple jet exhaust, not fitted when it was no. 271. 352 has been preserved at Francistown, Botswana, whilst 351, dumped for years at Bulawayo has recently been tendered for scrap.

Batch II These ten engines were fitted with a high, bulbous, front tank, which although looking much larger, held no more water than the normal tanks. The cab was wider than batch I, the first RR locomotives to carry this wide cab, also included later on the 16A and 20/20A classes. The bunker, also of ten tons capacity, had a fully radiussed rear, "streamlined" to match the front tank, with slightly turned in sides over the coal space. These bunkers were later increased in length, height, and top width, the turned-in portion being made vertical. Engine 361, the other involved in the head-on at Gado, also received at series III front tank. Apart from two left in Zambia, probably all received multiple jet exhausts except possibly 355 which was the first withdrawn. The original numbers of these were 275-80 and 290-93, of which only 275, 276, and 290 carried these numbers in service, being renumbered in January 1948. The remainder, placed in service 1948 were renumbered when erected and only saw service with their new numbers.

Batch III The twenty engines comprising this batch heralded the standard external form for the 15th class. Front tanks were of similar size and overall shape to batch I but had knife edge corners at the sides. the bunkers were also of modified and simplified shape, and held 12 1/2 tons of coal from the outset. Engines 364-83.

Batch IV These were basically identical to

batch III except for having 200 psi pressure and were classed 15A. Thirty engines, 384-413.

Batch V Again class 15A, they differed internally only, having Beyer Peacock's patent self adjusting pivots, and were built by Franco-Belge. Engines 414-423

Engine 424 Engine 404 from batch IV was notoriously trouble-prone, being involved in several serious accidents, finally killing its crew when overturning south of Wankie. For many years a numberplate from 404 was mounted on two sleepers at the spot, until disgracefully stolen, but the venue "404 curve" is well known to photographers and appears more than once in this book. Finally, 404 was renumbered 424 since when it has led a blameless life, being one of the last steam engines still in service on NRZ!

Distribution The 15th classes were mainly used in Southern Rhodesia, divided between Salisbury and Bulawayo sheds. Originally designed for the south line to Mafeking, none were ever stationed there as by the time the line was strengthened for their use, operation had changed to caboose working from Bulawayo. Similarly, in later days from the mid 1970s to the end of steam, Thomson Junction had half a dozen or so for shunting and working north to Victoria Falls but by then it was a sub shed to Bulawayo to where engines were returned roughly fortnightly for washouts and mechanical attention. None were ever allocated to Beira nor Umtali during RR and NRZ days, but several were loaned to Beira during the 1980s, as detailed, these again returning frequently to Zimbabwe whenever any sort of attention was needed.

Fireboxes Batch I had arch tubes only in the fireboxes, but subsequent batches had two thermic syphons flanked by a pair of arch tubes. From 1966 onwards new boilers with all-welded barrels, and lacking thermic syphons were introduced and it is believed that all engines refurbished had such boilers. Possibly the last two with syphons were 406 and 407, noted retaining them in Bulawayo dump about 1980. Engine diagrams were never altered to reflect this reality.

Chimneys All engines originally had typically Beyer Peacock flared chimneys when new. Sometime in the 1950s these were replaced by a rather stumpy chimney as is still used on the 16A class.

The Giesl experiment Following widespread success of this device, basically a multiple jet arrangement with all jets in line, exhausting through an oblong section chimney, Rhodesia Railways purchased two sets of this equipment from Messrs. Schoeller-Bleckman & Co. in Austria, licencees and manufacturers of the gear invented by the late Dr Adolph Giesl-Gieslingen. Engine 381 was fitted with the simple Giesl ejector, and 380 with ejector plus superheat booster, which was a weighted baffle calculated to increase gas flow through the superheater flues at lower steaming rates. At higher rates, passage of higher gas volumes lifted the baffle allowing more gas to pass through the lower plain tubes, having thus less effect. In practice the "booster" boosted steam temperatures and locomotive efficiency at lower rates only, leaving maximum steam temperatures unchanged at higher rates when they are normally at the maximum allowable by lubricating oils. Engine 381 was tested initially in April 1963 and engine 380 in June 1963. After testing, it was concluded that the Giesl ejector alone gave coal savings of 7,76% per ton-mile, with water savings of 3,33%. The combination of Giesl ejector plus superheater booster gave far better results, coal and water savings being 16,8% and 21,58% respectively. Both loco-

Allocations at selected dates were:

Date	Salisbury	Gwelo	Bulawayo	Wankie	Livingstone	Broken Hill	Nkana
6/1941	4	-	-	-	-	-	-
8/1948	12	-	2	-	-	-	-
6/1951	24	-	29	9	-	-	-
6/1955	23	-	32	9	7	-	-
6/1960	27	-	25	-	22	-	-
6/1967	-	-	63	-	7	2	2
						——— Z a m b i a ———	
6/1970	-	-	66	-		8	
7/1975	-	1	46	-		8	
6/1980	-	-	39	-		n/a	
	Beira*						
6/1984	3	1**	35	-		n/a	

* On loan from Bulawayo
** At Harare for training purposes

motives were fitted with the equipment some time before tests were carried out, 380 in July 1962 and 381 in September. In January 1965 it was decided that due to the superior performance of the engine with superheat booster, 381 was to be fitted with the booster off 380, and a new damper to be made for this latter, which still had thermic syphons at that date. The two sets of equipment later appeared on engines 382 and 419, surprisingly with different boilers than before, i.e. the equipment did not simply change locos due to boiler interchange. 419, by then a 15th class with 180 psi boiler, was fitted with the gear from 381 about March 1966, whilst 382 got 380s equipment in December 1966. By March 1971 it was decided not to continue the experiment, mainly due to the high royalty charges on its use (plus the fact that sanctions had intervened) and it was removed soon after, although correspondence does not provide exact removal dates which *seem* to be from 382 in September 1971 whilst in the P15 shop for a wheel job, and from 419 in August 1972 for the same reason.

Don Chapman, when CME, who had extensive experience of Giesl equipment in East Africa, told the writer that on Garratt locomotives the ejectors tended to get out of alignment as the boiler frame was less rigid than on a "straight" engine with its smokebox firmly held in the saddle formed by the cylinders, a reasonable statement.

In any case, by then Bulawayo had devised its own design of improved exhaust arrangement, needing no royalties.

Multiple jet exhaust To provide something like the free exhaust of the Giesl ejector, Bulawayo designed a multiple jet system, nicknamed a "pepper pot" exhaust, first applied to no. 376 about 1967, and noted by the writer in Mafeking, September 1967. This comprised six exhaust jets with nozzle diameter 63,5mm, exhausting through a larger diameter chimney similar to that then used on the 20th class. Most of the 15 series were so fitted, other than those in Zambia, which retained the "stumpy" chimney, and such early withdrawals as 352, 355, 362 and 364, all taken out of service in 1972-73. Strangely, the 16A class, which used the same boilers, retained the "stumpy" chimney to the end.

Refurbishment To counter oil shortages and sanctions, 34, 15th/15A locomotives from batches III to V were refurbished, when they were fitted with roller bearings on driving and coupled axles (already fitted on bogie axles) and given delightful animal and bird names in siNdebele.

15th class, first series, no 274 when still new. J. Dele-Hoffman collection

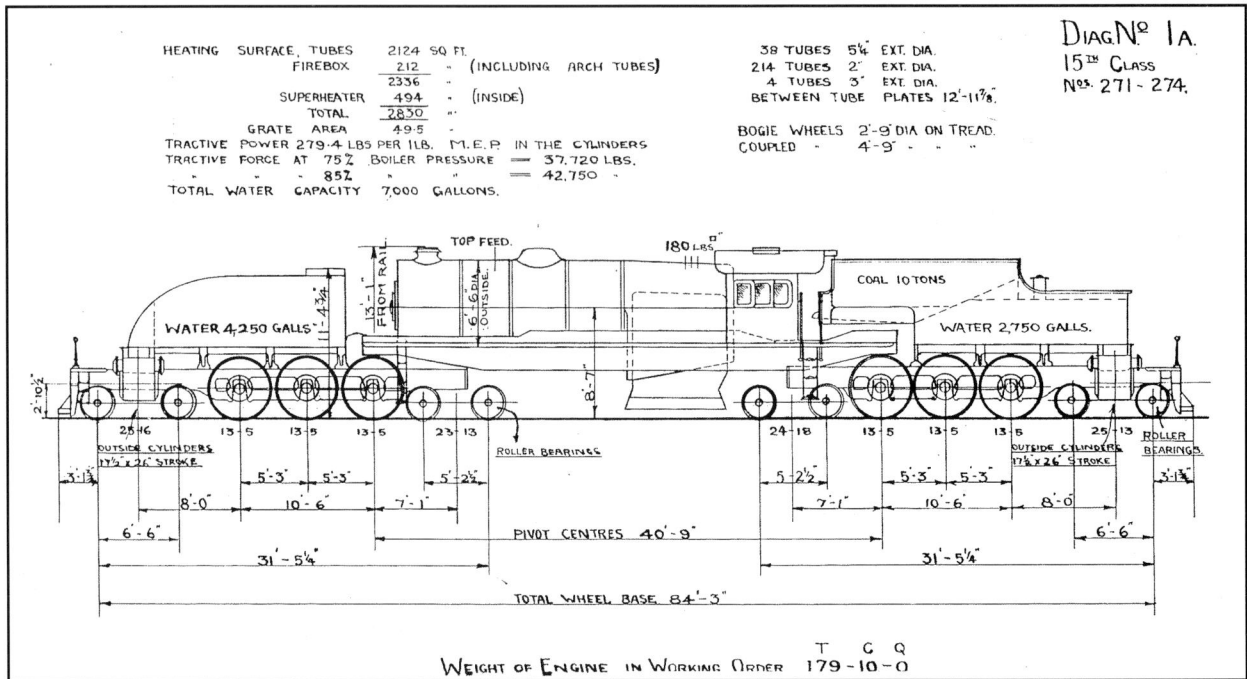

HEATING SURFACE, TUBES 2124 SQ.FT.
FIREBOX 212 " (INCLUDING ARCH TUBES)
  2336 "
SUPERHEATER 494 " (INSIDE)
TOTAL 2830 "
GRATE AREA 49.5 "
TRACTIVE POWER 279.4 LBS PER 1LB. M.E.P. IN THE CYLINDERS
TRACTIVE FORCE AT 75% BOILER PRESSURE = 37,720 LBS.
  " " 85% = 42,750 "
TOTAL WATER CAPACITY 7,000 GALLONS.

38 TUBES 5¼" EXT. DIA.
214 TUBES 2" EXT. DIA.
4 TUBES 3" EXT. DIA.
BETWEEN TUBE PLATES 12'-11⅞"

BOGIE WHEELS 2'-9" DIA ON TREAD.
COUPLED - 4'-9" " " "

DIAG. No. IA.
15ᵀᴴ CLASS
Nᵒˢ. 271 - 274.

WATER 4,250 GALLS. TOP FEED. 180 LBS COAL 10 TONS WATER 2,750 GALLS.

25.16 13.5 13.5 13.5 23.13 24.18 13.5 13.5 13.5 25.13
OUTSIDE CYLINDERS ROLLER BEARINGS OUTSIDE CYLINDER ROLLER BEARINGS
17½" x 26" STROKE 17½" x 26" STROKE

3-1¼ 5-3 5-3 5-2½ 5-2½ 5-3 5-3 3-1¼
8-0 10-6 7-1 7-1 10-6 8-0
6-6 PIVOT CENTRES 40'-9" 6-6
31'-5¼" 31'-5¼"
TOTAL WHEEL BASE 84'-3"

T C Q
WEIGHT OF ENGINE IN WORKING ORDER 179 - 10 - 0

15th class nos 272, 271, and 273 at Salisbury shed when new. RR

First series 15th class nos 273 and 274 doubleheading the Royal Train near Dibangombie, between Matetsi and Victoria Falls. RR

350 at Luveve in 1970, bringing into Bulawayo the passenger train from Victoria Falls.

351 in later condition, with stubby chimney and extended bunker, pilots a second series 15th class in Botswana. F. C. Butcher

352, with square bunker and third series front tank, near Khami in 1970 with the passenger train from South Africa.

First series no 353, with both front tank and rear bunker of third series design, heads a south line freight train at a wayside station in 1970.

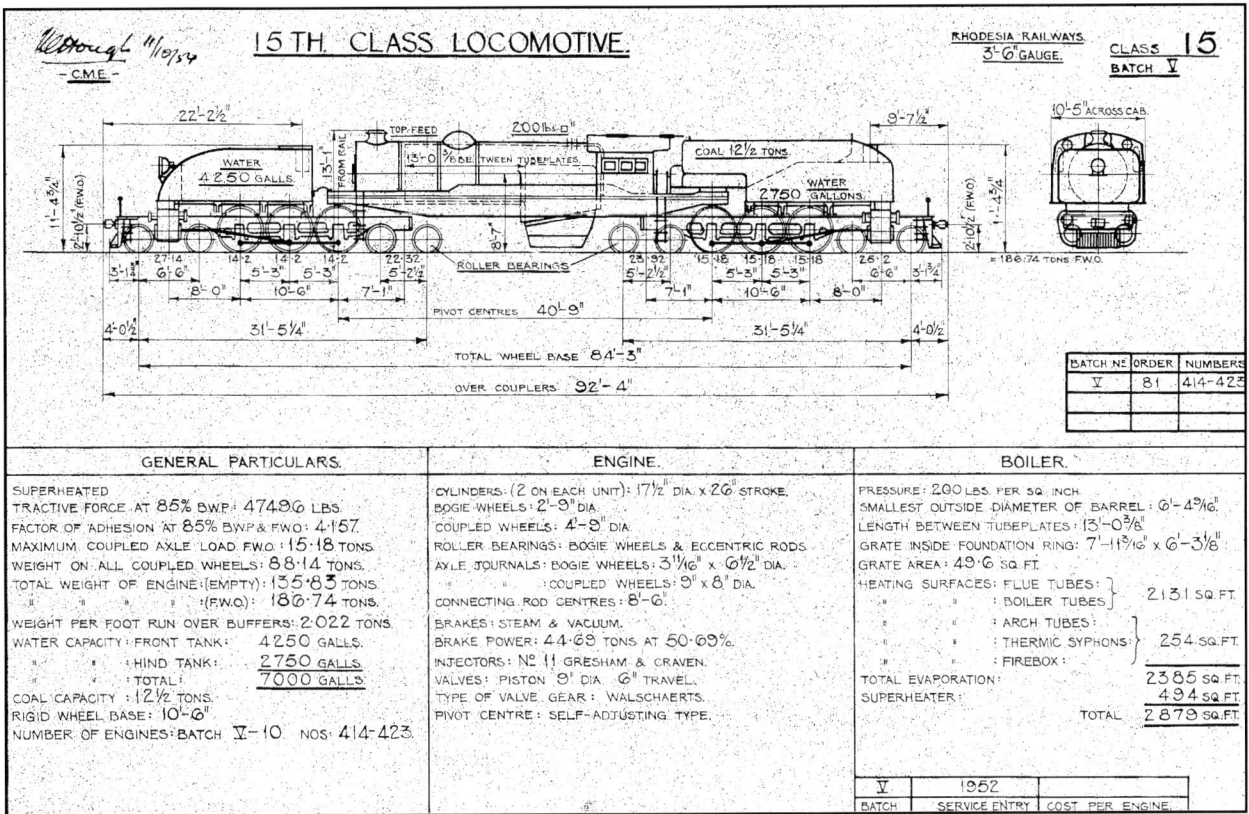

15TH CLASS LOCOMOTIVE.

W.H.Hough 11/10/51
C.M.E.

RHODESIA RAILWAYS.
3'-6" GAUGE.

CLASS **15**
BATCH **V**

22'-2½"
WATER 4250 GALLS.
TOP FEED
200 lbs.-0"
13'-0" 3/8" BETWEEN TUBEPLATES.
COAL 12½ TONS.
9'-7½"
10'-5" ACROSS CAB.
11'-4¾" (F.W.O.)
13'-1" FROM RAIL
2750 WATER GALLONS.
2'-10½" (F.W.O.)
2'-10½" (F.W.O.)
11'-4¾" (F.W.O.)
186·74 TONS F.W.O.

ROLLER BEARINGS
PIVOT CENTRES 40'-9"
TOTAL WHEEL BASE 84'-3"
OVER COUPLERS 92'-4"

31'-5¼"
31'-5¼"
4'-0½"
4'-0½"

BATCH No	ORDER	NUMBERS
V	81	414-423

GENERAL PARTICULARS.

SUPERHEATED
TRACTIVE FORCE AT 85% B.W.P. 47496 LBS.
FACTOR OF ADHESION AT 85% B.W.P. & F.W.O. 4·157
MAXIMUM COUPLED AXLE LOAD F.W.O. 15·18 TONS
WEIGHT ON ALL COUPLED WHEELS 88·14 TONS.
TOTAL WEIGHT OF ENGINE (EMPTY) 135·83 TONS.
" " " (F.W.O.) 186·74 TONS.
WEIGHT PER FOOT RUN OVER BUFFERS 2·022 TONS.
WATER CAPACITY FRONT TANK 4250 GALLS.
" HIND TANK 2750 GALLS.
" TOTAL 7000 GALLS.
COAL CAPACITY 12½ TONS.
RIGID WHEEL BASE 10'-6".
NUMBER OF ENGINES BATCH V-10 NOS. 414-423.

ENGINE.

CYLINDERS (2 ON EACH UNIT) 17½" DIA. x 26" STROKE.
BOGIE WHEELS 2'-9" DIA.
COUPLED WHEELS 4'-8" DIA.
ROLLER BEARINGS BOGIE WHEELS & ECCENTRIC RODS.
AXLE JOURNALS BOGIE WHEELS 3 11/16" x 6½" DIA.
" " COUPLED WHEELS 9" x 8" DIA.
CONNECTING ROD CENTRES 8'-6".
BRAKES STEAM & VACUUM.
BRAKE POWER 44·68 TONS AT 50·69%.
INJECTORS No 11 GRESHAM & CRAVEN.
VALVES PISTON 8" DIA. 6" TRAVEL.
TYPE OF VALVE GEAR WALSCHAERTS.
PIVOT CENTRE SELF-ADJUSTING TYPE.

BOILER.

PRESSURE 200 LBS. PER SQ. INCH.
SMALLEST OUTSIDE DIAMETER OF BARREL 6'-4 9/16"
LENGTH BETWEEN TUBEPLATES 13'-0 3/8"
GRATE INSIDE FOUNDATION RING 7'-11 9/16" x 6'-3 1/8"
GRATE AREA 49·6 SQ.FT.

HEATING SURFACES		
FLUE TUBES		
BOILER TUBES	}	2131 SQ.FT.
ARCH TUBES	}	254 SQ.FT.
THERMIC SYPHONS		
FIREBOX		
TOTAL EVAPORATION		2385 SQ.FT.
SUPERHEATER		494 SQ.FT.
TOTAL		2879 SQ.FT.

V	1952	
BATCH	SERVICE ENTRY	COST PER ENGINE

15th class, second series 277 as supplied by Beyer Peacock. This engine was renumbered 356 before being placed in service.

Engine 363 of the second series, at New Wankie in 1979, showing the modified contour of the enlarged bunker.

Engine no 359 of the second series 15th class, showing clearly the original bunker contour.
J. R. Lloyd

Engine 360 of the second series, at Bulawayo, emphasising the high and bulbous front tank.
F. C. Butcher

Second series no 361 with third series front tank, rounds the horseshoe curve near Tajintunda with the passenger train from Bulawayo, in 1978.

126

15 TH. CLASS LOCOMOTIVE.

RHODESIA RAILWAYS.
3'-6" GAUGE.

CLASS 15
BATCH II.

BATCH Nº	ORDER	NUMBERS
II		354-363

C.M.E.

GENERAL PARTICULARS
SUPERHEATED.
TRACTIVE FORCE AT 85% B.W.P. : 42,750 LBS.
FACTOR OF ADHESION AT 85% B.W.P. & F.W.O. : 4·351
MAXIMUM COUPLED AXLE LOAD : F.W.O. : 13·93 TONS.
WEIGHT ON ALL COUPLED WHEELS. F.W.O. : 83·04 TONS.
TOTAL WEIGHT OF ENGINE: (EMPTY) : 133·4 TONS.
    "   "   " : (F.W.O.) : 183·57 TONS.
WEIGHT PER FOOT RUN OVER BUFFERS : 1·989 TONS.
WATER CAPACITY : FRONT TANK : 4250 GALLS.
    "   "   : HIND TANK : 2,750 GALLS.
    "   "   : TOTAL : 7,000 GALLS.
COAL CAPACITY : 10 TONS.
RIGID WHEEL BASE : 10'-6"
NUMBER OF ENGINES : BATCH II—10. NOS. 354-363.

ENGINE
CYLINDERS : (2 ON EACH UNIT.) : 17½" DIA x 26" STROKE.
BOGIE WHEELS : 2'-3" DIA.
COUPLED WHEELS : 4'-9" DIA.
ROLLER BEARINGS : BOGIE WHEELS & ECCENTRIC RODS.
AXLE JOURNALS : BOGIE WHEELS : 160 MM. (ROLLER)
    "   " : COUPLED WHEELS : 9" x 8" DIA.
CONNECTING ROD CENTRES : 8'-6".
BRAKES : STEAM & VACUUM.
BRAKE POWER : 41 TONS AT 49·38%.
INJECTORS : Nº 11 GRESHAM & CRAVEN.
VALVES : PISTON 9" DIA. 6" TRAVEL.
TYPE OF VALVE GEAR : WALSCHAERTS.

BOILER
PRESSURE : 180 LBS.
SMALLEST OUTSIDE DIAMETER OF BARREL : 6'-4⁹⁄₁₆"
LENGTH BETWEEN TUBEPLATES : 13'-0⅜"
GRATE INSIDE FOUNDATION RING : 7'-11³⁄₁₆" x 6'-3⅛"
GRATE AREA : 49·6 SQ.FT.
HEATING SURFACES : FLUE TUBES :
    "   " : BOILER TUBES : } 2,131 SQ.FT.
    "   " : ARCH TUBES :
    "   " : THERMIC TUBES : } 254 SQ.FT.
    "   " : FIREBOX :
TOTAL EVAPORATION : 2385 SQ.FT.
SUPERHEATER : 494 SQ.FT.
              TOTAL : 2879 SQ.FT.

I	1947/48.	
BATCH	SERVICE ENTRY	COST PER ENGINE

389 at Mafeking in 1967, having already had the original flared chimney replaced by the stumpy type.

127

370 at Bulawayo shed in the 1980s, ex-works from ZECO and with multiple jet exhaust. Note also the antispill "dam" round the tank filler, which has discharge pipes other side.

Cabside of 381 INGWE (leopard) showing style of nameplate and NRZ number plate.

128

The six-jet blastpipe top as fitted to 15th class from 1967, and much later adopted for the 20/20A classes.

Loco 380 arriving at Bulawayo Westgate with the beautiful NRZ train used to "show the flag" on the weekly run to Johannesburg, 1988.

Engine 381, in NRZ days and after refurbishment, eases a heavy freight out of Lukosi siding after taking water on a winter's morning.

Close-up of 15th class Garratt 419, with the Giesl ejector and its distinctive chimney. Seen at Mafeking, 1970.

THE GIESL GARRATTS

As described in the text, two sets of Giesl ejector equipment, one with superheat booster, were ordered for RR 15th/15A class locomotives. Four different locomotives carried this equipment, as shown in the following illustrations.

380 with Giesl ejector, on a freight train near Dett. F. C. Butcher

381 with Giesl ejector. C. E. Rickwood

382 with Giesl ejector, at unknown location. F. C. Butcher

419, with Giesl ejector, stands in the shed yard at Mafeking, 1970.

15A 400, in early morning light, heads through the African bush with a loaded freight train.

With the daily mixed train in tow, a 15A Garratt rounds Wankie horseshoe curve on a cool winter morning, 1978.

The overnight passenger train from Bulawayo to Victoria Falls, running somewhat late, negotiates the double horseshoe curves before Zanguja behind a 15A Garratt.

409 INKAKHA, ex-works from ZECO the same week, hustles across the Deka river bridge at dawn, with train 16, timed at 06.45 ex Thomson Junction for Victoria Falls.

15A 417, slowing down for the water stop, is reflected in the still, early morning waters, of the Lukosi river.

15th/15A locomotives loaned to CFM for the Beira line

In the period 1984-88, several 15/15A Garratts were loaned to the Beira line to cover motive power shortages especially whilst Garratts from that line were under overhaul at ZECO in Bulawayo. The 15s were not as powerful as the locomotive they replaced, but were doubtless welcome as something working and available to haul traffic. None of these engines went on long term hire, but were returned to Zimbabwe whenever any sort of attention was needed, whether from wear and tear, neglect, or damage. Altogether twenty such locomotives went to Moçambique, some several times, and the main periods of loan are listed below:

Locomotive	Loan periods	Locomotive	Loan periods
370	10/1986 - 12/1987	391	6/1986 - 7/1987
371	6/1986 - 11/1986	392	1/1987 - 5/1987
376	1/1987 - 12/1987	394	1/1987 only
377	7/1985 - 10/1985	396	7/1986 - 3/1987, 12/1987 - 1/1988
380	12/1984 - 10/1985	397	2/1984 - 11/1987, (5 periods)
381	8/1986 - 11/1987	398	2/1986 - 10/1987, (3 periods)
385	8/1986 - 10/1986	400	8/1984 - 4/1987, (3 periods)
386	8/1986 - 10/1986	402	2/1984 - 8/1986, (3 periods)
387	9/1985 - 11/1985	406	5/1986 - 7/1986
389	5/1987 - 6/1987	409	5/1987 - 7/1987

Unsurprisingly, in view of the raging war, there seem to be no available photographs of these engines working in Moçambique.

Historical data:

First No	Second No	Beyer Peacock	Date Built	Date in Service	Date Refurbished	Name	Last Used	Disposal
Batch I								
271	350	6936	1940	4/1940	-	-	10/1973	Preserved, Kadoma
272	351	6937	1940	5/1940	-	-	10/1973	Scrapped 12/1994 cut up 4/1995
273	352	6938	1940	5/1940	-	-	9/1973	Preserved, Fancistown 9/1976
274	353	6939	1940	6/1940	-	-	2/1981	Scrapped 12/1994 cut up 4/1995
Batch II								
275	354	7228	1947	9/1947	-	-	9/1973	Tendered for scrap 1996
276	355	7229	1947	10/1947	-	-	8/1972	Scrapped 4/1981
(277)	356	7230	1947	1/1948	-	-	7/1978	Scrapped 12/1994
(278)	357	7231	1947	1/1948	-	-	6/1967	Zambia, scrapped Kabwe 9/1978
(279)	358	7232	1947	2/1948	-	-	10/1981	Tendered for scrap 1996
(280)	359	7233	1947	2/1948	-	-	6/1967	Zambia, derelict Ndola
290	360	7234	1947	12/1947	-	-	6/1975	Scrapped 12/1994 cut up 4/1995
(291)	361	7235	1947	2/1948	-	-	12/1980	Scrapped 12/1994 cut up 4/1995
(292)	362	7236	1947	1/1948	-	-	8/1973	Scrapped 7/1981
(293)	363	7237	1947	1/1948	-	-	8/1980	Tendered for scrap 1996
Batch III								
364	-	7260	1948	3/1949	-	-	9/1973	Tendered for scrap 1996

First No	Second No	Beyer Peacock	Date Built	Date in Service	Date Refurbished		Name	Last Used	Disposal
365	-	7261	1948	4/1949	-	-		6/1967	Zambia, scrapped Kabwe 9/1978
366	-	7262	1948	2/1949	-	-		3/1982	?
367	-	7263	1948	3/1949	-	-		8/1982	Scrapped 12/1994
368	-	7264	1948	2/1949	-	-		12/1976	Scrapped 12/1994
369	-	7265	1948	4/1949	-	-		4/1982	Scrapped 12/1994
370	-	7266	1948	3/1949	12/1981		Ibhalabhala	5/1993	Mothballed
371	-	7267	1949	5/1949	11/1981		Inkongolwane	-	In service
372	-	7268	1949	5/1949	12/1981		Umtshwayeli	5/1993	Scrapped 12/1994
373	-	7269	1949	5/1949	-	-		6/1967	Zambia, derelict Kabwe
374	-	7270	1949	6/1949	-	-		5/1981	Tendered for scrap 1996
375	-	7271	1949	6/1949	-	-		6/1981	Tendered for scrap 1996
376	-	7272	1949	7/1949	11/1981		Ingulungundu	4/1994	Scrapped 7/1996
377	-	7273	1949	6/1949	11/1981		Udwai	7/1993	
378	-	7274	1949	6/1949	-	-		9/1973	
379	-	7275	1949	7/1949	-	-		6/1981	Tendered for scrap 1996
380	-	7276	1949	7/1949	10/1981		Umahelwane	8/1993	Scrapped 12/1994
381	-	7277	1949	8/1949	10/1981		Ingwe	9/1994	
382	-	7278	1949	7/1949	2/1981		Iganyana	-	In service
383	-	7279	1949	8/1949	-	-		2/1981	Scrapped 12/1994

Batch IV

First No	Second No	Beyer Peacock	Date Built	Date in Service	Date Refurbished		Name	Last Used	Disposal
384	-	7326	1950	3/1950	-	-		/1975	Scrapped 9/1983
385	-	7327	1950	3/1950	12/1980		Ingwenya	4/1994	
386	-	7328	1950	3/1950	9/1981		Umayalene	3/1995	Museum, operable
387	-	7329	1950	4/1950	3/1981		Imvubu	7/1997	Scrapped collision 7/1997
388	-	7330	1950	4/1950	-	-		2/1981	Tendered for scrap
389	-	7331	1950	4/1950	2/1982		Umziki	7/1993	Scrapped 11/1994
390	-	7332	1950	4/1950	7/1991		-	8/1993	Scrapped 11/1994
391	-	7333	1950	5/1950	1/1981		Ingugama	6/1994	Derelict 7/1996
392	-	7334	1950	6/1950	5/1981		Ithaka	8/1993	Sold Wankie Collieries 1995 no10
393	-	7335	1950	6/1950	-	-		6/1967	Zambia, derelict Livingstone
394	-	7336	1950	5/1950	7/1981		Umzwazwa	9/1995	Museum, serviceable
395	-	7337	1950	5/1950	10/1991		-	9/1995	Serviceable
396	-	7338	1950	7/1950	-	-		6/1994	Wankie Col no9, 199A
397	-	7339	1950	7/1950	2/1981		Inyathi	8/1993	Scrapped 11/1994
398	-	7340	1950	7/1950	2/1982		Isidumuka	8/1993	Sold New Zealand, 1995
399	-	7351	1950	10/1950	-	-		6/1981	
400	-	7352	1950	10/1950	1/1982		Imbila	9/1995	
401	-	7353	1950	10/1950	-	-		6/1967	Zambia, Livingstone museum
402	-	7354	1950	11/1950	3/1981		Impofu	-	In service
403	-	7355	1950	12/1950	-	-		7/1984	Scrapped 8/1985
404	424	7356	1950	11/1950	6/1981		Isilwana	-	In service
405	-	7357	1950	12/1950	-	-		6/1967	Zambia
406	-	7358	1950	12/1950	9/1981		Ikolo	-	In service
407	-	7359	1950	11/1950	5/1981		Ukhozi	-	Serviceable
408	-	7360	1950	11/1950	-	-		6/1967	Zambia, scrapped Kabwe 12/1978
409	-	7361	1950	1/1951	6/1981		Inkhakha	7/1993	Scrapped 11/1994
410	-	7362	1950	1/1951	6/1981		Inkolomi	7/1993	Serviceable
411	-	7363	1950	1/1951	-	-		5/1981	Scrapped 11/1983
412	-	7364	1950	2/1951	-	-		6/1977	Scrapped 12/1994
413	-	7365	1950	2/1951	-	-		4/1981	Scrapped 7/1983

First No	Franco Belge	Beyer Peacock	Date Built	Date in Service	Date Refurbished	Name	Last Used	Disposal
Batch V								
414*	2963	7555	1952	4/1952	9/1981	Ubhejane	9/1995	Serviceable
415	2964	7556	1952	4/1952	7/1981	Itsheme	6/1994	Wankie Colliery no8
416	2965	7557	1952	4/1952	1/1982	Inungu	-	In service
417	2966	7558	1952	6/1952	1/1982	Umathebene	-	In service
418	2967	7559	1952	6/1952	3/1982	Umkhombo	5/1993	Serviceable
419	2968	7560	1952	6/1952	9/1979	Isambane	7/1993	
420*	2969	7561	1952	7/1952	8/1979	Indlovu	-	In service
421	2970	7562	1952	6/1952	1/1981	Intundhla	7/1993	Serviceable
422	2971	7563	1952	7/1952	9/1980	Inkonkoni	-	In service
423	2972	7564	1952	7/1952	10/1981	Idube	8/1993	Wankie Colliery 1995, no11

* Following a head-on collision at Dete in 1988, 414 was rebuilt with frames (probably front unit only) ex 411, and 420 with frames from 413. It is not certain whether the self adjusting pivots were retained.

15th class names

When refurbished, the 15th/15A locomotives so dealt with carried attractive names in siNdebele, the language of the Matabele through whose tribal areas they mainly operated. These are listed in the main data table for the class, but are repeated here with their English equivalents and Latin names, for interest.

Engine No	siNdebele	English	Latin
370	IBHALABHALA	Kudu	Tragelaphus strepisceros
371	INKONGWANE	Hartebeest	Alcephalus bucelaohus
372	UMTSHWAYELI	Sable Antelope	Hippotragus niger
376	UMGULUNGUNDU	Bush Pig	Potamochoerus porcus
377	UDWAI	Secretary bird	Sagittarius serpentarius
380	UMAHELWANE	African Goshawk	Accipiter tachira
381	INGWE	Leopard	Panthera pardus
385	INGWENYA	Crocodile	Crocodilus nilotica
387	IMVUBU	Hippopotamus	Hippopotamus amphibius
389	UMZIKI	Reed buck	Redunca arundinium
391	INGUGAMA	Gemsbok	Oryx gazella gazella
392	ITHAKA	Roan Antelope	Hippotragus equinus
394	UMZWAZWA	Yellow-billed Kite	Milvus migrans
397	INYATHI	Buffalo	Syncerus caffer
398	ISIDUMUKA	Waterbuck	Kobus ellipsiprymnus
400	IMBILA	Rock Hyrax	Procavia capensis
402	IMPOFU	Eland	Taurotragus oryx
406	IKOLO	Hornbill	(generic term)
407	UKHOZI	Eagle	(generic term)
409	INKHAKHA	Pangolin	Manis temmincki
410	INKOLOMI	Tsessebe	Damaliscus lunatus lunatus
414	UBHEJANE	Black Rhino	Dicerus bicornis
415	ITSHEME	Great Bustard	Otis kori
416	INUNGU	Porcupine	Hystrix africaeaustralis
417	UMATHABENE	Kestrel	(generic term)
418	UMKHOMBO	White Rhino	Ceratotherium simum
419	ISAMBANE	Ant bear	Orycteropus afer
420	INDLOVU	Elephant	Loxodonta africana africana
421	INTUNHLA	Giraffe	Giraffa cameleopardalis
422	INKONKONI	Wildebeest	Connochaetes taurinus
423	IDUBE	Zebra	Equus burchelli
424	ISILWANA	Lion	Panthera leo

Class 15E, 4-8-2

15E 2885 at Bulawayo in Rhodesia F. C. Butcher

Many years earlier, the CME, Major Sells, had proposed a large 4-8-2 similar to SAR's class 15F, and this proposal was nearly realised in 1970 when a severe locomotive shortage, probably caused by unreliable diesels, led to the hire of six class 15E heavy 4-8-2 from SAR. These were similar in most major dimensions to Sells' proposed 17th class (see p. 207) but had rotary cam poppet valves, the only such equipment used in Rhodesia. Six were hired from SAR of which no. 2878 was almost immediately replaced by 2886, due to "cracked cylinder". However, 2878 was a famous locomotive, much fêted as Henschel no 23000 when built, and there may be more to its return than a cracked cylinder, especially as it remains in SAR's museum fleet as the only operable 15E! Soon after being hired, the 15E were purchased by RR, retaining their original classification but having running numbers reduced by 2000, such that 2881 became RR 881, etc. In Rhodesia they were stationed only at Bulawayo, and used virtually exclusively on trains to and from Gwelo. After only two and a half year's service they were all withdrawn and scrapped, possibly due to unfamiliarity with the unorthodox valve gear. The same occurred in South Africa - when all were stationed at Bethlehem they gave sterling service, but after replacement, orphan examples sent to sheds unfamiliar with their maintenance (probably with no instruction material sent out) found them a problem and they were soon relegated to the scrap roads.

Historical data:

SAR Number	Builder	Builder's Number	Date in SAR Service	Date to RR	Last Used	
2878	Henschel	23000	10/1936	7/1970		7/1971
2881	Henschel	23103	11/1936	7/1970	2/1973 RR 881	Scrapped 7/1973
2882	Henschel	23104	1/1937	8/1970	1/1973 RR 882	Scrapped 7/1973
2883	Henschel	23105	2/1937	7/1970	3/1973 RR 883	Scrapped 7/1973
2885	Henschel	23107	2/1937	7/1970	3/1973 RR 885	Scrapped 7/1973
2886	Henschel	23108	3/1937	8/1971	12/1973 RR 886	Scrapped 7/1973
2898	Berliner	10589	1/1937	7/1970	5/1973 RR 898	Scrapped 7/1973

15E 2886 rolls out of Mpopoma towards Bulawayo. F.C. Butcher

Two Chris Butcher classics! 15E 2885 blasting out of Bulawayo station with a train for the Gwelo line.
F. C. Butcher

16th class, 2-8-2 + 2-8-2 Garratt

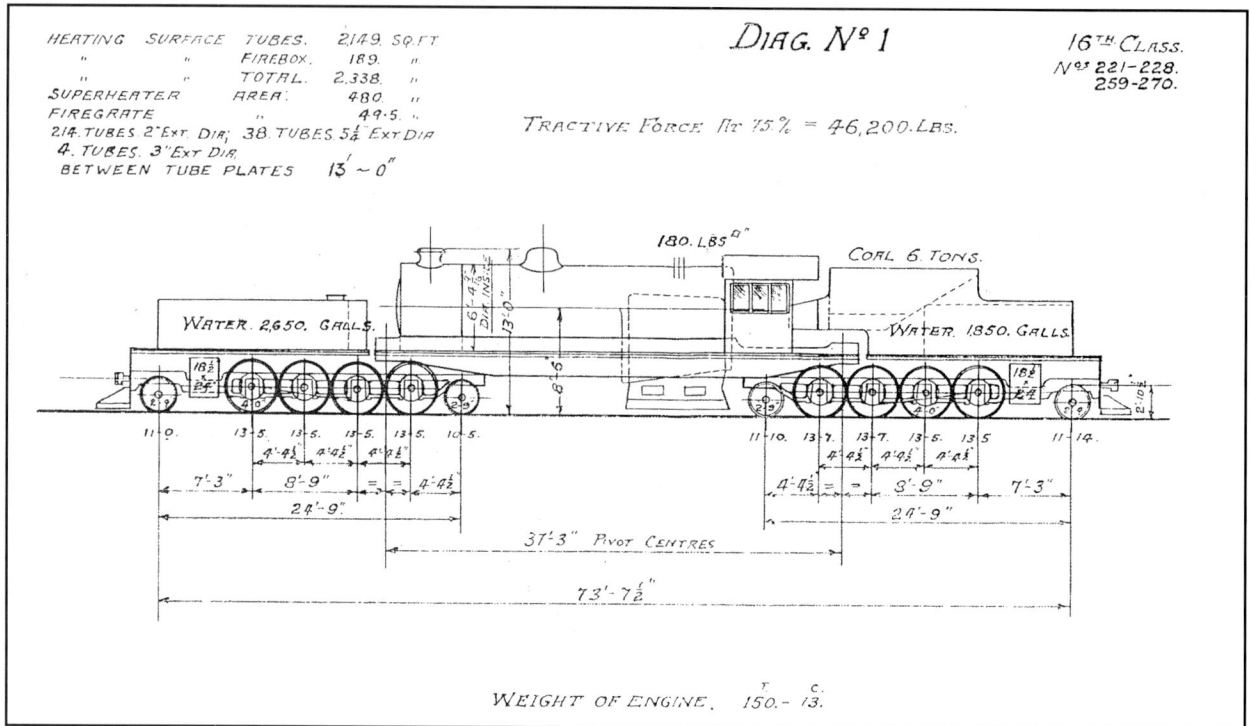

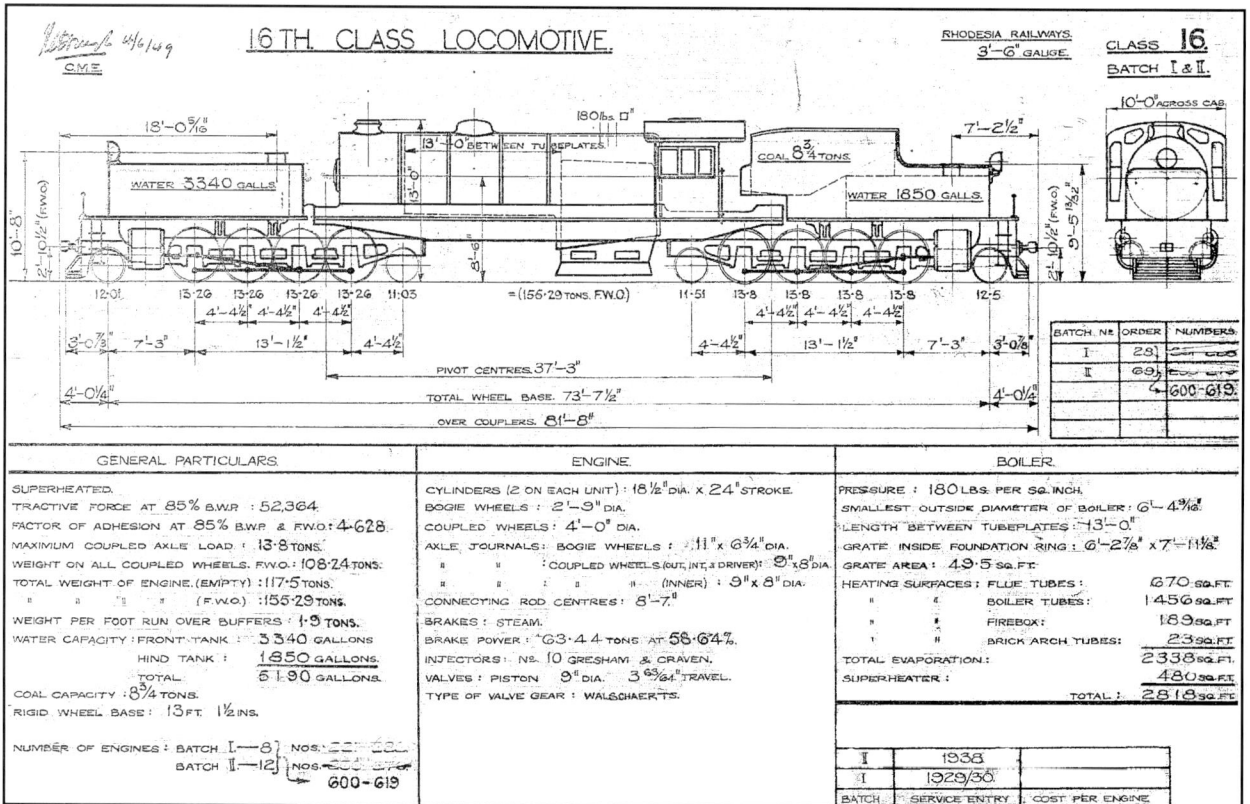

HEATING SURFACE TUBES. 2149. SQ.FT
" " FIREBOX. 189. "
" " TOTAL. 2.338. "
SUPERHEATER AREA. 480. "
FIREGRATE 49.5. "
214. TUBES 2" EXT DIA; 38 TUBES 5¼" EXT DIA
4. TUBES. 3" EXT DIA.
BETWEEN TUBE PLATES 13' ~ 0"

DIAG. N° 1

16TH CLASS.
N°S 221-228.
259-270.

TRACTIVE FORCE AT 75% = 46,200. LBS.

180. LBS □"

COAL 6. TONS.

WATER. 2,650. GALLS.

WATER. 1,850. GALLS.

11-0. 13-5. 13-5. 13-5. 13-5. 10-5. 11-10. 13-7. 13-7. 13-5. 13-5. 11-14.
4'-4½" 4'-9½" 4'-9½" 4'-4½" 4'-9½" 4'-4½"
7'-3" 8'-9" = 4'-4½" 4'-4½" = 8'-9" 7'-3"
24'-9" 24'-9"
37'-3" PIVOT CENTRES
73'-7½"

WEIGHT OF ENGINE. 150.- 13. T. C.

16TH. CLASS LOCOMOTIVE.

RHODESIA RAILWAYS.
3'-6" GAUGE

CLASS 16.
BATCH I & II.

10'-0" ACROSS CAB.

18'-0 5/16"

13'-0" BETWEEN TUBE PLATES 180 lbs. □"

7'-2½"

WATER 3340 GALLS.

COAL 8¾ TONS.

WATER 1850 GALLS.

12-0½ 13-26 13-26 13-26 13-26 11-03 = (155·29 TONS. F.W.O.) 11-51 13-8 13-8 13-8 13-8 12-5
4'-4½" 4'-4½" 4'-4½" 4'-4½" 4'-4½" 4'-4½"
3'-0⅝" 7'-3" 13'-1½" 4'-4½" 4'-4½" 13'-1½" 7'-3" 3'-0⅝"
4'-0¼" PIVOT CENTRES 37'-3" 4'-0¼"
TOTAL WHEEL BASE 73'-7½"
OVER COUPLERS 81'-8"

BATCH N°	ORDER	NUMBERS
I	28	221-228
II	69	
		600-619.

GENERAL PARTICULARS.

SUPERHEATED.
TRACTIVE FORCE AT 85% B.W.P : 52,364.
FACTOR OF ADHESION AT 85% B.W.P & F.W.O : 4·628
MAXIMUM COUPLED AXLE LOAD : 13·8 TONS.
WEIGHT ON ALL COUPLED WHEELS. F.W.O : 108·24 TONS.
TOTAL WEIGHT OF ENGINE. (EMPTY) : 117·5 TONS.
" " " " (F.W.O.) : 155·29 TONS.
WEIGHT PER FOOT RUN OVER BUFFERS : 1·9 TONS.
WATER CAPACITY : FRONT TANK : 3340 GALLONS.
HIND TANK : 1850 GALLONS.
TOTAL : 5190 GALLONS.
COAL CAPACITY : 8¾ TONS.
RIGID WHEEL BASE : 13 FT. 1½ INS.

NUMBER OF ENGINES : BATCH I—8 } NOS. 221-228
BATCH II—12 } NOS. 600-619.

ENGINE.

CYLINDERS (2 ON EACH UNIT) : 18½" DIA. x 24" STROKE.
BOGIE WHEELS : 2'-3" DIA.
COUPLED WHEELS : 4'-0" DIA.
AXLE JOURNALS : BOGIE WHEELS : 11" x 6¾" DIA.
" " : COUPLED WHEELS (OUT, INT, & DRIVER) : 9" x 8" DIA.
" " " (INNER) : 9" x 8" DIA.
CONNECTING ROD CENTRES : 8'-7".
BRAKES : STEAM.
BRAKE POWER : 63·44 TONS AT 58·64%.
INJECTORS : N° 10 GRESHAM & CRAVEN.
VALVES : PISTON 9" DIA. 3 63/64" TRAVEL.
TYPE OF VALVE GEAR : WALSCHAERTS.

BOILER.

PRESSURE : 180 LBS PER SQ. INCH.
SMALLEST OUTSIDE DIAMETER OF BOILER : 6'- 4 3/16"
LENGTH BETWEEN TUBEPLATES : 13'-0".
GRATE INSIDE FOUNDATION RING : 6'-2⅞" x 7'-11⅛"
GRATE AREA : 49·5 SQ. FT.
HEATING SURFACES : FLUE TUBES : 670 SQ. FT.
" " BOILER TUBES : 1456 SQ. FT.
" " FIREBOX : 189 SQ. FT.
" " BRICK ARCH TUBES : 23 SQ. FT.
TOTAL EVAPORATION : 2338 SQ. FT.
SUPERHEATER : 480 SQ. FT.
TOTAL : 2818 SQ. FT.

BATCH	SERVICE ENTRY	COST PER ENGINE
I	1938	
II	1929/30	

The 16th class were a direct enlargement of the 14th class, with units having eight-coupled wheels apiece, providing about one third more power. All mechanical features, bar frames, round topped firebox, and ultra-short steam lap and valve travel remained. Their original task was a stop-gap job, conveying ever increasing coal traffic north, and copper south, between Wankie and Monze, and of the first batch 221-4 were allocated to Wankie and 225-8 to Livingstone. This was the original pioneer route, out of Wankie up the Katuna river valley, and to Fuller from Matetsi with gradients of 1 in 50 uncompensated for 7 chain curves, equal to 1 in 37 straight gradi-

16th class in early condition. No 227, first number, with small tank and bunker, and flared chimney. RR

ents. The Katuna bank had a severe S-bend (sometimes mistakenly described as a horseshoe curve) and this route may still be traversed by what is called the Bingwa loop road, through delightfully wild terrain even today. Meanwhile the Deka to Victoria Falls deviation was under construction enabling heavy loads to be hauled by 12th class up mere 1 in 120 gradients, after which the 16th were transferred to Salisbury for working the heavy road to Umtali.

It was on these duties the coal and water capacities were found inadequate, and both were increased in two stages. The original front tank held 2650 gallons, but this was raised about six inches to provide 3200 gallons capacity, increased later again to 3340 gallons. Meanwhile the original six ton bunker was firstly raised to hold 8 3/4 tons of coal, and later again lengthened to carry eleven tons. Now all railways have a natural departmental battle between the traffic men and both civil and mechanical engineers. Traffic want more powerful engines to haul greater loads over longer distances, which the CME can provide easily were it not for the civil engineer who naturally lays down restrictions on both axle loads and all-up weight for his beloved track and structures! However, the 16th class are a good example of how official figures are "adjusted" (sounds better than "fiddled") to meet these conflicting criteria. As built, with their original and smallest capacities weight in full working order was quoted, probably truthfully, as 150,65 tons. After adding 550 gallons (2,45 tons) of extra water, 5 tons of additional coal, and perhaps half a ton of plating to hold these additions, totalling about 8 tons in all. The final weight on the last diagram issued showed an all-up weight of 155,29 tons. Nearly 3 1/2 tons had been "lost" during these processes,

but as no disasters were attributable to this camouflaged obesity, everybody remained happy!

A second batch of 16th class were placed in service during 1938, enabling several engines to be allocated to the North line for coal and copper traffic, their original *raison d'etre*, and it was the earlier batch which returned to their old ground, typically, as at November 1938, seeing Bulawayo with 226, Wankie with 221-22, and Livingstone with 223/27, although the two batches soon began to mix. By 1950 most were again at Salisbury, and in June 1951 221 was renumbered 600, some months elapsing before the remainder became 601-19. By the end of 1955 Salisbury and Bulawayo had ten each, then by mid 1956 all were at Bulawayo presumably handling heavy traffic on the north line whilst the 20th class were on order. After the 20th/20A class were commissioned they drifted back to Salisbury where most utilisation was on the branches north of the city.

The 16th class were the first big Garratts rendered redundant by dieselisation, but being sturdy and powerful machines they were in demand elsewhere, nine being sold to the Benguela Railway in Angola, where their principal dimensions almost exactly matched the standard CFB Garratts of 4-8-2 + 2-8-4 wheel arrangement. Two only were scrapped by RR, eight sold to collieries in South Africa, and the first engine, no 600, is preserved in the Bulawayo museum. No 605, sold to Landau colliery where it operated in maroon livery, was also preserved privately after withdrawal, although unfortunately badly vandalised after being left unattended for several years.

An interesting modification was made to no 612 whilst in South African colliery service, where it was fitted with a Giesl ejector. This is believed to have been fitted whilst working at either Enyati or Vryheid Coronation, but was first noted by the author when working at Durnacol, Dannhauser, by which time the boiler unit with Giesl ejector had been mated with engine units from 604, formerly of Apex colliery, near Witbank. These colliery engines were purchased by Dunn's Locomotive Works, Witbank, and mainly hired out to various mines, where they usually worked with their RR insignia and original numbers.

As the 16th class in South Africa were mainly owned by Dunn's it is possible that there were one or two short term users not recorded in the accompanying table. Those sold to the Benguela Railway (CFB) in Angola seem to have been renumbered probably in order of issuing to traffic. They were classified at the end of the standard Garratts, as "10a class E" and converted to wood firing, a large cage substituting for the former coal bunker. Weight in working order was given on the CFM diagram book as 155,15 metric tonnes, rather lighter than before, but whether this represents an actual reduction due to the lower specific gravity of Eucalyptus relative to coal, or whether it was an "adjustment" to suit the local civil engineer will probably never now be known! They worked mainly in the upper,

easterly, sections of the CFB, largely around Luso, and the late F.C. Butcher seems the only person who obtained good photographs of the CFB locomotives.

Renumbering

All were given their new numbers in 1951, 600 in June, 604/07/12 in July and the remainder in August.

Double 16th workings

The 16th class were used in pairs not infrequently, making a formidable Garratt combination totalling over 100 000 pounds of tractive effort, and more than 100 square feet of grate area, figures more in line with practice in the USA!. From Salisbury, doubleheaders sometimes worked on the Shamva and Sinoia branches, and these would occasionally have been worked by two 16th class. In Angola pairs of 16th class worked out of Luso in an operation described by the CFB authorities as a "dupla", with one engine leading and another cut in halfway down the train. Finally, at Douglas Colliery, South Africa, the author arrived early one morning to find two ex-RR 16th in steam only to find that during the night shift one had hauled trains whilst the other acted as banker! In daylight, only one engine was used, to his great frustration.

Historical data:

First Number	Second Number	Beyer Peacock	Date Built	Date in Service	Last Used	Disposal
221	600	6562	1929	12/1929	9/1967	Bulawayo museum
222	601	6563	1929	1/1930	7/1963	CFB 9/1964 no 388
223	602	6564	1929	1/1930	8/1964	CFB 9/1964 no 381
224	603	6565	1929	1/1930	4/1963	Dunn's 5/1963. Douglas Colliery, Dunn's 11/1975
225	604	6566	1929	1/1930	3/1968	Dunn's 3/1971. Apex, then Douglas. Engine units to Durnacol for 612
226	605	6567	1929	1/1930	3/1963	Dunn's 6/1963 Landau 3 colliery no 1 Preserved
227	606	6568	1929	1/1930	4/1963	Dunn's 6/1963 Enyati, later Vryheid Coronation Co
228	607	6569	1929	1/1930	10/1963	CFB 9/1964 no 389
259	608	6877	1938	5/1938	10/1963	Darwendale collision. Scrapped 8/1964
260	609	6878	1938	5/1938	12/1970	Dunn's 3/1971. Transvaal Navigation Colliery
261	610	6879	1938	5/1938	6/1964	CFB 9/1964 no 382
262	611	6880	1938	5/1938	9/1963	CFB 9/1964 no 385
263	612	6881	1938	6/1938	6/1968	Dunn's 2/1971. Douglas, later Durnacol collieries
264	613	6882	1938	6/1938	3/1967	Scrapped 4/1972
265	614	6899	1938	6/1938	3/1967	Dunn's 5/1971. Cannibalised for spare parts
266	615	6900	1938	7/1938	7/1964	CFB 9/1964. no 383
267	616	6901	1938	7/1938	8/1963	CFB 9/1964. no 386
268	617	6902	1938	7/1938	7/1963	CFB 9/1964. no 384
269	618	6903	1938	7/1938	5/1970	Dunn's 3/1971. Enyati Colliery
270	619	6904	1938	7/1938	6/1963	CFB 9/1964. no 387

16th class 618 in final condition, at Salisbury, the second last of its class in RR service.
Author's collection

A rare doubleheader at Willoughby's siding, near Gwelo. 16th class 609 leads 20th class 704 on a freight for Bulawayo.
F. C. Butcher

Another Butcher rarity, 16th class 613 leads a 16A class at an unknown location, possibly Mount Hampden Junction.
F. C. Butcher

Class 16A, 2-8-2 + 2-8-2 Garratt

GENERAL PARTICULARS

SUPERHEATED
TRACTIVE FORCE AT 85% B.W.P. : 58,183 LB.
FACTOR OF ADHESION AT 85% BWP= 4·51.
MAXIMUM COUPLED AXLE LOAD F.W.O. : 14·64 TONS
WEIGHT ON ALL COUPLED WHEELS: 117·12 TONS FND.
TOTAL WEIGHT OF ENGINE (EMPTY): 127·8 TONS.
"   "   "   "   (F.W.O.) 169·18 TONS.
WEIGHT PER FOOT RUN OVER BUFFERS: 2·05 TONS
WATER CAPACITY : FRONT TANK: 3,045 GALLS.
"   "   : HIND TANK: 1,955 "
"   "   : TOTAL : 5,000 GALLS.
COAL CAPACITY : 8½ TONS.
RIGID WHEEL BASE : 13'-1½"
NUMBER OF ENGINES: BATCH I-30. Nos. 620-649.

ENGINE

CYLINDERS: (2 ON EACH UNIT) 18½" DIA. × 24" STROKE.
BOGIE WHEELS : 2'-9" DIA.
COUPLED WHEELS : 4'-0" DIA.
ROLLER BEARINGS: {ECCENTRIC ROD.
{BOGIE BOXES-ENG. Nos 640-649.
AXLE JOURNALS {PLAIN BOGIE WHEELS : 11" × 6¾ DIA.
{   : COUPLED   : 9" × 8" DIA.
CONNECTING ROD CENTRES: 8'-3"
BRAKES: STEAM AND VACUUM.
BRAKE POWER : 51·41 TONS AT 43·9%
INJECTORS : Nº 11 GRESHAM & CRAVEN
VALVES : PISTON. 9" DIA. × 6" TRAVEL.
TYPE OF VALVE GEAR: WALSCHAERTS.

BOILER

PRESSURE : 200 LB. PER SQ. INCH.
SMALLEST OUTSIDE DIA. OF BARREL: 6'-4 9/16"
LENGTH BETWEEN TUBEPLATES: 13'-0⅜"
GRATE INSIDE FOUNDATION RING: 6'-3⅛" × 7'-11¾₆"
GRATE AREA: 49·6 SQ. FT.
HEATING SURFACES : FLUE TUBES : } 2,131 SQ.FT.
"   " : BOILER TUBES: }
"   " : ARCH TUBES: } 212 SQ.FT.
"   " : FIREBOX : }
TOTAL EVAPORATION : 2,343 SQ.FT
SUPER HEATER : 494 SQ.FT
TOTAL : 2,837 SQ.FT

BATCH	SERVICE ENTRY	COST PER ENGINE
I	1953	

16A class 625, as built with flared chimney. Beyer Peacock

The 16A class were, as might be expected, a modernised version of the older 16th class. The design was thoroughly revised throughout and externally was notable for the "streamlined" tanks and bunkers, while the cab was widened to the maximum possible below waistrail, with inwardly sloping panels above. Internally they had long travel, long lap, valve gear, roller bearings on pony truck axles, separate boxes on the earlier engines but cannon boxes on most, and higher boiler pressure. This latter gave them a tractive effort equal to the former 18th class, to which they were mechanically vastly superior.

Between 1957 and 1958 they suffered several problems, mainly boiler, due to rather shoddy manufacture, as happened also to the later 20th class. It appears that Beyer Peacock, in its later years, instead of former proud traditions of management by engineers, and work performed by craftsmen, had descended to the modern malaise of management by accountants of radical trade union "workers", a situation which led eventually to the firm's closure. In May 1957 nine of the 16As were stopped for repairs, increasing to fifteen (just half the class) by July, and it was not until October 1958 that all were back into normal service. The new 20th class suffered similar problems, and this affected the distribution of the 16A class which were withdrawn from their originally intended work in the copperbelt and used around Bulawayo to cover duties intended for the 20th class. Boiler problems recurred for a while in 1967.

Despite these problems, the 16A were finally excellent machines and those remaining in Rhodesia after the independence of Zambia were, with the exception of three loaned to Beira in Moçambique, included in the refurbishment programme which included roller bearings on driving and coupled axles, and a somewhat piecemeal replacement of tanks and bunkers by units of larger capacity. A survey carried out by the author, and checked by the late Chris Butcher, showed the following variations as refurbished.
Original tank and bunker: 601, 606, 609
New tank, old bunker: 604 (unique)
New tank and bunker:
602/03/05/07/08/10/11/12/14/15.
608 and 615 at one time carried longer, 14A type, chimneys, but these were later replaced by standard.

No new diagram was ever issued to cover the refurbished 16A which, with their various improvements will be heavier than that as built, but some pencilled figures on the original diagram as reproduced possibly indicate the estimated new weights which will, as described, vary from engine to engine.

Although built for low speed, slogging, work, the 16A were surprisingly versatile, especially after fitting with roller bearings on the main axles. In their later years they were not infrequently used on passenger trains and despite their four foot wheels, speeds of well over 50 mph

(80km/h) were easily attained. They also seemed to have greater reliability than the 15th classes, and during 1989, when a strike by artisan staff caused serious disruptions to services, it was the good old 16As which, released from slogging over the 1 in 40 gradients of the West Nicholson branch during the week, were available for passenger service, replacing 15As, on the Plumtree line over the weekend!

Three 16A, 627, 634 and 639 were loaned to Moçambique for the Beira line in November 1975, returning June 1981. It was originally intended to include these in the refurbishment programme, when they would have been renumbered 616-18, but their condition as returned from Beira prevented this. 639 was never used again, but 627 and 634 were utilised on shunting only until scrapped in 1983. Those refurbished were renumbered as shown in the table, the first few refurbished engines re-entering service with their old numbers for a short while.

Of the engines left in Zambia, all were gradually run into the ground, as was normal policy in that unfortunate country, but two engines, 620 and 623, were purchased by the ZCCM for their mine at Kitwe/Nkana. 620 was sent to ZECO in Bulawayo for refurbishment and sent to Kitwe where it enjoyed several years use. 623 although ZCCM property, never moved from Livingstone, where it was dumped. The last stage in the 16A saga, is the purchase of 615 by Transnet Museum, South Africa, for use as backup and other power for the restored GEA Garratt especially over the Montagu pass out of George. To fit the South African loading gauge, 615 will need its cab reducing in width to a similar profile to the original 16th class. Nevertheless it was moved to Millsite in January 1997 without problems, and in March despatched to the Cape!

16A class distribution

Date	Salisbury	Gwelo	Bulawayo	Broken Hill	Ndola	Nkana
1/1954	7	-	8	14	-	-
1/1958	-	-	16	-	-	-
10/1958	-	-	19	2	5	2
6/1960	-	-	22	-	3	2
6/1965	9	-	4	-	-	15
6/1967	5	-	5	1	-	10
					———— Z a m b i a ————	
6/1970	12	1	5		10	
6/1975	-	9	8		11	
	B e i r a					
6/1979	3*	6	5		n/a	
6/1982	-	-	16		n/a	
Thence all Bulawayo. (15 locos)						

* On loan to CFM.

Historical data:

First Number	Second Number	Date Re-numbered	Beyer Peacock	Date Built	Date in Service	Date Refurb.	Last Used	Disposal
620	-	-	7498	1952	1/1953	-	6/1967	Zambia. sold ZCCM Kitwe, out of use, 1994.**
621	-	-	7499	1952	1/1953	-	6/1967	Zambia, derelict Livingstone.
622	-	-	7500	1952	1/1953	-	6/1967	Zambia, derelict Livingstone.
623	-	-	7501	1952	2/1953	-	6/1967	Zambia, sold ZCCM, not refurbished.***
624	-	-	7502	1952	2/1953	-	6/1967	Zambia, scrapped Kabwe 3/1979.
625	601	6/81	7503	1953	3/1953	7/1979	8/1993	Museum, operable.
626	602	11/80	7504	1953	3/1953	6/1980		Awaiting scrap instructions.
627	*	-	7505	1953	3/1953	-	7.1983	To CFM Beira 11/1975. Scrapped 8/1983.
628	603	6/81	7506	1953	3/1953	4/1980	10/1991	Stationary boiler, loco shed.
629	604	6/81	7507	1953	4/1953	3/1980		In service.
630	-	-	7508	1953	4/1953	-	6/1967	Zambia, derelict Kabwe
631	605	6/81	7509	1953	4/1953	3/1980		In service.
632	606	6.81	7510	1953	4/1953	10/1979	9/1994	Tendered for scrap.
633	607	6/81	7511	1953	4/1953	2/1980	8/1993	Museum.
634	*	-	7512	1953	5/1953	-	12/1982	To CFM Beira 11/1975. Scrapped 8/1983.
635	608	6/81	7513	1953	5/1953	5/1980		In service.
636	609	6/81	7514	1953	5/1953	6/1979	10/1990	Scrapped 9/1991.
637	610	7/80	7515	1953	5/1953	7/1980	8/1995	Museum.
638	611	7/80	7516	1953	5/1953	7/1980		Museum.
639	*		7517	1953	5/1953	-	11/1975	To CFM Beira 11/1975, scrapped 10/1982.
640-	-	-	7518	1953	5/1953	-	6/1967	Zambia, scrapped Kabwe 9/1978.
641	-	-	7519	1953	6/1953	-	6/1967	Zambia, derelict Livingstone.
642	-	-	7520	1953	6/1953	-	6/1967	Zambia, scrapped Kabwe 9/1978.
643	612	6/81	7521	1953	7/1953	6/1979		In service, allotted to Museum.
644	-	-	7522	1953	7/1953	-	6/1967	Zambia, scrapped Kabwe 9/1978.
645	613	1/81	7523	1953	7/1953	11/1979		Museum.
646	-	-	7524	1953	7/1953	-	6/1967	Zambia, derelict Kabwe.
647	614	9/80	7525	1953	8/1953	9/1980	4/1993	Mothballed.
648	615	10/80	7526	1953	8/1953	10/1980	5/1993	Sold to Transnet, 1995.
649	-	-	7527	1953	8/1953	-	5/1967	Scrapped Zambia 1/1970 (collision).

* Engines 627/34/39 loaned to CFM Beira 11/1975. Returned 6/1981. Provisionally allocated numbers 616-18 after refurbishment, but in poor condition and not refurbished.

** 620 Refurbished ZECO 1991.

*** 623 to Livingstone Museum 1995-6

New capacities and weights:

The original water and coal capacities of the 16A locomotives was 3045 gallons in the front tank plus 1955 in the rear, making 5000 gallons. Coal capacity was 8 1/2 tons. Maximum axle load was 14.64 tons. Pencilled into the author's diagram are figures increasing front and rear tanks by 400 and 200 gallons respectively, with coal increased to 11 tons, making a total extra weight of 6 1/2 tons, plus (say) half a ton for platework, making 7 tons in all. Engine weight is up from 169.18 to 180 tons, the remainder probably being accounted for the roller bearings and especially their cannon box housings. Actual extra capacities from the detail drawings are 499 gallons for the front tanks, and 384 gallons rear, but evidently all this was not utilised. No official amended diagrams were ever issued, and with the variations in front and rear tanks as applied, the actual weights of individual engines may be "guesstimated" from the above!

Renumbering:

The fifteen engines remaining in Zimbabwe were renumbered 601 to 615 in a rather piecemeal fashion, with six engines done from July 1980 to January 1981, the remainder following in June 1981. Thus several were refurbished whilst retaining their original numbers. The three engines on loan to Beira were to have become 616-18 after refurbishing, but being in poor condition were neither refurbished nor renumbered.

Roller bearing insignia:

Goods wagons, in Rhodesia and Zimbabwe, when fitted with roller bearings carried painted insignia, comprising three rings in line, to denote this. This was to prevent maintenance staff applying the old thick "goo" in error. The first few 16A with roller bearings, perhaps a few other locos, also originally carried this logo.

Postscript:

In July 1997, 601 was noted with new front tank, and 604 with larger bunker.

16A 635 (old number) at Glendale, with the mixed train from Salisbury to Shamva in 1968. Here the engine prepares to depart.

A pair of 16A, led by 628, roll into Balla Balla station with the cross tripper working, before returning with a full load of limestone.
F.C. Butcher

149

A pair of 16A, led by 632, thunder up Mulungwane bank with a fully loaded "crosstripper" bound for Cement and Mpopoma. F. C. Butcher

Engine 601, which still retained its original smaller tank and bunker, seems particularly popular as a passenger engine. Here it leaves Coldridge siding with the Botswana train in 1989.

Departing Mbalabala with a short load, 615 with enlarged tank, is well on its way for the climb ahead.

The formerly unique 604, with enlarged front tank but original bunker, roars up Mulungwane with a full load in 1987.

With exemplary timing, 612 on a northbound limestone train, which has been audible for many minutes, thunders into the rising sun at Big Ben Road seconds after the shadow cleared!

609, still with small tank and bunker, erupts from Hwange tunnel with a southbound freight in 1981.

The first few 16A were not renumbered until after refurbishment. 628 is seen here after refurbishment but with original number.

602 storms out round "Christine's curve", with a southbound coal train, 16A were quite common on the north line while the 20/20A classes were being refurbished.

Putting on a full fire after easing off for the tunnel, 614 bellows well on a southbound coal train in 1981.

On another occasion, with water tanks for Lukosi, whose pump had failed, 614 rolls through "Chris' Vista", named after the late Chris Butcher who discovered the spot. It was a long walk to get there, and there were lion in the vicinity, but a quiet growl from the bush was the worst that ever happened!

17th class, 4-6-4 + 4-6-4 Garratt

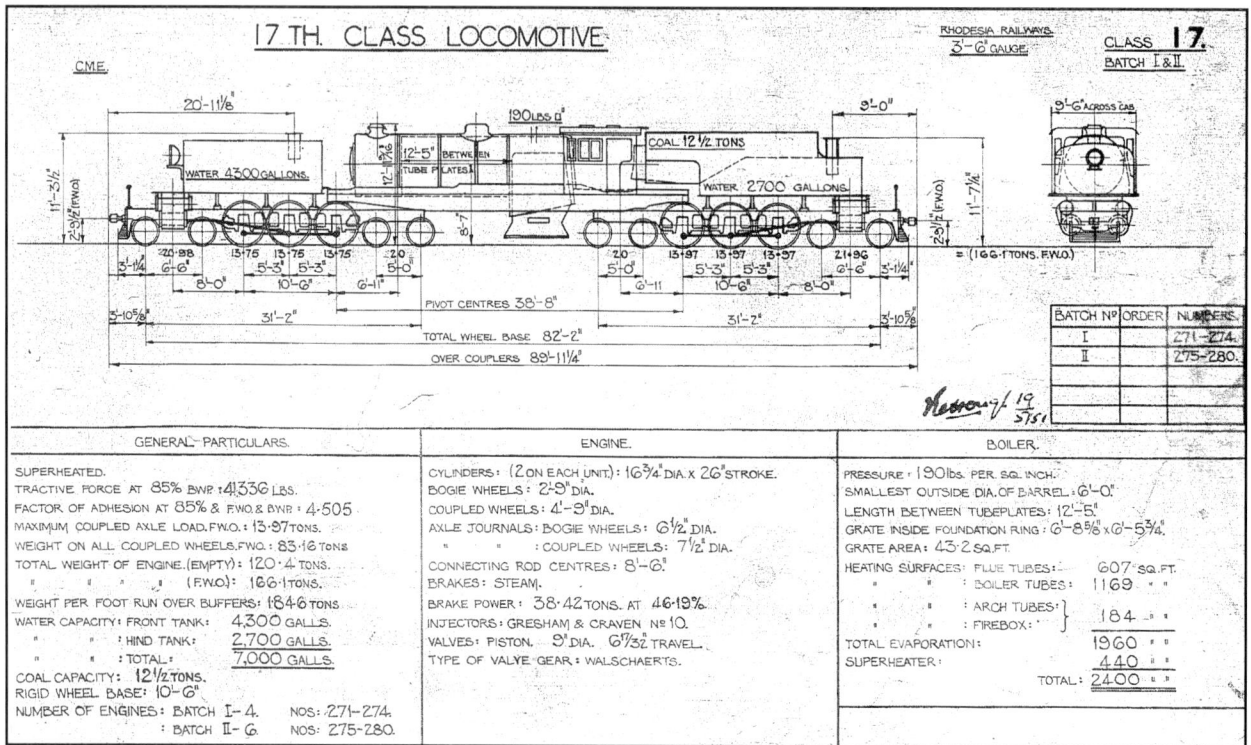

17. TH. CLASS LOCOMOTIVE

RHODESIA RAILWAYS. 3'-6" GAUGE — CLASS 17. BATCH I & II.

BATCH Nº	ORDER	NUMBERS
I		271-274
II		275-280

GENERAL PARTICULARS.	ENGINE.	BOILER.
SUPERHEATED.	CYLINDERS: (2 ON EACH UNIT): 16¾" DIA. x 26" STROKE.	PRESSURE: 190 lbs. PER. SQ. INCH.
TRACTIVE FORCE AT 85% BWP: 41,336 LBS.	BOGIE WHEELS: 2'-9" DIA.	SMALLEST OUTSIDE DIA. OF BARREL: 6'-0".
FACTOR OF ADHESION AT 85% & F.W.O. & BWP: 4.505	COUPLED WHEELS: 4'-3" DIA.	LENGTH BETWEEN TUBEPLATES: 12'-5".
MAXIMUM COUPLED AXLE LOAD. F.W.O.: 13.97 TONS.	AXLE JOURNALS: BOGIE WHEELS: 6½" DIA.	GRATE INSIDE FOUNDATION RING: 6'-8⅝" x 6'-5¾".
WEIGHT ON ALL COUPLED WHEELS. F.W.O.: 83.18 TONS	" : COUPLED WHEELS: 7½" DIA.	GRATE AREA: 43.2 SQ. FT.
TOTAL WEIGHT OF ENGINE. (EMPTY): 120.4 TONS.	CONNECTING ROD CENTRES: 8'-6".	HEATING SURFACES: FLUE TUBES: 607 SQ. FT.
" " " (F.W.O.): 166.1 TONS.	BRAKES: STEAM.	" " : BOILER TUBES: 1169 " "
WEIGHT PER FOOT RUN OVER BUFFERS: 1.846 TONS.	BRAKE POWER: 38.42 TONS. AT 46.19%.	" " : ARCH TUBES: } 184 " "
WATER CAPACITY: FRONT TANK: 4,300 GALLS.	INJECTORS: GRESHAM & CRAVEN Nº 10.	" " : FIREBOX: }
" " : HIND TANK: 2,700 GALLS.	VALVES: PISTON. 9" DIA. 6⅞" TRAVEL.	TOTAL EVAPORATION: 1960
" " : TOTAL: 7,000 GALLS.	TYPE OF VALVE GEAR: WALSCHAERTS.	SUPERHEATER: 440 " "
COAL CAPACITY: 12½ TONS.		TOTAL: 2400 " "
RIGID WHEEL BASE: 10'-6".		
NUMBER OF ENGINES: BATCH I- 4. NOS: 271-274.		
" : BATCH II- 6. NOS: 275-280.		

Sudan Railways Garratt No 252, later RR 17th class 273. Beyer Peacock advertisment

The 17th class were the first 4-6-4 + 4-6-4 Garratts ever built, and possibly led to the use of that unique wheel arrangement on Rhodesia Railways. Originally built for the Sudan Government Railways, for hauling heavy traffic over lightly laid lines, as were so many Garratts, their downfall was the sandy conditions of that desert country. Track was "ballasted" with indigenous sand, and in the days before wide-spread use of roller bearings, the dust kicked up by the leading engine unit played havoc with the bearings of the following unit, leading to heavy maintenance costs. They were eventually superceded by straight 4-8-2 tender engines.

At the time of their availability, Rhodesia was in the grip of the post-war locomotive shortage and thankfully purchased what seemed to be a bargain in what was similar to the native 15th class. In terms of axle load, total weight, and nominal tractive effort the 17th class were close equivalents to the 15ths, but boiler capacity was much less. Boiler diameter was the same as a

14th class, and grate area nearer to a 14th than a 15th, such that hopeful rostering of a 17th to a 15th class duty produced disappointing results. As such, they became unpopular, and this was exacerbated by a stuffy cab with inadequate ventilation. Cabs were slightly modified before going into service, but the complaints remained (one wonders how hot they were in Sudanese conditions, perhaps another factor in their being sold). Had they been rostered for lower grade jobs, they may have been more successful, as they had good valve events, but a hard pressed roster clerk in a locomotive shortage was too easily tempted to specify them for jobs they could not do! As a result, they were downgraded largely to shunting, for which they were hardly suited and, purchased in an emergency, they were happily sold to the Beira line in Moçambique who later experienced a similar shortage of motive power.

The first four engines, after erection, were allocated to Bulawayo, but very soon were sent to Livingstone, where 272-7 were allocated late 1950. By early 1951 they had all been returned to Bulawayo and over the next few years, from 1951 to 1957, one or two were sent out to Gwelo where, under sufference they were allocated to local goods duties. By early 1958 most were at Salisbury, on what duties seem unknown, but where they were fairly handy for flogging to the innocent Moçambiquans when they needed more power for the Beira line. Thus the whole class was available for sale when needed in 1964/5, spending probably at least another ten years at work on the lower section between Beira and Vila Machado, from whence the larger, eight-coupled, Garratts took over for the two escarpment sections between there and Umtali. The 17th class in Moçambique were often used on passenger trains, which they shared with the ex-SAR GF Garratts, but were otherwise mainly used for freight trains.

Historical data:

| Sudan G. Rlys | | | | | | | CFM Estado | |
First Number	Second Number	RR Number	Beyer Peacock	Date Built	Date in RR Service	Last Used	Sold	Number
250	100	271	6798	1936	3/1950	5/1963	9/1964	921
251	101	272	6799	1936	2/1950	5/1964	8/1964	922
252	102	273	6800	1936	1/1950	5/1964	10/1964	923
253	103	274	6801	1936	5/1950	3/1963	11/1964	924
254	104	275	6870	1937	6/1950	5/1963	7/1964	925
255	105	276	6871	1937	7/1950	9/1964	3/1965	926
256	106	277	6872	1937	9/1950	5/1963	11/1964	927
257	107	278	6873	1937	10/1950	1/1965	3/1965	928
258	108	279	6874	1937	12/1950	7/1963	1/1965	929
259	109	280	6875	1937	12/1950	5/1964	7/1964	930

Sudan Railways Garratt No 100, just arrived at Bulawayo. Note ACFI feed heating equipment removed.
J. R. Lloyd

17th class No 277 poses at Bulawayo. F. C. Butcher

A rare shot of 17th class No 278 hauling a train at an unknown location. NRZ

18th class, 2-8-2 + 2-8-2 Garratt

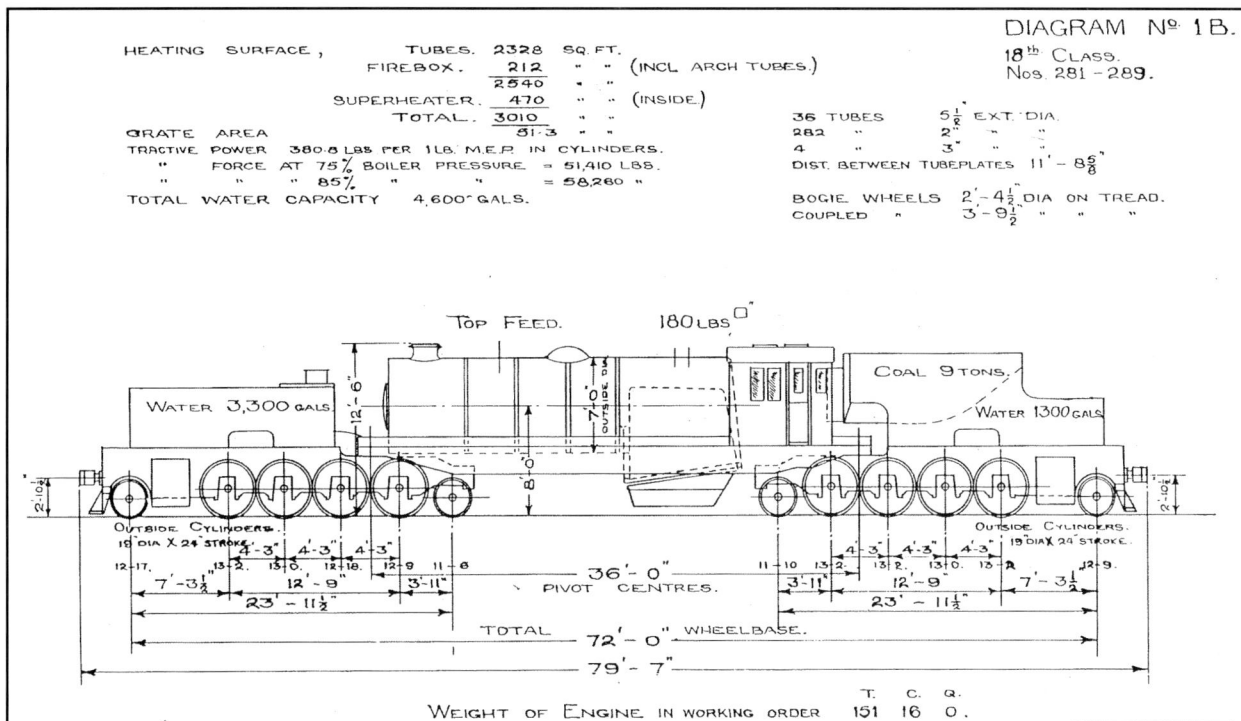

DIAGRAM Nº 1 B.
18ᵗʰ Class.
Nos. 281 – 289.

HEATING SURFACE,
TUBES. 2328 SQ. FT.
FIREBOX. 212 " " (INCL ARCH TUBES.)
2540 " "
SUPERHEATER. 470 " " (INSIDE.)
TOTAL. 3010 " "
GRATE AREA 51·3 " "
TRACTIVE POWER 380·8 LBS PER 1 LB. M.E.P. IN CYLINDERS.
" FORCE AT 75% BOILER PRESSURE = 51,410 LBS.
" " " 85% " " = 58,260 "
TOTAL WATER CAPACITY 4,600 GALS.

36 TUBES 5⅛ EXT. DIA.
282 " 2⅛ "
4 " 3" "
DIST. BETWEEN TUBEPLATES 11' – 8⅝"

BOGIE WHEELS 2' – 4½ DIA ON TREAD.
COUPLED " 3' – 9½ " " "

TOP FEED. 180 LBS
WATER 3,300 GALS
COAL 9 TONS.
WATER 1300 GALS

OUTSIDE CYLINDERS. 19 DIA X 24 STROKE.
OUTSIDE CYLINDERS. 19 DIA X 24 STROKE.

7' – 3½" 12' – 9" 3' – 11"
23' – 11½"
36' – 0" PIVOT CENTRES.
3' – 11" 12' – 9" 7' – 3½"
23' – 11½"
TOTAL 72' – 0" WHEELBASE.
79' – 7"

T. C. Q.
WEIGHT OF ENGINE IN WORKING ORDER 151 16 0.

18th class lettered and numbered RR281, but still carrying the 'WD 4409' identity. Beyer Peacock

During World War II, from 1939-45, haulage of munitions and other war supplies was in great demand, and the major powers turned out vast numbers of heavy freight engines, often to "austerity" designs lacking all frills in the expectation of short lives. Britain built mainly 2-8-0, Americans 2-8-0 and 2-8-2, whilst Germany built thousands of 2-10-0. It is a tribute to the Garratt concept that it was considered suitable in such days for wartime construction and use, and two basic groups were built, metre gauge with ten ton axle load for the far East, and larger engines with 13 ton axle load for Africa. Of these latter seven were 4-8-2 + 2-8-4 of metre gauge for Kenya, and the remaining eighteen were 3'6" gauge 2-8-2 + 2-8-2 for central Africa, six to the Gold Coast, three

for the Congo Ocean Railway, and nine for Rhodesia. The design was based on the South African GE class, with plate frames and small wheels, but as a wartime expedient did the job designed for. In fact, on each railway used, they were at the time the most powerful engines on the system.

All had British War Department numbers, but each railway numbered and classified them within its own system after delivery. The Rhodesian batch were classed 18th, and were placed immediately into the North line service, hauling coal and copper, the initial allocation being Bulawayo 282/9, Wankie 281/3/4 and Broken Hill 285-8. From mid 1947 Umtali started to have some allocated, and they were all there by August 1948, working down into Moçambique in conjunction with the earlier 14th class. No doubt by then negotiations were under way for selling the Beira section to Moçambique, and by allocating these War orphans to the line, a class which did not conform to Rhodesian standards was conveniently jettisoned! However, the CFM seemed happy enough with them and subsequently purchased the three which went to the Congo-Ocean Railway, to make up the dozen. As built they were designed down to a 12'6" high loading gauge, but presumably to improve steaming extensions were added to the short chimneys. By the time the author first saw them in Moçambique, shapely chimneys of greater height had been fitted, but it has not been possible to establish whether this was an RR or CFM modification. The three ex-C-O locos were also fitted after sale to CFM. A few of the Moçambique survivors were noted dumped at Gondola in November 1993, but had evidently not been used for several years, the others presumably having been scrapped.

Historical data:

War Dept. Number	RR Number	Beyer Peacock	Date Built	Date in Service	Sold to CFM	CFM Number	Disposal
4409	281	7066	1943	10/1943	10/1949	981	Scrapped
4410	282	7067	1943	10/1943	10/1949	982	Gondola
4411	283	7068	1943	10/1943	10/1949	983	Gondola
4412	284	7069	1943	1/1944	10/1949	984	Scrapped
4413	285	7070	1944	5/1944	10/1949	985	Gondola
4414	286	7071	1944	5/1944	10/1949	986	Scrapped
4415	287	7072	1944	5/1944	10/1949	987	Scrapped
4416	288	7073	1944	6/1944	10/1949	988	Scrapped
4417	289	7074	1944	6/1944	10/1949	989	Scrapped

982/3/5 derelict Gondola Oct 1993. No later information available.

An interesting transition. W. D. heavy Garratt running as RR Mashonaland No 287, and fitted with German style chimney extension, This loco later went to Moçambique, and was fitted with a permanent chimney of taller proportions. W. H. C. Kelland

19th class, 4-8-2

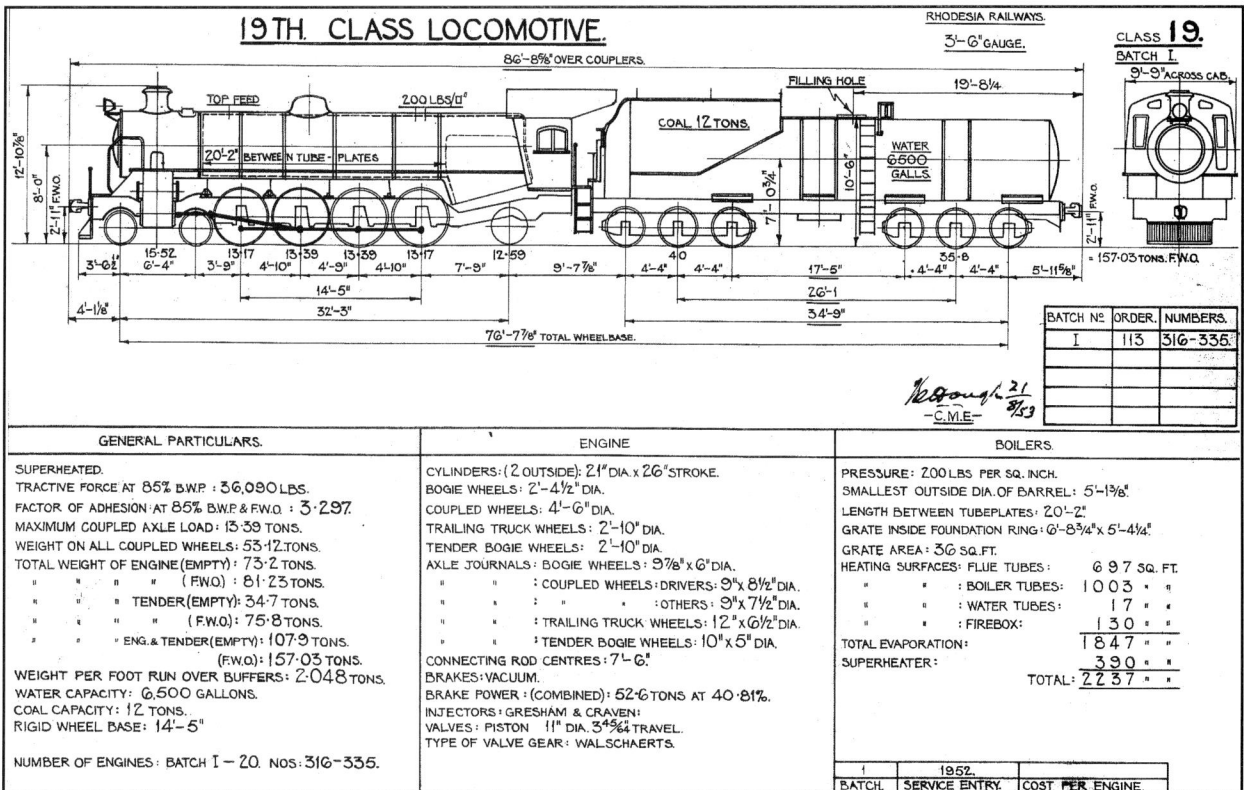

19TH. CLASS LOCOMOTIVE.

RHODESIA RAILWAYS.
3'-6" GAUGE.

CLASS **19.**
BATCH I.

86'-8⅝" OVER COUPLERS.

FILLING HOLE
19'-8¼"
TOP FEED
200 LBS/☐"
COAL 12 TONS.
WATER 6500 GALLS.
9'-9" ACROSS CAB.

20'-2" BETWEEN TUBE-PLATES.

= 157.03 TONS. F.W.O.

76'-7⅞" TOTAL WHEELBASE.

BATCH N⁰	ORDER.	NUMBERS.
I	113	316-335.

—C.M.E.

GENERAL PARTICULARS.

SUPERHEATED.
TRACTIVE FORCE AT 85% B.W.P. : 36,090 LBS.
FACTOR OF ADHESION AT 85% B.W.P. & F.W.O. : 3·297.
MAXIMUM COUPLED AXLE LOAD : 13·39 TONS.
WEIGHT ON ALL COUPLED WHEELS : 53·12 TONS.
TOTAL WEIGHT OF ENGINE (EMPTY) : 73·2 TONS.
   "   "   " (F.W.O.) : 81·23 TONS.
   "   "   " TENDER (EMPTY) : 34·7 TONS.
   "   "   " (F.W.O.) : 75·8 TONS.
   "   " ENG. & TENDER (EMPTY) : 107·9 TONS.
           (F.W.O.) : 157·03 TONS.
WEIGHT PER FOOT RUN OVER BUFFERS : 2·048 TONS.
WATER CAPACITY : 6,500 GALLONS.
COAL CAPACITY : 12 TONS.
RIGID WHEEL BASE : 14'-5"

NUMBER OF ENGINES : BATCH I — 20. NOS. 316-335.

ENGINE

CYLINDERS : (2 OUTSIDE) : 21" DIA. x 26" STROKE.
BOGIE WHEELS : 2'-4½" DIA.
COUPLED WHEELS : 4'-6" DIA.
TRAILING TRUCK WHEELS : 2'-10" DIA.
TENDER BOGIE WHEELS : 2'-10" DIA.
AXLE JOURNALS : BOGIE WHEELS : 9⅞" x 6" DIA.
   "   " : COUPLED WHEELS : DRIVERS : 9" x 8½" DIA.
   "   "   " : OTHERS : 9" x 7½" DIA.
   "   " : TRAILING TRUCK WHEELS : 12" x 6½" DIA.
   "   " : TENDER BOGIE WHEELS : 10" x 5" DIA.
CONNECTING ROD CENTRES : 7'-6".
BRAKES : VACUUM.
BRAKE POWER : (COMBINED) : 52·6 TONS AT 40·81%.
INJECTORS : GRESHAM & CRAVEN :
VALVES : PISTON 11" DIA. 3⁴⁵⁄₆₄ TRAVEL.
TYPE OF VALVE GEAR : WALSCHAERTS.

BOILERS.

PRESSURE : 200 LBS PER SQ. INCH.
SMALLEST OUTSIDE DIA. OF BARREL : 5'-1⅜".
LENGTH BETWEEN TUBEPLATES : 20'-2".
GRATE INSIDE FOUNDATION RING : 6'-8¾" x 5'-4¼".
GRATE AREA : 36 SQ. FT.

HEATING SURFACES :	FLUE TUBES :	697 SQ. FT.
"	" : BOILER TUBES :	1003 "
"	" : WATER TUBES :	17 "
"	" : FIREBOX :	130 "
TOTAL EVAPORATION :		1847 "
SUPERHEATER :		390 "
	TOTAL :	2237 "

BATCH.	SERVICE ENTRY.	COST PER ENGINE.
1	1952.	

19th class 331 pauses at Nyamandhlovu (elephant meat) station in 1968, heading a northbound train.

By 1950 the 10th class, the oldest of which had been worked hard through two World wars, were becoming due for replacement. Much of their work through Bechuanaland had been carried out with South African crews who in later days had become used to SAR's 19D class light 4-8-2, known affectionately as "Dollies". the fairly new CME, Hough, evidently thought that whatever was good for the SAR goose was good enough for the RR gander, and twenty 19D were ordered from Henschel & Sohn in 1951. It is difficult to understand why this happened. Certainly the 19D were slightly more powerful than the old 10th class, but then so were the RR 12A and 12B classes, which had much better boilers, shorter, fatter, and with Belpaire fireboxes. True, their driving wheels were 5 percent smaller for what it was worth but any decent drawing office could soon have designed a 4'6" wheeled 12B, retaining RR standards throughout. It is not that Henschel had drawings and patterns of 19D to hand — they had never built "Dollies" for SAR, so tooling up for the job was just as difficult as would have been an improved 12B. Nevertheless, the 19D were ordered, and by coincidence the next vacant class number on RR was the 19th class which

they took. Tenders were similar to the long SAR "torpedo" type, on six wheel bogies, but had plate frames, independently spring axleboxes, instead of the "Buckeye" cast steel, compensated, SAR type, perhaps to avoid royalty payments.

The 19th class were never popular on RR, and despite what was a theoretically better cylinder design, with the longest valve travel in Rhodesia, the 19th class were never so free running, and the exhaust from a well wound up 12th class was audibly much superior. The 19th class were built mainly for the Mafeking line, where fifteen went when new, the other five going to Livingstone where they lasted only six months before joining the remainder at Mafeking. All stayed there until August 1966 after which they were transferred to Bulawayo and their duties taken over by 15th class Garratts working from the Matabeleland capital on the 1550 km round trip with two crews and caboose. Bulawayo tried to make use of them, mainly on local goods turns both north and east, but Garratts displaced by dieselisation soon caused them to be set aside and most were scrapped, six being sold to industrial users, and one retained for the museum where it remains as an operable locomotive.

Historical data:

Number	Henschel Number	Date Built	Date in Service	Last Used	Disposal
316	27386	1952	3/1952	6/1973	Scrapped 2/1976
317	27387	1952	3/1952	6/1973	Scrapped 2/1976
318	27388	1952	3/1952	3/1975	Scrapped 7/1980
319	27389	1952	3/1952	2/1975	Selebi-Pikwe No III
320	27390	1952	4/1952	7/1973	Wankie Colliery No 5
321	27391	1952	4/1952	4/1973	Scrapped 2/1976
322	27392	1952	4/1952	9/1973	Selebi-Pikwe No IV
323	27393	1952	4/1952	7/1973	Scrapped 2/1976
324	27394	1952	4/1952	7/1973	Scrapped 2/1976
325	27395	1952	4/1952	4/1973	Wankie Colliery No 6
326	27396	1952	6/1952	4/1973	Wankie Colliery No 7
327	27397	1952	6/1952	6/1973	Scrapped 7/1980
328	27398	1952	6/1952	1/1979	Selebi-Pikwe, not used
329	27399	1952	6/1952	10/1979	Scrapped
330	27400	1952	6/1952	5/1980	Museum, operable
331	27401	1952	6/1952	6/1973	Scrapped 2/1976
332	27402	1952	6/1952	6/1973	Scrapped 2/1976
333	27403	1952	5/1952	9/1973	Scrapped 11/1979
334	27404	1952	8/1952	5/1973	Scrapped 11/1979
335	27405	1952	8/1952	6/1973	Scrapped 2/1976

Those sold to Wankie Colliery had their superheaters removed, baffles being placed opposite the empty flues, to restrict gas flow. They joined four 19th class built unsuperheated which remain at work, but the desuperheated 19th class are out of service, and were cut up 1996.

With a substantial mixed freight 332 accelerates out of Nyamandhlovu in 1968.

Wankie Colliery No 7, formerly RR 326, between duties within the mine complex.

Bamangwato Concessions Limited, Selebi Phikwe, Botswana, 19th class ex-works from Zeco, still with RR number 319 ZECO.

329 heads north at Nyamandhlovu with a featherweight freight, in 1968.

Class 19B, 4-8-2

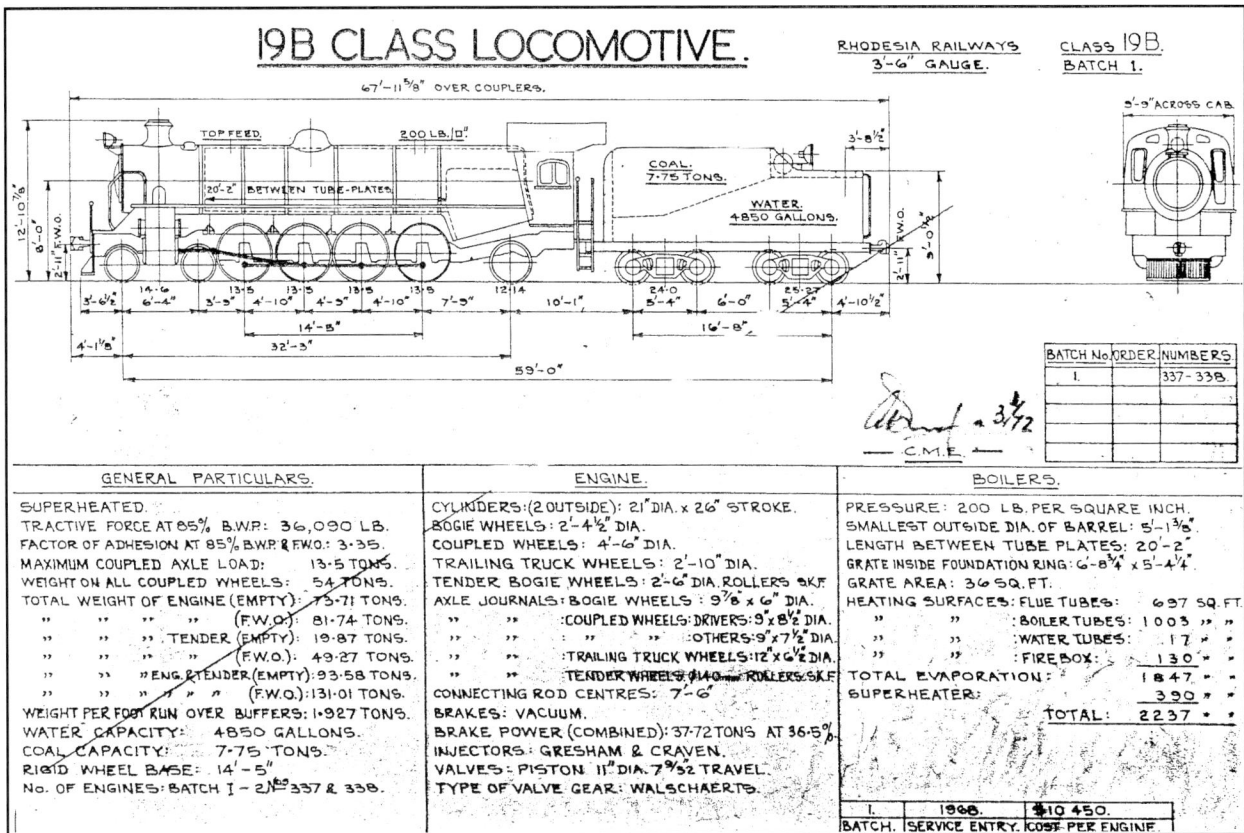

19B CLASS LOCOMOTIVE.

RHODESIA RAILWAYS 3'-6" GAUGE. **CLASS 19B. BATCH 1.**

67'-11⅝" OVER COUPLERS.

TOP FEED. 200 LB/☐" COAL 7·75 TONS. WATER 4850 GALLONS.

20'-2" BETWEEN TUBE-PLATES.

5'-9" ACROSS CAB

C.M.E.

BATCH No.	ORDER NUMBERS
1.	337 - 338

	GENERAL PARTICULARS.	
SUPERHEATED.		

GENERAL PARTICULARS.

SUPERHEATED.
TRACTIVE FORCE AT 85% B.W.P.: 36,090 LB.
FACTOR OF ADHESION AT 85% B.W.P. & F.W.O.: 3·35.
MAXIMUM COUPLED AXLE LOAD: 13·5 TONS.
WEIGHT ON ALL COUPLED WHEELS: 54 TONS.
TOTAL WEIGHT OF ENGINE (EMPTY): 73·71 TONS.
  " " " " (F.W.O.) 81·74 TONS.
  " " " TENDER (EMPTY): 19·87 TONS.
  " " " " (F.W.O.): 49·27 TONS.
  " " " ENG. & TENDER (EMPTY): 93·58 TONS.
  " " " " " (F.W.O.): 131·01 TONS.
WEIGHT PER FOOT RUN OVER BUFFERS: 1·927 TONS.
WATER CAPACITY: 4850 GALLONS.
COAL CAPACITY: 7·75 TONS.
RIGID WHEEL BASE: 14'-5".
No. OF ENGINES: BATCH I - 2 N°s 337 & 338.

ENGINE.

CYLINDERS: (2 OUTSIDE): 21" DIA. x 26" STROKE.
BOGIE WHEELS: 2'-4½" DIA.
COUPLED WHEELS: 4'-6" DIA.
TRAILING TRUCK WHEELS: 2'-10" DIA.
TENDER BOGIE WHEELS: 2'-6" DIA. ROLLERS SKF
AXLE JOURNALS: BOGIE WHEELS: 9⅞" x 6" DIA.
  " " : COUPLED WHEELS: DRIVERS: 9" x 8½" DIA.
  " " : " " : OTHERS: 9" x 7½" DIA.
  " " : TRAILING TRUCK WHEELS: 12" x 6½" DIA.
  " " : TENDER WHEELS 9 1·0 " ROLLERS SKF
CONNECTING ROD CENTRES: 7'-6".
BRAKES: VACUUM.
BRAKE POWER (COMBINED): 37·72 TONS AT 36·5%
INJECTORS: GRESHAM & CRAVEN.
VALVES: PISTON 11" DIA. 7⁹⁄₃₂ TRAVEL
TYPE OF VALVE GEAR: WALSCHAERTS.

BOILERS.

PRESSURE: 200 LB. PER SQUARE INCH.
SMALLEST OUTSIDE DIA. OF BARREL: 5'-1⅜".
LENGTH BETWEEN TUBE PLATES: 20'-2".
GRATE INSIDE FOUNDATION RING: 6'-8¾" x 5'-4¼".
GRATE AREA: 36 SQ. FT.
HEATING SURFACES: FLUE TUBES: 697 SQ. FT.
  " " : BOILER TUBES: 1003 " "
  " " : WATER TUBES: 17 " "
  " " : FIREBOX: 130 " "
TOTAL EVAPORATION: 1847 " "
SUPERHEATER: 390 " "
                 TOTAL: 2237 " "

BATCH.	SERVICE ENTRY.	COST PER ENGINE.
1.	1988.	$10 450.

RR 338, ex Rhokana Corporation, at Bulawayo. These two 19B were restricted to the Bulawayo-Gwelo section, due to tender axleloading. F. C. Butcher

These two locomotives were built for the Nkana copper mines, Northern Rhodesia, owned by the Rhokhana Corporation. The locomotives themselves were identical to the 19th class built by Henschel for RR at the same time, but as the high capacity "torpedo" tenders were not needed, they had standard eight-wheeled tenders of the same design as several locomotives recently built for Moçambique. After dieselisation at Nkana, they were purchased at bargain prices by RR, who ran them for five years before again replacing them by diesels. Quixotically, they were then sold to Bamangwato Concessions Limited for their mines at Selebi-Pikwe, Botswana, where this time they replaced diesels! Incidentally, when at Nkana, they were latterly used on the ore haulage from Mindola shaft to the main reduction plant.

Historical data:

Nkana Number	RR Number	Henschel Number	Date Built	Date in RR Service	Last Used	Disposal
107	337	27409	1952	8/1968	6/1973	Selebi-Pikwe I, 10/197
108	338	27410	1952	2/1968	4/1973	Selebi-Pikwe II, 10/197

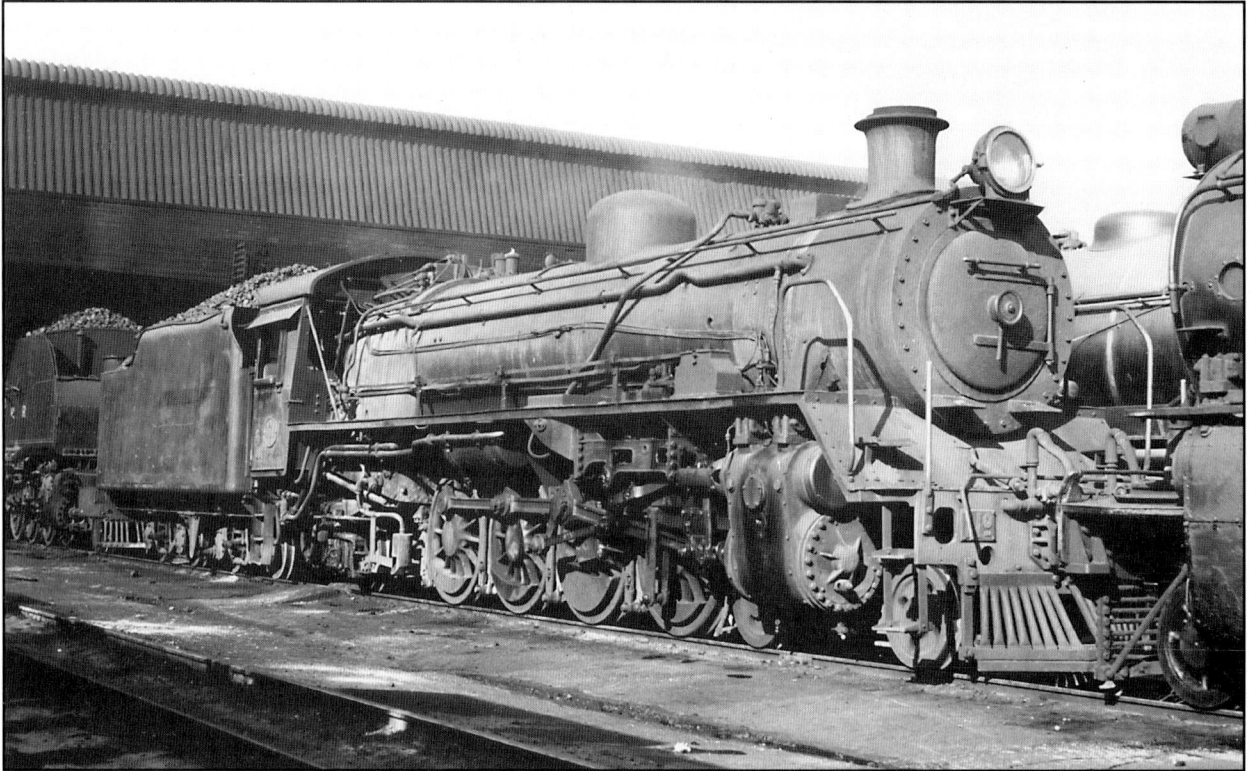

Right hand side of 19B 338, at Bulawayo shed. F. C. Butcher

Rhokana Corporation's class 19B at their shed, presumably when new. No107, it became RR No 337.

Class 19C, 4-8-2

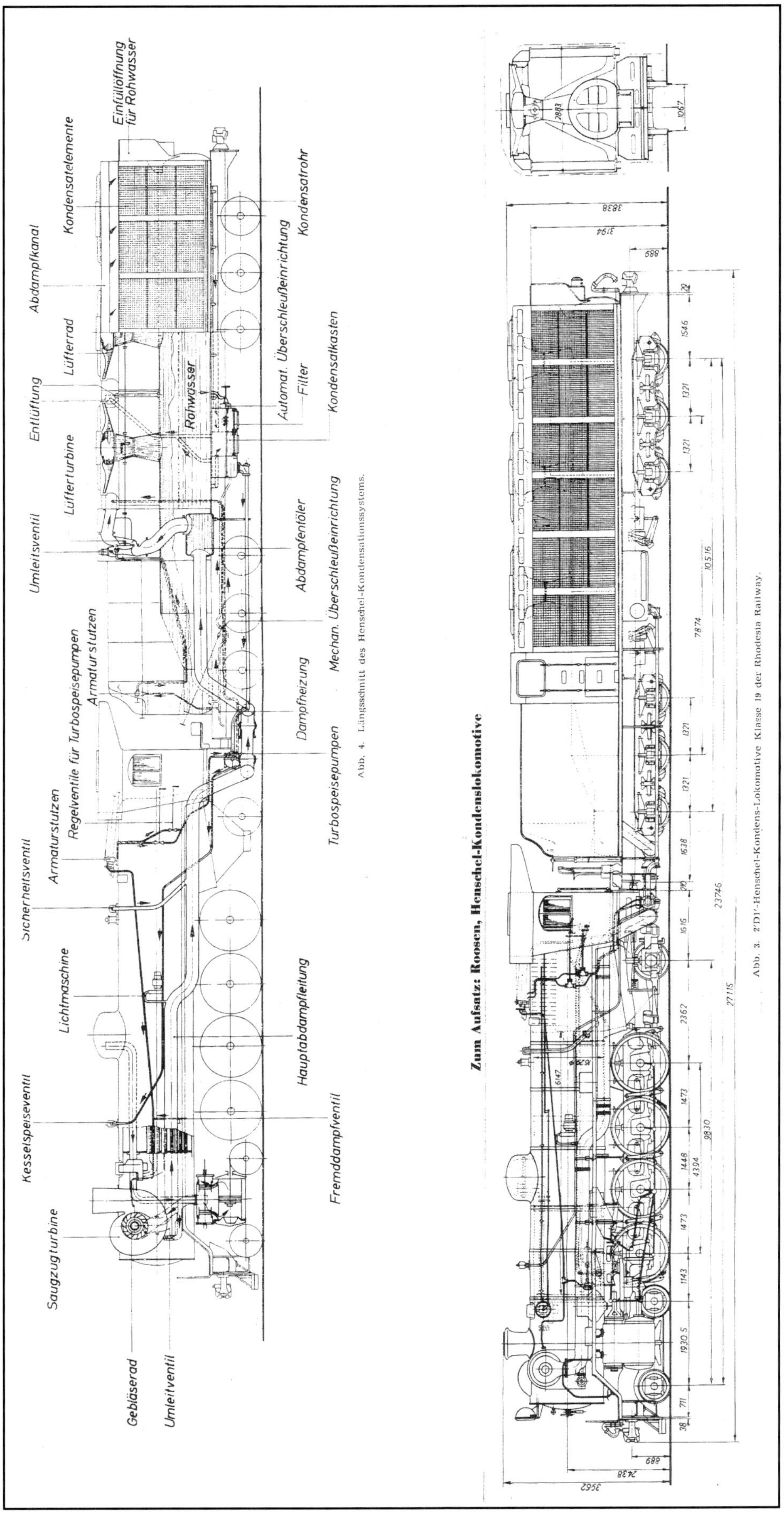

Abb. 4. Längsschnitt des Henschel-Kondensationssystems.

Zum Aufsatz: Roosen, Henschel-Kondenslokomotive

Abb. 3. 2'D1'-Henschel-Kondens-Lokomotive Klasse 19 der Rhodesia Railway.

Rhodesian class 19C condensing locomotive, as originally built by Henschel. Henschel

Condensing and re-using exhaust steam from a locomotive's propulsion units (cylinders or turbines) has always had the interest of locomotive engineers. It is standard equipment on steam ships, which had limitless cooling water available under their hulls, and equally for power stations which were either situated on rivers for cooling water, or had enormous towers to hold air-cooling apparatus. With locomotives, due to their mobility there were no built-in rivers, nor was there space within the average loading gauge for cooling towers, such that cooling equipment had to be compact. The arguments for condensing were several. Thermally condensation into a vacuum, as on ships and power stations, increased both power and efficiency due to back pressure being negative. Impurities in the feed water were largely removed first time round, such that water of greater purity was theoretically fed into the boiler, although make-up water to combat losses would still include impurities, whilst there would be additional contamination by lubricating oil. A condensing locomotive is more complicated and thus more expensive than a simple type, both in first cost and in maintenance, and the theoretical thermal improvements are insufficient to justify these additional costs.

Justification of these costs is usually only in desert regions where water supplies are both scarce and of poor quality, and the elimination of one or more water stops, and the costly boiler maintenance resulting from bad water usage, can sometimes make the use of condensing steam locomotives a viable proposition. The line through Bechuanaland (now Botswana) is in such a category, and RR decided to try out a 19th class fitted with condensing equipment. Henschel & Sohn of Germany started thinking seriously about condensing equipment in the 1920s, and in 1928 converted a standard P8 4-6-0 in which exhaust steam from the cylinders firstly drove four tender wheels through a turbine, whilst the residual heat was dissipated in an air-cooled condenser mounted on the tender. The exhaust steam turbine, a form of compounding, saw no further application (it would be interesting to read an honest account of its trials and tribulations!), but evidently the condensing gear itself showed promise of development. In 1931 a condensing-only set of equipment was supplied to Argentina and fitted to engine 7034, a standard metre gauge 2-8-2, and on test in 1932 this hauled an 1100 tonne load 759 km without replenishing water, over the dry country between Santa Fé and Tucuman. As a result six larger 4-8-2 with condensing equipment were placed in service during 1938. Meanwhile, an experimental 0-10-0 was supplied to Russia and during the 1939-45 war some 200 German "Kriegslok" wartime 2-10-0 were supplied with condensers for the Russian campaign.

After the war, one of a group of South African officials, sent to America to study various developments, returned via Argentina to study their condensing locomotives and his report led to the conversion of the class 20, 2-10-2, into an experimental condensing engine, and ultimately to construction of the famous 25 class condensers. Thus

RR had a good background to their own experiment, which was of the same basic configuration as similar engines elsewhere. Exhaust from the cylinders passed to the tender, and en route a portion of this exhaust was used to drive a small turbine which drove an induced draught fan in the smokebox, replacing the normal blast through the chimney. Once in the tender, further fans were driven by exhaust steam, drawing cooling air through radiators in the tender side. The whole concept conformed to the Stephensonian principles in being automatic - the harder the engine worked, the greater the draught in both the smokebox and tender fans. No additional controls were needed, and the locomotive could be driven like a normal non-condensing machine. However, there was a price to pay in maintenance, mainly in the smokebox which is not the best place to situate moving machinery. Gritty and hot exhaust gases abraded the smokebox fan, not only reducing its effectiveness, but sometimes unevenly causing out-of-balance. The bearings supporting this rapidly revolving equipment were almost impossible to keep clean from the all-pervading grit, and were subject to rapid wear and failure. Today it might be possible to overcome these problems, with perhaps ceramic fans and bearings with better seals, but the technology of forty years ago could not cope and following a collision with another locomotive, RR's 19C was laid aside for over a year and eventually converted into a standard 19th class, although its tender,

shortened from the original, was different in several dimensions, leading to 336 in its final form having a diagram of its own. Absence of the normal exhaust beat, replaced by a continuous whine from the chimney, led to 19C 336 being known as "Silent Suzie", although "Whining Winnie" might have been more appropriate! The soft exhaust from the fan, without its normal steam component, caused problems with drifting smoke, and more than one form of smoke deflector was allegedly tried, although no evidence of these remain. Eventually the engine was given outsize "elephant ears" of German design, which remained whilst operating as a condenser.

In December 1956 336 was involved in a collision between Daisyfield and Wida, and was sent to Bulawayo shops. Some considerable time was spent in deciding her fate, such that eventually rebuilding to non-condensing form was the verdict, then further time elapsed whilst the tender was rebuilt, resulting in an ex-works date of February 1958. After a brief period at Bulawayo, she joined her sisters at Mafeking, later returning to Bulawayo until scrapped.

Historical data:

Engine no. 336, Henschel no. 27411, built 1953. (note that the Henschel number is consecutive with 19B nos. 337-8, built two years earlier). Date in service 1/1954, last used 4/1974, scrapped 11/1979.

In service the condensing 19C was found to need smoke deflectors, and this outsize pair was soon applied, RR

20th and 20A classes, 4-8-2 + 2-8-4 Garratts

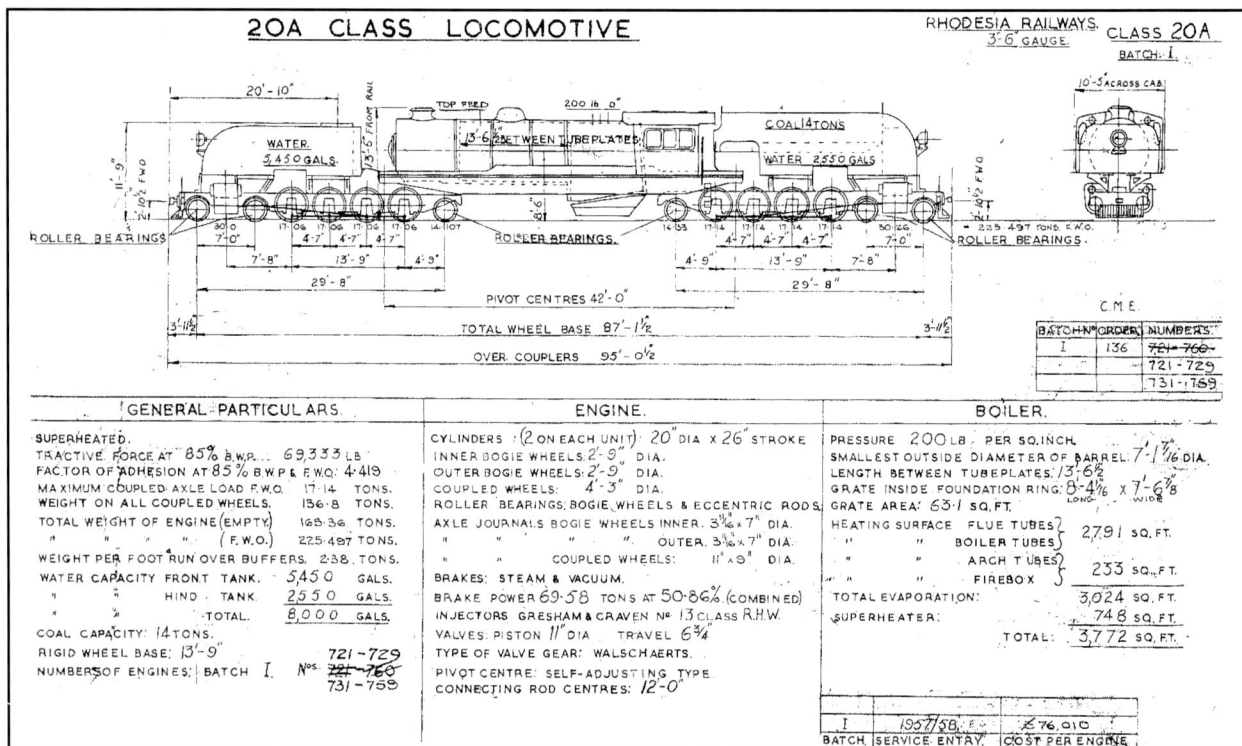

20A CLASS LOCOMOTIVE   RHODESIA RAILWAYS. 3'-6" GAUGE. CLASS 20A BATCH I.

GENERAL PARTICULARS.	ENGINE.	BOILER.
SUPERHEATED.	CYLINDERS : (2 ON EACH UNIT) 20" DIA x 26" STROKE	PRESSURE 200 LB. PER SQ.INCH.
TRACTIVE FORCE AT 85% B.W.P. 69,333 LB.	INNER BOGIE WHEELS. 2'-9" DIA.	SMALLEST OUTSIDE DIAMETER OF BARREL. 7'-1 7/16 DIA.
FACTOR OF ADHESION AT 85% B.W.P.& F.W.O. 4.418	OUTER BOGIE WHEELS. 2'-9" DIA.	LENGTH BETWEEN TUBEPLATES. 13'-6½
MAXIMUM COUPLED AXLE LOAD F.W.O. 17.14 TONS.	COUPLED WHEELS: 4'-3" DIA.	GRATE INSIDE FOUNDATION RING: 8-4⅞ LONG x 7'-6⅞ WIDE
WEIGHT ON ALL COUPLED WHEELS. 136.8 TONS.	ROLLER BEARINGS, BOGIE WHEELS & ECCENTRIC RODS.	GRATE AREA: 63.1 SQ.FT.
TOTAL WEIGHT OF ENGINE (EMPTY) 185.36 TONS.	AXLE JOURNALS BOGIE WHEELS INNER. 3⁹⁄₁₆ x 7" DIA.	HEATING SURFACE FLUE TUBES
" " " (F.W.O.) 225.487 TONS.	" " " OUTER. 3⁹⁄₁₆ x 7" DIA.	BOILER TUBES 2,791 SQ. FT.
WEIGHT PER FOOT RUN OVER BUFFERS. 2.38 TONS.	" COUPLED WHEELS: 11" x 9" DIA.	" " ARCH TUBES
WATER CAPACITY FRONT TANK. 5,450 GALS.	BRAKES: STEAM & VACUUM.	" " FIREBOX 233 SQ. FT.
" " HIND TANK. 2,550 GALS.	BRAKE POWER 69.58 TONS AT 50.86% (COMBINED)	TOTAL EVAPORATION: 3,024 SQ. FT.
" " TOTAL. 8,000 GALS.	INJECTORS GRESHAM & CRAVEN Nº 13 CLASS R.H.W.	SUPERHEATER: 748 SQ. FT.
COAL CAPACITY: 14 TONS.	VALVES: PISTON 11" DIA TRAVEL 6¾"	TOTAL: 3,772 SQ. FT.
RIGID WHEEL BASE: 13'-9"	TYPE OF VALVE GEAR: WALSCHAERTS.	
NUMBERS OF ENGINES: BATCH I. Nᴼˢ 721-760 731-759	PIVOT CENTRE: SELF-ADJUSTING TYPE	
	CONNECTING ROD CENTRES: 12'-0"	

BATCH	SERVICE ENTRY	COST PER ENGINE
I	1957/58.	£76,010

20th class No 703, outshopped at Gorton works, with flared chimney. Beyer Peacock

With the relaying of Rhodesian Railways' main line from Beira to the copper belt with heavy rail (80lb./yd.), the way was open for introducing heavier and more powerful locomotives, of which the 20th classes were the biggest and unfortunately the last built. They were also in the author's opinion, the best looking, due in a large way to the chamfered sides of the front tank, which somehow adds an air of rakish classiness. Only three types of Garratt had this feature, the New South Wales 60 class of 1952 which were the first, followed by the East African 59 and RR 20th classes, almost simultaneously in 1954-55. Interestingly a model 20th class exhibited in

Bulawayo museum lacks this feature, having a slab sided tank, which may have been in error, but possibly indicates the originally intended form, before design was finalised for production.

In many major dimensions the 20th classes can be likened to a Garratt built from a pair of 12th chassis, but with few, if any, interchangeable components as the 20th class frame and motion was thoroughly redesigned, with more modern cylinders and long lap, long travel valve gear, whilst long connecting rods drove the third coupled axle. Roller bearings were fitted to bogie axleboxes and return cranks, although the driving and coupled axleboxes were still on plain

RR had a good background to their own experiment, which was of the same basic configuration as similar engines elsewhere. Exhaust from the cylinders passed to the tender, and en route a portion of this exhaust was used to drive a small turbine which drove an induced draught fan in the smokebox, replacing the normal blast through the chimney. Once in the tender, further fans were driven by exhaust steam, drawing cooling air through radiators in the tender side. The whole concept conformed to the Stephensonian principles in being automatic - the harder the engine worked, the greater the draught in both the smokebox and tender fans. No additional controls were needed, and the locomotive could be driven like a normal non-condensing machine. However, there was a price to pay in maintenance, mainly in the smokebox which is not the best place to situate moving machinery.Gritty and hot exhaust gases abraded the smokebox fan, not only reducing its effectiveness, but sometimes unevenly causing out-of-balance. The bearings supporting this rapidly revolving equipment were almost impossible to keep clean from the all-pervading grit, and were subject to rapid wear and failure. Today it might be possible to overcome these problems, with perhaps ceramic fans and bearings with better seals, but the technology of forty years ago could not cope and following a collision with another locomotive, RR's 19C was laid aside for over a year and eventually converted into a standard 19th class, although its tender,

shortened from the original, was different in several dimensions, leading to 336 in its final form having a diagram of its own. Absence of the normal exhaust beat, replaced by a continuous whine from the chimney, led to 19C 336 being known as "Silent Suzie", although "Whining Winnie" might have been more appropriate! The soft exhaust from the fan, without its normal steam component, caused problems with drifting smoke, and more than one form of smoke deflector was allegedly tried, although no evidence of these remain. Eventually the engine was given outsize "elephant ears" of German design, which remained whilst operating as a condenser.

In December 1956 336 was involved in a collision between Daisyfield and Wida, and was sent to Bulawayo shops. Some considerable time was spent in deciding her fate, such that eventually rebuilding to non-condensing form was the verdict, then further time elapsed whilst the tender was rebuilt, resulting in an ex-works date of February 1958. After a brief period at Bulawayo, she joined her sisters at Mafeking, later returning to Bulawayo until scrapped.

Historical data:

Engine no. 336, Henschel no. 27411, built 1953. (note that the Henschel number is consecutive with 19B nos. 337-8, built two years earlier). Date in service 1/1954, last used 4/1974, scrapped 11/1979.

In service the condensing 19C was found to need smoke deflectors, and this outsize pair was soon applied, RR

20th and 20A classes, 4-8-2 + 2-8-4 Garratts

20th class No 703, outshopped at Gorton works, with flared chimney. Beyer Peacock

With the relaying of Rhodesian Railways' main line from Beira to the copper belt with heavy rail (80lb./yd.), the way was open for introducing heavier and more powerful locomotives, of which the 20th classes were the biggest and unfortunately the last built. They were also in the author's opinion, the best looking, due in a large way to the chamfered sides of the front tank, which somehow adds an air of rakish classiness. Only three types of Garratt had this feature, the New South Wales 60 class of 1952 which were the first, followed by the East African 59 and RR 20th classes, almost simultaneously in 1954-55. Interestingly a model 20th class exhibited in

Bulawayo museum lacks this feature, having a slab sided tank, which may have been in error, but possibly indicates the originally intended form, before design was finalised for production.

In many major dimensions the 20th classes can be likened to a Garratt built from a pair of 12th chassis, but with few, if any, interchangeable components as the 20th class frame and motion was thoroughly redesigned, with more modern cylinders and long lap, long travel valve gear, whilst long connecting rods drove the third coupled axle. Roller bearings were fitted to bogie axleboxes and return cranks, although the driving and coupled axleboxes were still on plain bearings, an over conservative feature compared with their contemporaries in South Africa, East Africa, and Australia. However, this was eventually remedied in those locomotives refurbished at Bulawayo during 1979-82. The boiler was of course very much larger than previous classes, and almost identical with those of the SAR GMA/M classes and the NSW 60 class. Alone of all RR locomotives, it was mechanically stoked, being too large for hand firing.

The 20th class were built essentially for the heavy mineral traffic of the North line, coal traffic north and south of Wankie, and copper south from the Northern Rhodesian copper belt. The designed duties of these splendid machines was the haulage of 1400 short tons (2000lb) equal to 1250 imperial tons over compensated gradients of 1 in 64.5 between Kafue and Broken Hill. Over easier gradients between Bulawayo and Gwelo (1 in 80) they hauled 1650 short tons, and between Wankie and Bulawayo over easy grades of 1 in 130, loads were 1950 short tons (1740 imperial tons) which latter was limited mainly by train length. For most of their lives they were limited to these sections of line, except after 1988 when, after steam replaced diesel between Bulawayo and Plumtree, they appeared with ever increasing frequency on this line and were in great demand for the heavy grain traffic for drought relief, from Plumtree to Bulawayo.

Although designed for heavy freight, they were no strangers to passenger work but were rarely rostered for such duties unless more suitable engines were unavailable, and a "twenty" in good condition could move over the road surprisingly fast!

The original 20th class, and to a lesser extent the 20A class fell victim to the shoddy workmanship which befell Beyer Peacock in their last days of steam construction, following on directly from similar problems experienced with the16A class. By January 1959, eleven engines, 701/2/6-14 were in Bulawayo shops, and the following month were recorded as "stabled, awaiting material". This position was exacerbated with some early 20A engines, 716-20 and 732, which were similarly staged by August the same year. For a railway coping with booming traffic, the staging of their largest and latest locomotives was an embarrassing situation which took two or three years to rectify, and the last of the defective engines was 732, a 20A, which was only admitted to shops in March 1962 and returned to service the following month, having been out of service for nearly three years. These were early victims of the current malaise of management by accountants, combined with radical trade unionism, which has been the cause of much of the world's poor economic performance since the age of steam rail-

way dominance.

Five years after the last defective locomotive was returned to service Northern Rhodesia became independent as the Republic of Zambia, within which two thirds of the 20th/20A class were allocated. Initially, Zambian locomotives returned to Bulawayo for heavy repairs, but when this new country failed to pay its bills the practice ceased, and several 20th/20A engines from Zambia remained south of the Zambezi, which considerably prolonged their active lives. A locomotive workshop was belatedly erected at Kabwe, formerly Broken Hill, but there were no trained staff to operate it other than a floating population of expatriate employees on contract, and these fine, modern, locomotives, like most other infrastructure in Zambia, steadily fell out of use. There were three attempts to get some working again, in 1980 when Livingstone shed did some up for local operation, followed by a more comprehensive scheme to fully refurbish some with not only roller bearing axleboxes but crankpins also, but the Zambians did not have their hearts in it, and if fell through. Finally, in 1988, it was schemed to get sixteen locomotives, chosen from the best remaining 16A, 20th, and 20A locomotives, back into operation, but this again fell by the wayside - it was so much easier to beg new diesels from over enthusiastic donors!

Two "twenties" were prematurely scrapped due to collisions, the first, 700, only two years old after a head on at Kasavasa, Northern Rhodesia, and the last, 760 after a similar incident at Magoye also NR. Those remaining in Southern Rhodesia were included in the refurbishment programme and fitted with roller bearings to driving and coupled axles, whilst the bunker was increased in capacity by perhaps an extra tonne of coal, although this was not specified. Actually, the enlarged bunker was originally authorised in 1965 for locomotives working in the Livingstone - Broken Hill section, and the prototype, 744, fitted January 1968. 707/11/14/24/28/31/52 were also fitted in 1970 after which no more were done until the refurbishment programme when those with original bunkers were brought into line.

The twenties were worked hard until 1993 when a combination of new diesels plus a drop in traffic put them all out of work. Unlike previous practice, when locomotives languished for long periods out of use, and despite the presence of numerous older hulks due for scrap, these fine engines were tendered for scrap almost immediately, and it is thought that this was due to the presence of Canadian consultants, afraid that any upswing in traffic would lead to a return to traffic of the "twenties", jeopardizing plans to sell NRZ more diesels! There is no other explanation why these fine locomotives, some in excellent condition, should be scrapped with such unseemly haste. Whilst this was in progress, the author tendered for no. 736 and was successful, outbidding the scrap vultures, and this engine currently resides in the NRZ museum, Bulawayo. The only difference between a 20th and a 20A was in the wheel diameter of the inner pony truck, the 20th class having 2'9" wheels as with other Garratts, whilst the 20A had smaller wheels (2'4 1/2") standard with the outer bogies. This seemed hardly sufficient to warrant a separate classification, but such it was.

Multiple jet exhausts.

In 1983 the late Chris Butcher and the author were staying at the famous Baobab Hotel, Hwange, from whose bedrooms could be heard Garratts as they climbed south with heavy coal or copper trains. By then, the 15th/15A classes had long been fitted with multijet exhausts, which gave a mushy exhaust beat which will be familiar to those who have experienced modern motive power. This night, at some ungodly hour, the author was awoken by a hard working Garratt with mushy exhaust like a "fifteen", but deep, reverberating knock as with a "twenty", whose long connecting rods rang with a noise reminiscent of the lower chords of a Beethoven piano concerto, played on a grand piano! Next morning Chris was asked if he also heard it, as he did, and upon our usual 05.30 descent into the running shed at TJ, we confirmed that the only possible departure was indeed a "twenty", 749. Chris later confirmed the fitting of multiple jet to this locomotive, and fairly soon after it became standard, probably fitted in the running shed, as no chimney change was included. More recently, with the help of Brian Noble, chief draughtsman, drawings for this application were dug out, and found to be exactly the same as the "fifteen" application, but with larger diameter orifii. Orifice diameter for a 20th class was 67mm, compared with 63,5mm on a 15th class, an 11,13 percent increase in nozzle area whereas the grate area was 27,5 percent more than a 15, giving the multi-jet twenties a considerably fiercer blast than the smaller engines.

Allocations

Date	Bulawayo	Thomson Junction	Livingstone	Kafue	Broken Hill
6/1955	-	-	-	2	13
6/1960	2	1	10	-	24
6/1965	3	-	17	-	30
6/1967	12	-	12		27
6/1970	17	-		Zambia 40	

Thence virtually unchanged. From the 1970s to the end of steam, two or three 20/20A were usually sub-shedded at Thomson Junction for working north to Victoria Falls.

Renumbered 742 and named Gwaai, at Bulawayo shed 1991. Note enlarged bunker, and "dam" round the tank filler.

Refurbished 16A no 614 heads south from Hwange with a train probably loaded with copper from Zambia.

174 *The unique 16A no 604, with large tank but original bunker, bellows out of the cutting near Entuba with a southbound coal train.*

▲   Rounding the curves at Upper Zanguja, maroon 20th 730 hauls the 1992 Transnet "Union Limited Zambesi" early morning en route from Thomson Junction to Victoria Falls.

▼   Now owned by the author, 20th Class no 736 restarts from a halt in typical Zimbabwean bush country, in autumn colours.

175

▲ A afternoon coal train, headed by 20A 749, passes the tumbled rock formations between Nchokomela and Mambanje, nearby an elephant could be heard tearing down vegetation.

▼ At Lukosi River, a 20th Class trundles north whilst local people fish for Bream from the still waters.

78 *In Rhodesian days, before refurbishment, a 20th Garratt smokes out of the railways only tunnel, near Wankie, with a Bulawayo bound coal train. Note the Baobab tree on the hillside.*

▲ The classic scene of a 20th Class roaring round "404 curve" with southbound coal. Foreground are the two sleepers to which were affixed the number plate from the ill-fated no 404.

▼ An afternoon coal train thunders south from Lukosi - before long it will be dark and the train will be amid the Hwange National Game Reserve.

▲ A southbound special passenger to Johannesburg rounds the s-bend at Lobatse, Botswana, in 1973, headed by a 15A Garratt.

▼ Despite the drought, this 15A is reflected in water at Ramoutsa, Botswana, as it starts an afternoon train bound for Mafeking South Africa. Within a month or so, the line was dieselised.

Historical data:

First Number	Second Number	Beyer Peacock	Date Built	Date in Service	Date Refurb.	Name	Last Used	Disposal
20th class								
700	-	7685	1954	1/1955	-	-	10/1955	Scrapped 4/1956. Head on 702
701	-	7686	1954	11/1954	-	-	5/1967	Zambia, derelict Livingstone
702	-	7687	1954	12/1954	-	-	6/1967	Zambia, derelict Ndola
703	-	7688	1954	1/1955	-	-	6/1967	Zambia, derelict Lusaka
704	-	7689	1954	2/1955	-	-	6/1967	Zambia, derelict Lusaka
705	730	7690	1954	2/1955	9/1981	Insuga	11/1992	Bulawayo museum, operable
706	-	7691	1954	2/1955	-	-	6/1967	Zambia, derelict Kabwe
707	731	7692	1954	2/1955	12/1981	Induba	11/1990	Scrapped 11/1993
708	-	7693	1954	2/1955	-	-	6/1967	Zambia, Livingstone museum
709	732	7694	1954	3/1955	11/1982	Amavani	11/1992	Scrapped 11/1993
710	733	7695	1954	3/1955	3/1981	Imbizo	11/1989	Scrapped 10/1990
711	-	7696	1954	3/1955	-	-	6/1967	Zambia, derelict Kabwe
712	-	7697	1954	3/1955	-	-	6/1967	Zambia, derelict Livingstone
713	-	7698	1954	2/1955	-	-	6/1967	Zambia, presumed scrapped
714	734	7699	1954	3/1955	6/1982	Ihlathi	2/1988	Scrapped 4/1995
715	-	7780	1957	5/1957	-	-	6/1967	Zambia, derelict Livingstone
716	735	7781	1957	5/1957	2/1983	Isiziba	9/1992	Scrapped 11/1993
717	736	7782	1957	5/1957	7/1982	Enxa	10/1992	Purchased by AED, Bulawayo museum
718	737	7783	1957	6/1957	10/1980	Ingubu	12/1992	Scrapped 11/1993
719	-	7784	1957	6/1957	-	-	6/1967	Zambia, derelict Livingstone
720	-	7785	1957	7/1957	-	-	6/1967	Zambia, derelict Livingstone
20A class								
721	-	7786	1957	7/1957	-	-	6/1967	Zambia, derelict Mufilira mine
722	-	7787	1957	8/1957	-	-	6/1967	Zambia, derelict Livingstone
723	740	7788	1957	8/1957	9/1982	Ingwezi	12/1992	Bulawayo museum, operable
724	741	7789	1957	8/1957	1/1983	Bubi	8/1991	Scrapped 11/1993
725	-	7790	1957	8/1957	-	-	6/1967	Zambia, derelict Livingstone
726	742	7791	1957	8/1957	5/1980	Gwaai	11/1992	Bulawayo, derelict
727	743	7792	1957	9/1957	5/1982	Shangani	8/1991	Scrapped 8/1994
728	-	7793	1957	9/1957	-	-	6/1967	Zambia, derelict Livingstone
729	744	7794	1957	9/1957	5/1982	Umguza	12/1992	Scrapped 11/1993

First Number	Second Number	Beyer Peacock	Date Built	Date in Service	Date Refurb.	Name	Last Used	Disposal
730	-	7795	1957	9/1957	- -		1966?	Zambia, Kabwe, no boiler
731	-	7796	1957	9/1957	- -		6/1967	Zambia, derelict Kabwe
732	-	7797	1957	10/1957	- -		6/1967	Zambia, derelict Kabwe
733	-	7798	1957	10/1957	- -		6/1967	Zambia, derelict Lusaka
734	-	7799	1957	11/1957	- -		6/1967	Zambia, scrapped
735	-	7800	1957	12/1957	- -		6/1967	Zambia, derelict Ndola
736	-	7801	1957	1/1958	- -		6/1967	Zambia, derelict Livingstone
737	-	7802	1957	12/1957	- -		6/1967	Zambia, derelict Kabwe
738	745	7803	1957	1/1958	8/1982	Insiza	4/1992	Scrapped 3/1994
739	-	7804	1957	12/1957	- -		6/1967	Zambia, derelict Kitwe
740	-	7805	1957	1/1958	- -		6/1967	Zambia, derelict Ndola
741	-	7806	1957	1/1958	- -		6/1967	Zambia, derelict Ndola
742	-	7807	1957	1/1958	- -		6/1967	Zambia, derelict Livingstone
743	-	7808	1957	2/1958	- -		6/1967	Zambia, derelict Livingstone
744	-	7809	1957	2/1958	- -		6/1967	Zambia, derelict Livingstone
745	-	7810	1957	3/1958	- -		6/1967	Zambia, derelict Kabwe
746	-	7811	1957	3/1958	3/1983	Tuli	10/1991	Scrapped 9/1994
747	-	7812	1958	3/1958	10/1982	Jumbo	10/1992	Scrapped 3/1994
748	-	7813	1958	3/1958	- -		6/1967	Zambia, derelict Ndola
749	-	7814	1958	4/1958	4/1983	Umzimgwane	10/1992	Scrapped 3/1994
750	-	7815	1958	4/1958	- -		6/1967	Zambia, derelict Livingstone
751	-	7816	1958	4/1958	- -		6/1967	Zambia, derelict Livingstone
752	-	7817	1958	4/1958	- -		6/1967	Zambia, derelict Livingstone
753	748	7818	1958	5/1958	8/1982	Lukosi	6/1967	Scrapped 4/1995
754	-	7819	1958	5/1958	- -		6/1967	Zambia, derelict Livingstone
755	-	7820	1958	7/1958	- -		6/1967	Zambia, derelict Livingstone
756	750	7821	1958	7/1958	6/1982	Bembezi	12/1992	Scrapped 11/1993
757	-	7822	1958	7/1958	- -		6/1967	Zambia, derelict Livingstone
758	-	7823	1958	7/1958	- -		6/1967	Zambia, scrapped
759	-	7824	1958	7/1958	- -		6/1967	Zambia, derelict Kabwe
760	-	7825	1958	9/1958	- -		7/1962	Scrapped 4/1964, collision damage

Note: Most probably all locomotives at Livingstone have been cut up.

20A No 740, in blue livery, poses on Victoria Falls bridge for photography by steam enthusiasts, in 1993. Photo taken from helicopter

20A 745 crosses the Lukosi river with a northbound train, opening up for the slight climb out of the river valley.

A rare working at Pasipas in 1988, with 20A 740 bringing in the overnight passengers from Victoria Falls, no doubt due to the normal 15A having failed.

20A class No 738, the last to retain the original Beyer Peacock flared chimney, approaches New Wankie station with a coal train in 1975.

Negotiating the lower horseshoe between Sambawisi and Zanguja 20A 745 thunders upgrade with train 120 in the winter of 1988.

The upper level view at "404 curve", in 1981, with an unrefurbished 20 or 20A Garratt heading south with a heavy coal train.

Early morning in winter, at Thomson Junction, and 20th class 737 with cylinder cocks open, eases itself round the turning triangle, 1991.

Wankie winter! For those willing to rise before dawn. A 20th class is silhouetted and reflected in the still waters of the Lukosi river, whilst the winter sun crosses the horizon.

The mixed train, 07.30 from Thomson Junction in 1978, winds round the horseshoe curve behind a splendid 20th class.

20th class 736, somewhere in the African bush, heading south with a train of copper. The author has now purchased this magnificent machine, residing in Bulawayo museum.

If there was a doubleheader to be had, Chris Butcher usually managed to find it! Here 20A 757 leads a 14A in an unrecorded operation. F. C. Butcher

"MMBA"-miles and miles of bloody Africa-was our nickname for this wonderful photographic location, with the topography sloping down towards the Zambezi in the background.

Somewhere between Gwelo and Bulawayo, another doubleheader with 20A 749 ahead of a 15A, on mixed freight.
F. C. Butcher

The ultimate Rhodesian doubleheader, a pair of massive 20th class Garratts rolls through the Luveve area on a mixed freight. F. C. Butcher

Locomotives on Hire

Over the years, indeed from the very beginning, locomotives were hired from other administrations to operate lines in Rhodesia, its constituents, and its subsequent owners. Most of these were hired from South Africa, beginning with Cape Government Railways engines hired first to the Bechuanaland Railway Company, which ran from Vryburg in the northern Cape through Bechuanaland into Bulawayo. Some of these Cape locomotives were photographed as far north as Victoria Falls, whilst others hired to Paulings, the main construction contractors are known to have crossed the Kafue river. However, details of these early hirings are scant, and the author has included items gleaned from the annual General Manager's reports of the Cape Government Railways, by no means uniform in its year-by-year treatment of hirings. Later hirings, to Rhodesia Railways, National Railways of Zimbabwe, and Zambian Railways are better documented and more complete information is presented.

Early hirings.

The Bechuanaland Railway Company, as will have been seen on pages 9-11 initially ordered their own locomotives but sold them to the Cape Government Railways from whom motive power was then hired. Paulings, the main contractors also hired CGR locomotives, and during the often chaotic conditions inevitable with operating traffic under construction conditions it was probably sometimes difficult to know whose engines were whose. A few photographs exist from these early days, and on two occasions the annual General Manager's report of the Cape Government Railways details locomotives used on the northerly extending tracks. In 1896 the following were listed as "working on the Mafeking-Bulawayo Extension".

Ex-Western Cape:

2-6-0 12,	BP 1576/1875 1st class	
0-4-0ST	43 Huns	271/1882
	44 Huns	272/1882
	45 Huns	280/1882
	46 MW	494/1874
4-6-0	62 RS 2834/1882 4th class	
	63 RS 2835/1882 4th class	
4-4-0	85 Neils 2931/1883 Four coupled Joy	
4-4-0T	90 Neils 2795/1882 Wynburg Tank	
	93 Neils 2798/1882 Wynburg Tank	
4-4-0	107 Dubs 2538/1889 3rd class	
	113 Dubs 2544/1889 3rd class	

Cape Midland:
289 This locomotive unidentifiable!

Eastern Cape:

4-4-0	10 Neils 2557/1880 1st class	
4-6-0T	29 RS	2387/1880 4th class
4-6-0	38 RS	2475/1882 4th class
	39 Neils 2951/1883 4th class	
	48 Neils 2983/1883 4th class	

A motley collection of engines, not all of which will have worked into Bulawayo, or even beyond Mafeking, but we will probably never know which engines went where.

The GM's report for 1898 lists more simply the locomotives used during 1897, as follows:

1st class	1 (probably the 2-6-0)	
2nd class	9 (details unknown)	
4th class		2 4-6-0
5th class		1 4-6-0
6th class		15 4-6-0
Total		28

Cape 3rd class No 114, at Bulawayo.
J. Dele-Hoffman collection

192

Another Cape 3rd 4-4-0, on Victoria Falls bridge. Collection R. Menzigo, photo by his father

The train de Luxe, Cape Town to Bulawayo, hauled by a Cape 6th class 4-6-0. Photo probably in South Africa (note fencing) but similar trains and locos ran to Bulawayo. Transnet

The Katanga "Mikados"

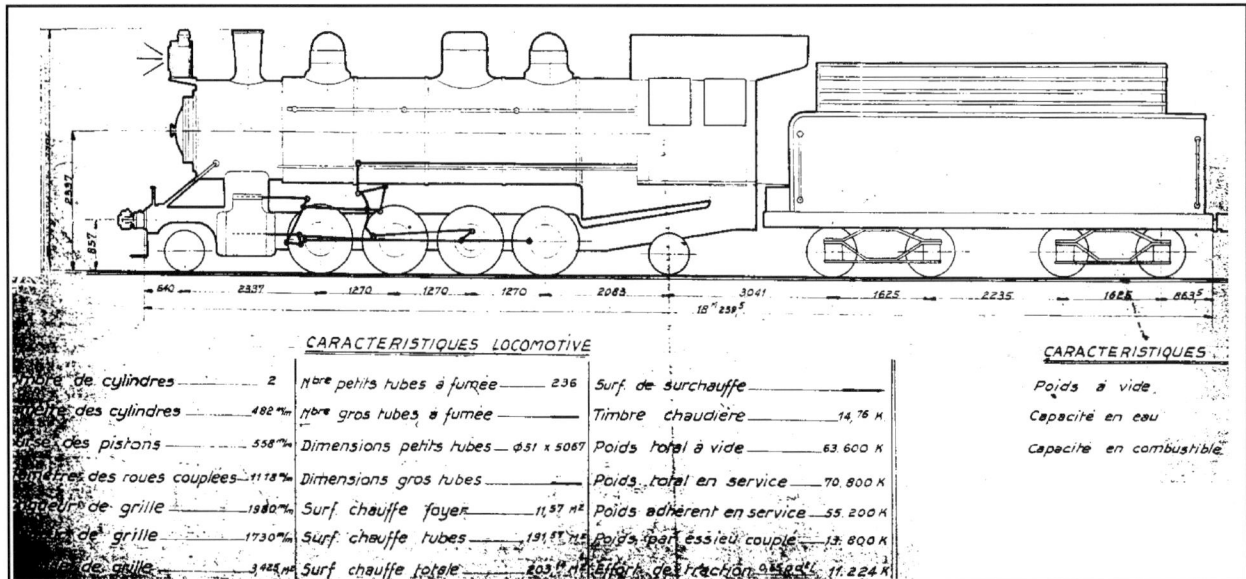

CARACTERISTIQUES LOCOMOTIVE

...bre de cylindres — 2	N^{bre} petits tubes à fumée — 236	Surf. de surchauffe —
...tre des cylindres — 482 ™	N^{bre} gros tubes à fumée —	Timbre chaudière — 14,76 K
...rse des pistons — 558 ™	Dimensions petits tubes — φ51 x 5067	Poids total à vide — 63.600 K
...mètres des roues couplées — 1118 ™	Dimensions gros tubes —	Poids total en service — 70.800 K
...eur de grille — 1980 ™	Surf. chauffe foyer — 11,57 m²	Poids adhérent en service — 55.200 K
...r de grille — 1730 ™	Surf. chauffe tubes — 191,57 m²	Poids par essieu couplé — 13.800 K
...des grille — 3,425 m²	Surf. chauffe totale — 203,14 m²	Effort de traction 0,85d²... 11.224 K

CARACTERISTIQUES
Poids à vide
Capacité en eau
Capacité en combustible

H. K. Porter 2-8-2 for the Katanga railway, Belgian Congo, six of which were hired to the Beira line about 1917-18. This engine 202, but actual engines used on the Beira line are unknown. Author's collection

During 1917, when traditional suppliers were unavailable due to the 1914-18 war, H.K. Porter of Pittsburg, Pennsylvania, USA, built twenty-four 2-8-2 locomotives for the *Chemins de Fer du Bas Congo á Katanga* in Belgian Congo. Due to both South Africa and Rhodesia being also critically short of motive power, six were hired to the South African Railways and another half dozen to the Beira Mashonaland Railway, these latter being used on the Beira line where with larger grate and more adhesion they must have proved very useful substitutes for the native 9th class. The Belgian diagram is of course metric, but a comparison of some key dimensions show how effective they were:

Dvg. wheels	3'8"	4'0"
Boiler pressure	210 psi	175 psi
Tractive effort	24 750lb.	29 750lb.
Grate area	37 sq. ft.	31.2 sq. ft.
Loco weight	69.7 tons	66.0 tons
Adhesion	54.3 tons	51.35 tons
Axle load	13.6 tons	12.9 tons

The engines were BCK numbers 201-24, Porter 5993-6016 of 1917, but which individual engines worked on the Beira line are unknown. No photographs of them at work in Rhodesia (or rather Moçambique) seem to have survived, but a very small builder's catalogue shot, and a later photograph on home territory show their appearance. For their time, they were rather primitive, being unsuperheated and having slide valves compared with the superheated, piston valve, 9th class.

Locomotive	BCK 2-8-2	RR 9th class
Cylinders	19" x 22"	20" x 24"

Rhodesia Railways Engineering Dept, ex-SAR 13 class. 4-8-0T +T.

For building the southeast line from Bannockburn to Malvernia, RR's civil engineering construction department purchased from SAR five old 13th class 4-8-0 tank engines with tenders, originally built as 4-10-2T to Natal design, for the Imperial Military Railways during the Anglo-Boer war. Soon after service they were converted to their later form by cutting off the rear section and adding an old tender, both reducing the coupled wheelbase for easier curving and increasing coal and water capacities to extend their working range. As such they were used on branch lines and shunting. They were taken over after the war by the Central South African Railways and thirty of the 35 locos converted to tank plus tender. The five engines sold to RR were as follows:

Hamer records them as working in Rhodesia from 1952, but SAR records show them as being sold October 1954, so they may have initially been on hire. In service they carried small letters "C.E." on cabsides, below which was a number, details of which seem not to hand. They were never RR running stock engines, and the numbers carried were probably plant or equipment numbers, mixed up with other less interesting plant such as bulldozers! It is believed they were disposed of, after contract completion, to a scrap yard in the Khami Road, Bulawayo.

IMR/CSAR No	SAR No	Builder	Date	Works No
225	1314	Dubs	1901	4091
229	1318	Dubs	1901	4095
237	1323	Neilson Reid	1902	6198
238	1324	Neilson Reid	1902	6199
241	1327	Neilson Reid	1902	6202

Old SAR 13th class, as purchased by the Chief Engineer's department for construction work. F. C. Butcher

SAR class 14R, 4-8-2

When the SAR GMAM Garratts proved unsuitable for Zimbabwean conditions, a new tack was taken in hiring nominally twenty class 14R for shunting work, thus releasing NRZ Garratts for main line duty. This occurred for a period of nearly two years, at the latter stage of the refurbishment programme, with two or three allocated to Thomson Junction shed, Hwange, whilst the majority shunted around Bulawayo. The only line work performed was in transfer trips between yards. Whether they hauled trains to or from Thomson Junction seems unknown, but probably they were hauled dead in the train.

Most were scrapped after return to South Africa, but three have survived into preservation at different sites, whilst two were sold to Grootvlei Proprietary Gold Mines, Springs, where one remains operable and the other is cannibalized for spares. Two of these 14R also worked in Swaziland, one before going to Zimbabwe, and the other after its return.

The SAR class 14R were all rebuilds with standard boilers from older classes 14, 14A and 14B, which became identical as rebuilt.

SAR class 14R No 1921 brings a train of coal into Bulawayo station in 1981.

SAR Number	Builder	Works Number	Date in Service	Date in Zimbabwe	Notes
1579	North British	20571	8/1914	5/1981 - 10/1982	Scrapped
1580	North British	20572	8/1914	2/1981 - 3/1982	Scrapped
1581	North British	20573	8/1914	5/1981 - 3/1982	Scrapped
1588	North British	20580	9/1914	2/1981 - 10/1982	Scrapped
1591	North British	20583	10/1914	2/1981 - 8/1982	Scrapped
1703	R. Stephenson	3545	1913	4/1981 - 3/1982	Scrapped
1706	R. Stephenson	3548	1913	4/1981 - 3/1982	Scrapped
1707	R. Stephenson	3549	1913	6/1982 - 10/1982	Scrapped
1709	R. Stephenson	3551	1913	7/1982 - 10/1982	Swaziland 1978-80 scrapped
1712	R. Stephenson	3554	1914	4/1981 - 11/1982	Scrapped
1715	R. Stephenson	3557	1914	10/1981 - 8/1982	Scrapped
1725	R. Stephenson	3609	2/1915	9/1981 - 8/1982	Scrapped
1728	R. Stephenson	3612	2/1915	10/1981 - 11/1982	Scrapped
1731	R. Stephenson	3630	6/1915	2/1981 - 10/1982	Scrapped
1733	R. Stephenson	3632	6/1915	7/1981 - 4/1982	Pres. Millsite
1745	R. Stephenson	3644	10/1915	9/1981 - 10/1982	Pres. Hilton
1747	Beyer Peacock	5878	4/1915	9/1981 - 7/1982	Scrapped
1751	Beyer Peacock	5882	4/1915	2/1981 - 7/1982	Scrapped
1757	Beyer Peacock	5888	4/1915	4/1981 - 7/1981	GVPM (spares)
1758	Beyer Peacock	5889	4/1915	4/1981 - 3/1982	Scrapped
1909	North British	20830	12/1914	4/1981 - 6/1982	Pres. SANRASM
1916	North British	20837	1/1915	9/1981 - 10/1982	Scrapped
1921	North British	20842	1/1915	6/1981 - 6/1982	Swaziland 1982-83 GVPM No 3

SAR class 15F, 4-8-2

15F 3066 sits beside Rhodesian class 20A Garratt in Bulawayo shed yard in 1979. The SAR loco is already disconnected, and ready for towing back home.

Rhodesia's policy of dieselisation, in the face of international oil sanctions can be seen as largely an act of bravado. A country with ample supplies of excellent coal, but no oil, should have stayed on the steam standard and developed new designs. Several countries were willing to risk the opprobrium of sanctions-breaking in order to secure contracts for diesel locomotives, but when, later, a few spare parts were wanted, they could not be bothered. Thus Rhodesia suffered a motive power shortage eventually leading to the refurbishment of 87 Garratts. The first power shortage occurred in 1978, and six class 15F were hired from SAR to do exactly the same job as the six 15E scrapped only five years before! However, local drivers prefer Garratts, and when large numbers of GMAM Garratts became available, the 15F were returned. Apart from having piston valves and standard Walscheart's valve gear, these 15F were distinguished from the 15E by having large, twelve wheeled, tenders, taken from scrapped 23 class locos. The 15F lasted only nine months on RR, and spent their local lives working between Bulawayo and Gwelo.

SAR Number	Builder	Works Number	Date in Service	Date in Rhodesia
3000	North British	25539	6/1945	11/1978 - 8/1979
3031	North British	25570	11/1945	10/1978 - 8/1979
3066	North British	25950	5/1947	10/1978 - 8/1979
3072	North British	25956	8/1947	10/1978 - 8/1979
3094	North British	25978	11/1947	10/1978 - 8/1979
3126	North British	26010	3/1948	11/1978 - 6/1979

All were returned to service in South Africa.

SAR GMAM 4-8-2 + 2-8-4 Garratts

A South African GMAM Garratt at Bulawayo shed in 1981. Note the extended bunker, and bullet-proof plating obscuring cabside number plate. Stencilled number is 4103.

From August 1979 to the end of 1981, whilst NRZ's Garratt refurbishment was in full swing, numerous GMAM Garratts were hired from the South African Railways. Unlike South Africa, where they were mostly used cab-first, Zimbabwe crews were used to running Garratts in the forward direction, i.e. chimney - first, and did so with the "foreigners". In all major dimensions, the SA Garratts were closely equivalent to the native 20th/20A classes, and could haul the same loads. However, probably due to the crude exhaust arrangements, with a heavy "cross" across the blast pipe, leading to an audibly harsh exhaust, the GMAMs were very heavy on coal and despite extensions to the bunkers, frequently ran dangerously low in fuel, with resultant dumping of trains while engines ran light to shed for refuelling. Towards the end they were limited to the same loads as an NRZ 16A, in order to conserve coal. Their main use was on the North line, from Bulawayo to Thomson Junction and Victoria Falls, but they also appeared East as far as Gweru. No sluggards, the GMAM were used on both passenger and freight trains. Although running repairs were carried out at Bulawayo, they returned to South Africa for any major work, and were nominally allocated to Capital Park, Pretoria, whilst on hire to Zimbabwe. Thus the periods of hire quoted below included gaps where engines were home in South Africa, sometimes being replaced with other similar engines whilst away. Due to their unpopularity, they were later replaced by smaller 14R class 4-8-2 which were used on the shunts, releasing NRZ Garratts for the main line. After returning to South Africa, most were taken straight out of service and not used again, although several were hired to Moçambique, Beira line, some sold to South African industrial users, whilst two have been preserved, 4112 as a static exhibit in Scotland, and 4070 still as an operating locomotive at Voorbaai, South Africa. Two almost had an interesting further life in Western Australia but the deal fell through mainly due to the cost of transporting them overseas.

SAR Number	Builder	Works Number	Date in Service	Date in Rhodesia/Zimbabwe		Disposal
4059	Henschel	28688	1/1954	12/1979 -	7/1981	REGM No 16
4060	Henschel	28689	2/1954	8/1979 -	9/1981	Scrapped
4064	Henschel	28693	3/1954	8/1979 -	5/1981	Scrapped
4065	Henschel	28694	3/1954	8/1979 -	3/1981	Scrapped
4070	Henschel	28699	4/1954	8/1980 -	2/1981	Preserved SAR
4071	Henschel	28700	5/1954	12/1979 -	9/1980	CFM 1981-83, REGM for spares
4087	Beyer Peacock	7753	1/1957	8/1979 -	9/1981	Scrapped
4089	Beyer Peacock	7755	2/1957	8/1979 -	10/1980	REGM for spares
4090	Beyer Peacock	7756	2/1957	12/1979 -	9/1980	Bloemfontein works*
4098	Beyer Peacock	7764	3/1957	1/1980 -	9/1981	Scrapped
4099	North British	27691	11/1956	12/1979 -	3/1981	CFM 1982-83, Scrapped
4102	North British	27694	1/1957	9/1980 -	5/1981	Scrapped
4103	North British	27695	1/1957	12/1979 -	2/1981	Scrapped
4111	North British	27769	8/1957	2/1980 -	2/1981	Scrapped
4112	North British	27770	9/1957	8/1979 -	10/1980	Preserved, UK
4117	North British	27775	10/1957	6/1980 -	2/1981	Scrapped
4120	North British	27778	11/1957	8/1979 -	10/1980	Scrapped
4121	Beyer Peacock	7836	7/1958	12/1979 -	9/1981	Scrapped
4125	Beyer Peacock	7840	9/1958	8/1979 -	4/1980	Tweefontein No 2
4126	Beyer Peacock	7841	9/1958	12/1979 -	1/1980	CFM 1982-83, Tweefontein No 3
4129	Beyer Peacock	7844	10/1958	3/1979 -	10/1980	Bloemfontein works*
4134	North British	27786	1/1958	8/1979 -	10/1980	Scrapped
4135	North British	27787	2/1958	8/1979 -	2/1981	CFM 1982-83, REGM No R14
4137	North British	27789	3/1958	8/1979 -	9/1980	Scrapped
4139	North British	27791	6/1958	8/1979 -	8/1981	Scrapped
4140	North British	27792	6/1958	12/1979 -	8/1981	Scrapped

CFM: Caminhos de Ferro de Moçambique (hired)
REGM: Randfontein Estates Gold Mines (sold)
* Retained for sale to Western Australia, deal failed to materialise.

SAR 12R class, 4-8-2. Hired to Zambia

During 1980, ten SAR 12R class were hired to Zambian Railways. All were from Germiston shed and travelled up via Mafeking. None lasted more than a few months, but they were used for shunting at Livingstone, Choma, Kafue, Kabwe, and Ndola. After return to South Africa, all but one were scrapped. The hiring dates shown are from and to Mafeking, from SAR records. Details are:

Loco	Builder	Works no.	Date built	Date ex Mafeking	Returned to Mafeking	Scrapped
1495	North Brit.	19594	1912	2/1980	7/1980	4/1988
1500	North Brit.	19686	1912	2/1980	7/1980	7/1987
1501	North Brit.	19687	1912	3/1980	6/1980	1986
1503	North Brit.	20174	1913	2/1980	?	2/1986
1504	North Brit.	20175	1913	2/1980	5/1980	10/1987
1510	North Brit.	20812	1915	2/1980	5/1980	Sold Umgala, 1981
1940	Baldwin	52691	1920	2/1980	5/1980	1984
1944	Baldwin	52713	1920	3/1980	6/1980	1984
1950	Baldwin	52757	1920	2/1980	6/1980	1984
1954	Baldwin	52761	1920	2/1980	6/1980	?

RR and NRZ Locomotives sold to other countries

A good number of Rhodesian and Zimbabwean steam locomotives have been sold out of use to other countries, mainly in Africa, and details of these are to be found in the historical tables accompanying each class of locomotive. However, a brief summary of these engines, country by country, will be useful together with further photographs which could not be fitted into the main text.

Angola.
Nine 16th class Garratts were sold to the Benguela Railway (CFB).

Botswana.
Three 14A Garratts three 19th and two 19B sold to the Selebi-Phikwe mines.

Congo Belge.
Mashonaland locos 5 and 6, plus three 7th class, sold to the former Belgian Congo.
The Katanga Railways (BCK) also adopted the 7th class in RR form, with Belpaire firebox, for locomotives built in Belgium.

Great Britain.
7 class 993 from the Zambesi Sawmills Railway was given to wildlife painter David Shepherd and is now in England. This was originally a Cape, and later South African engine, and not built for Rhodesia. At least two narrow gauge engines from the Selukwe Peak Light Railway are also in Britain.

Moçambique.
Numerous RR locomotives of the 7th, 11th, 11A, 12A, 12B, 14th., 17th and 18th class were sold to the CFM at different times.

Nyasaland.
One 7th class sold to the Shiré Highlands Railway, a forerunner of the Nyasaland Railway.

South Africa.
Several 7th class sold to SAR in 1915, together with some narrow gauge "Lawley" 4-4-0 from the former Beira Railway. The 7th class were for use in the South West Africa campaign, and two of the "Lawleys" are preserved in South Africa. A number of 16th class Garratts were sold to coal mining companies in the 1960s and in 1995 a 14A and 16A Garratt here been sold to the Transnet Heritage Foundation for operation from their centre at George.

Swaziland.
No direct sales to Swaziland, but many locomotives sold to Moçambique saw service on the Swaziland Railway.

New Zealand.
A 15A Garratt has been sold to a buyer in New Zealand, and is intended for operation.

Angola CFB 386, ex RR 16th class 616 heads a "dupla", cut into which can be seen another of the same class.
F. C. Butcher

Botswana, Selebi-Phikwe mines. Engine No 2, ex RR class 19B no 338, at Phikwe shed, 1986.

Botswana, Selebi-Phikwe mines. 14A Garratt No L0810, Ex NRZ 523, hauling ore from Selebi North shaft in February 1996.

Moçambique. CFM 462, ex RR 11A class 315, at Matsapha, Swaziland, in 1969.

Moçambique. CFM 492, ex RR 12A class No 213, at Sidvokodvo, Swaziland, 1970.

Moçambique. CFM 476, ex RR 12B class 266, at Sidvokodvo, Swaziland, 1969.

Moçambique. Beira line No 903, ex RR 14th class No 217, at Gondola 1969.

Moçambique. Beira line No 922, ex RR 17th class No 272. At Dondo Entroncamanto (Junction), 1968.

Moçambique. Beira line No 982, ex RR 18th class No 282. At Gondola. 1968.

Moçambique. 7th class No 10, ex RR No 32, at Beira in 1969. This loco has now been preserved at the dock entrance.

Moçambique. CFM, 445 ex RR 11th class No 151, shunting at Lourenço Marques in 1967.

South Africa. For some odd reason RR 7th class No 63 (ex No 1) was numbered out of sequence when sold to SAR in 1915, becoming their No 949, shown here.
Author's collection

Several South African coal mines used second hand RR 16th class Garratts. Here is Landau 3 colliery, near Witbank, No 1 ex RR 605, in maroon livery.

The fifth RR loco to carry a Giesl ejector, fitted after sale from Rhodesia. 612, at Durnacol mine, Dannhauser, with Giesl ejector, and engine units ex 604.

7th class No 69, with Belpaire firebox, is seen on the Zambezi Sawmills Railway in 1970.
P. F. Bagshawe

ZR 9B No 84 on hire to Zambian Broken Hill Development Co in 1970.
P. F. Bagshawe

10th class 156 on the ZSR at Mulobezi in 1971. This engine was donated to David Shepherd, the wildlife artist, and is now in Livingstone Railway Museum, operable.
P. F. Bagshawe

Proposed 17th class, 4-8-2

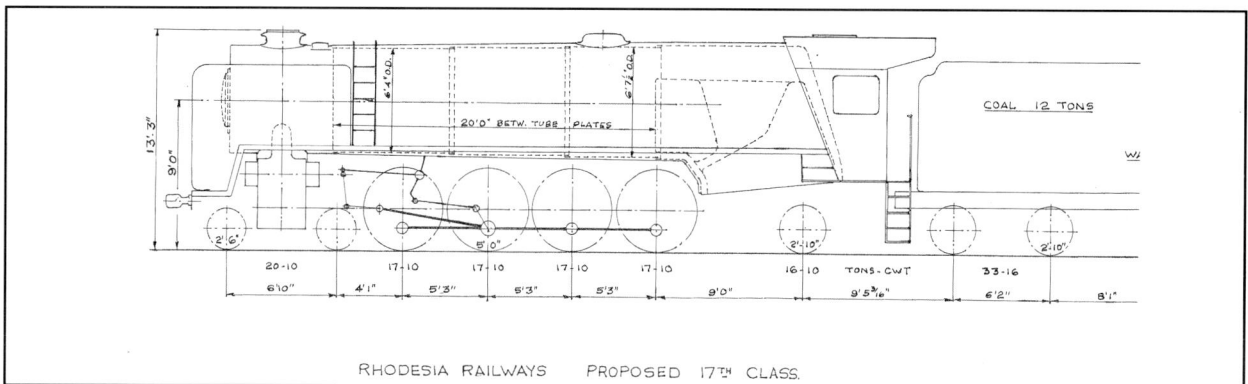

RHODESIA RAILWAYS   PROPOSED 17ᵀᴴ CLASS.

During 1944-45, when World War II was coming to an end, Rhodesia Railways were naturally planning their post-war motive power requirements, and the consulting engineers, Messrs Freeman Fox and Partners, had proposed an enlarged 15th class 4-6-4 + 4-6-4 Garratt with cylinders 19 1/2 x 26 inches, five foot driving wheels, and boiler with 64.8 square feet of grate area. Estimated weight with two thirds coal and water was 184 tons, a rather optimistic under estimate, as the engine will have been much the same size as the later 20th class. Tractive effort at 85 percent boiler pressure will have been 50 420 lb. It is probable that the proposal diagram for this resides in the Beyer Peacock archives, but attempts by the author to exhume this have so far not materialised.

Major Sells, the then CME, was against this proposal, and thought that a large 4-8-2, similar to the SAR 15F, would be a more viable alternative, and prepared such a scheme, redrawn as above from a rather crude sketch in the author's possession. From this it will be seen that the 15F design was very closely followed, but the boiler had a combustion chamber and short tubes, which will have been an advantage. The boiler was also pitched slightly lower and with a taller loading gauge a handsome chimney was incorporated. Bearing in mind the actual 15F figures, the weight, and especially the maximum axle load, was decidedly optimistic, but no doubt these figures would have been suitably "adjusted" had the locomotive materialised.

In correspondence with Mr. (later Dr.) M.M. Loubser of SAR, some interesting figures were provided in a letter dated 27 December 1944, and a precis of these, covering the most nearly relevant classes, showed the following:

The GH and U classes were "Union-Garratts", and the above figures show clearly why they were not adopted further. However, the GM Garratt type was very favourable, especially as it was of similar age to the 15F and 23 classes, and evaluating these figures as presented, one finds for these three more modern types, the following:

Class	Tractive effort lb. per £ capital cost	Maintenance, tractive effort per pence/ mile cost
15F	3.66	7494
23	3.41	5589
GM	3.45	6430

Relative to tractive effort, a convenient but certainly not exhaustive comparison figure, the three types, which had closely similar grate areas, show the 15F as being the least expensive in capital and having the lowest maintenance costs. The GM Garratt is similar to the 23 class in capital, but shows better maintenance costs.

All in all, Major Sells seems not to have made out his case to the RR management, who decided to proceed with their Garratt policy, although neither the 17th class 4-8-2 nor the competing large 4-6-4 + 4-6-4 (which would presumably have also been 17th class) were proceeded with, and further orders were for the 15th class. Maintenance costs "per mile" can be very misleading, especially if engines are on dissimilar work, and the GM Garratt costs, slogging over 1 in 40 gradients which reduce speed and thus the cost denominator, show up very well against the tender engines on fast, main line, work. Clearly RR saw through this, but certainly in later days this obvious truth evaded SAR authorities.

Loco Class	Tractive Effort	Capital Cost	Average maintenance cost pence/mile, 1941-44	Type
15F	42340	£11 567	5.65	4-8-2
23	43200	£12 669	7.73	4-8-2
GH	44490	£14 526	14.20	4-6-2+2-6-4
U	50050	£12 141	23.01	2-6-2+2-6-2
GM	60700	£17 578	9.44	4-8-2+2-8-4

The Cook ten-coupled proposal

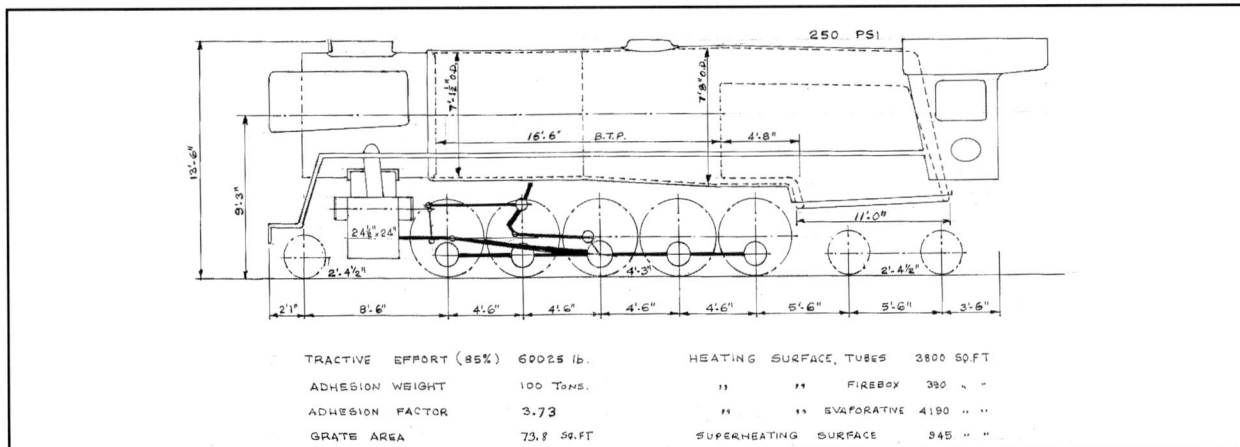

TRACTIVE EFFORT (85%) 60025 lb.   HEATING SURFACE, TUBES 3800 SQ.FT
ADHESION WEIGHT 100 Tons.   " " FIREBOX 390 " "
ADHESION FACTOR 3.73   " " EVAPORATIVE 4190 " "
GRATE AREA 73.8 SQ.FT   SUPERHEATING SURFACE 945 " "

Somewhere about 1977, when planning and designs for refurbishing the Garratt fleet were under way, and the disastrous mix of "sanction-busting" diesels were giving increasing trouble, Derek Cook the then Assistant Chief Mechanical Engineer of Rhodesia Railways, conceived the idea of building one hundred new steam locomotives for RR. Brian Noble, chief draughtsman, remembers Derek bursting into the drawing office with a freehand sketch of the new engine, not even to scale, with instructions to "design me an engine like this!" The writer, then manager of SKF's Railway division in South Africa was brought into the picture when Derek wanted to discuss possible roller applications for his new brainchild, what he did not realise until the interview was that the SKF representative was a full-blown steam engineer with a Swindon training - just what the CME wanted as he was basically a diesel man. The usual half hour interview thus stretched out for a whole morning as we discussed steam design in general and in detail. Derek's idea was for a ten-coupled loco, 2-10-2 or 2-10-4 according to the interview, with twenty ton axle load to provide "about 70 000 pounds tractive effort, and equal a 20th class". As will be seen later, these figures simply do not gel. Derek wanted to use all possible existing patterns and flanging blocks to save time and cost, and had the idea to mount the back end on a standard Issels wagon bogie. A boiler pressure of 250 psi was proposed, and all the Wardale modifications as used on 19D 2644 were to be incorporated. In 1995 Brian Noble discovered the original Cook sketches, which had been misfiled, and these show a 2-10-4 with, on a second page, an even less practical 4-10-4 version.

From these sketches, plus figures in correspondence, and memories of the conversation, the author has reconstructed a diagram showing what the beast may have looked like. This uses the four foot wheels and 250 psi pressure specified by Cook, together with a boiler using the front flanging block for a 20th class Garratt. The Cook sketch shows 16 feet between tubeplates with a combustion chamber three feet long, but a better design, when drawn to scale, is to increase the combustion chamber to five feet long, with Cook's other firebox dimensions unchanged. The freight car bogie, spaced twelve feet from the trailing coupled axle was clearly impracticable, and the diagram has been drawn using a South African 25NC class trailing truck, whose patterns will have been available from SAR, probably at Salt River works. With one hundred tons adhesion, the maximum practical tractive effort works out to about 60 000 pounds and bearing in mind the use of roller bearing crankpins combined with four foot wheels, cylinder dimensions have been reduced from the Cook figures of 26" x 26" to 24" x 24". Even so, it may well have been necessary to increase wheel size to 4'3" or even 4'6" to give sufficient radial clearance for roller bearing rods, but all these were standard tyre sizes on RR and no problem.

Cook's idea was to build one hundred such machines, at a rate of twenty per annum commencing 1981. A great deal of assistance from South Africa must have been assumed, especially for such major components as the main frames, but much detail work plus the final erection was certainly possible in Rhodesia. Before anything could be fully detailed and implemented, Rhodesia became Zimbabwe, and the salesmen from GM probably flew in on the first plane! One cannot begrudge Zimbabwe its independence, but there is always the nagging thought...if only that 2-10-4 scheme could have got off the ground before independence!

How would the Cook 2-104 have performed? On a maximum tractive effort basis, its starting capacity was somewhat less than a 20th class Garratt. However, the large boiler with ample grate area presupposed a much higher horsepower, and had the Wardale features later incorporated in the "Red Devil" been included, we are talking about a 5000 horsepower machine with 35 percent more starting capacity than the "Red Devil" itself - an item of motive power which the French, including the great André Chapelon would have pronounced *formidable!*

The 25NC project

During 1988 a severe motive power shortage was experienced by the NRZ and discussions with South Africa revealed that numerous class 25NC 4-8-4, had been recently withdrawn from service and were available for either hire or purchase. NRZ decided to investigate the purchase of twenty, or possibly 25 of these locomotives for a short term basis, the idea being to operate them for a few years only and then scrap them once finished with. What was thus required were locomotives in the best possible condition such that minimum repairs would be needed, for virtually immediate issuing to traffic. A team of three were sent down from Bulawayo comprising Mr A. Mabena, then assistant CME (now general manager) together with mechanical and boiler inspectors. The author was appointed by the Ministry of Industry and Technology, Harare on a short term consultancy, to accompany the inspection team and submit an independent report on the locomotives' condition and suitability for purchase, within the terms of reference laid down. He also provided details and descriptions of these engines together with their capabilities as traffic machines. A total of fifty locomotives were inspected by the team, at Warrenton and De Aar, with full co-operation from the South African Transport Services, who provided such important details as the dates of last heavy overhaul, and due dates for boiler certificate renewals, all of which needed balancing against any damage, or missing components. The author also independently inspected locomotives at Bethleham and Bloemfontein.

The author, in his report, categorised the locomotives into three groups, according to the time expected to elapse before heavy repairs were needed, and enthusiasts will be interested to know which locomotives were so considered.

Category A
locomotives with five or more years before heavy overhaul.

Warrenton:	3438, 3442, 3445, 3453, 3457, 3459, 3504, 3508, 3519
De Aar:	3428
Bethlehem:	3404, 3410, 3422
Bloemfontein:	3479

Total 14 locomotives

Category B
needing heavy repairs by 1993-94

Warrenton:	3464, 3490, 3498, 3520, 3537
De Aar:	3424, 3473, 3507
Bloemfontein:	3412, 3475, 3518

Total 11 locomotives

Category C
locomotives needing heavy repairs in 1992

Warrenton:	3439, 3446
De Aar:	3515

Total 3 locomotives

25NC 3404, a one-time candidate for sale to NRZ, was later returned to SAR service and is regularly used on the "Trans Karoo" express. Here it is seen heading a freight out of Springs, where the author resides.

Thus 28 locomotives were submitted from which it would be possible to choose twenty, or twenty-five, or any lesser number which might be needed.

It was proposed to use these engines not only on the main line North, but also East to Gweru, thus releasing diesels which could then be concentrated in the eastern areas where no steam facilities remained. In the end, the deal did not materialise, which was a pity as a number of fine locomotives would have been given a new lease of life, although Zimbabwe would have lost its status as being an "all Garratt" railway over the steam sections. As an amusing aside, although no degree of secrecy was ever mentioned, the author felt that being involved he should not report what was going on to the railway press at that time. However, such things invariably leak out and one writer, notorious for "jumping the gun" published an article claiming that twenty-five class 25NC had already been purchased by NRZ! There was never any apology nor retraction when they failed to appear in Zimbabwe!

Although these engines never ran in Zimbabwe, they were a distinct possibility, and one of the Category A locomotives is illustrated as an example.

Several of those chosen as Zimbabwe possibles have subsequently been resuscitated and found new owners, as below:

3404	Prestige locomotive, Braamfontein
3410	Prestige locomotive, Bloemfontein
3422	Prestige locomotive, Braamfontein
3442	Rovos Rail, Pretoria, awaiting renovation
3508	sold to Enyati Colliery, later sold to Mr I. Welch, New Zealand.

A possible 21st class, 4-10-2 + 2-10-4 Garratt

The author's professional association with Rhodesia and Zimbabwe included the period of the World Oil Crisis, which slowed down the replacement of steam in several countries and actually reversed it in Zimbabwe. The world at the time was full of schemes to reduce oil consumption, and a number of schemes, some horrifically impracticable, were produced and aired to show the possibilities of modern steam traction. In South Africa, David Wardale had modified class 19D no. 2644 with good results, and was working out details for his "Red Devil" 4-8-4, 3450, which emerged in 1981. Meanwhile, the author in 1979 read a paper entitled "STEAM LOCOMOTION, a reappraisal for an oil-starved world", to the Rhodesian Institution of Mechanical Engineers, in Bulawayo, winning an award from the Institution in London. Soon after,

Rhodesia became Zimbabwe, and another steam paper was delivered, also in Bulawayo. After a year or two, by which time the Wardale "Red Devil" had been operated and tested in service, a third paper was commenced, to describe these good results and to show what could really be done with steam under conditions in Zimbabwe. By then, all main lines were capable of withstanding a twenty tonne axle load and the DE8 class diesels, whatever their other shortcomings, were demonstrating that such an axle load was perfectly practicable.

The "21 class" was designed in metric units, unlike all other steam engines in the country, designed in imperial units. Nevertheless, it is interesting to convert some of the key dimensions and compare with the 20A class, the largest and most powerful to run on the system.

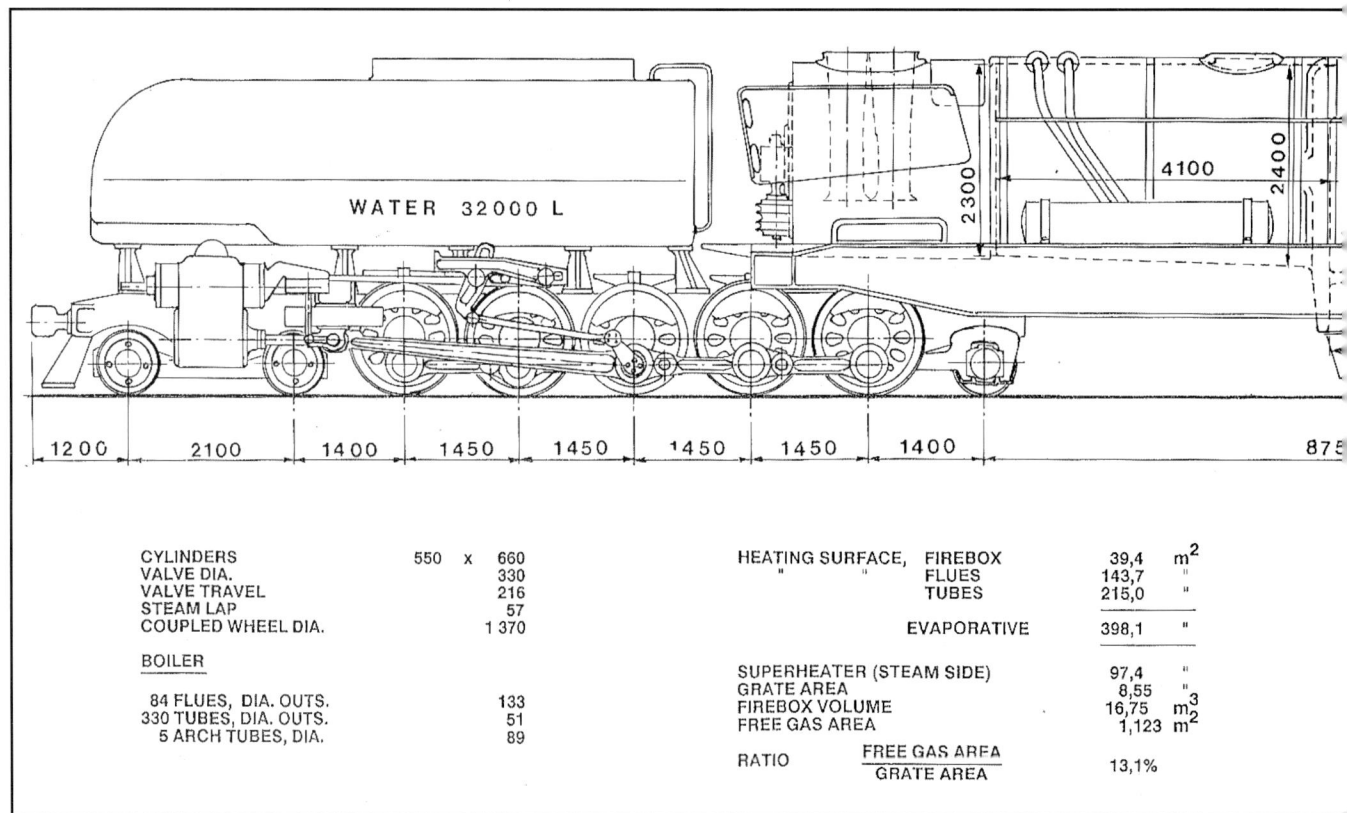

WATER 32000 L

4100   2400   2300

1200   2100   1400   1450   1450   1450   1450   1400   875

CYLINDERS	550 x 660	
VALVE DIA.	330	
VALVE TRAVEL	216	
STEAM LAP	57	
COUPLED WHEEL DIA.	1 370	
BOILER		
84 FLUES, DIA. OUTS.	133	
330 TUBES, DIA. OUTS.	51	
5 ARCH TUBES, DIA.	89	

HEATING SURFACE,	FIREBOX	39,4	m^2
" "	FLUES	143,7	"
	TUBES	215,0	"
	EVAPORATIVE	398,1	"
	SUPERHEATER (STEAM SIDE)	97,4	"
	GRATE AREA	8,55	"
	FIREBOX VOLUME	16,75	m^3
	FREE GAS AREA	1,123	m^2
RATIO	$\dfrac{\text{FREE GAS AREA}}{\text{GRATE AREA}}$	13,1%	

Engine class	20A	21	Increase, percent
Cylinder dimensions (inches)	20x26	21.65 x 26	17.2 (Volume)
Driving wheels (feet/inches)	4.3	4.6	5.8
Boiler pressure psi	200	256	28
Valve diameter (inches)	11	13	18
Valve travel (inches)	6.75	8.5	26
Grate area, sq. ft.	63.2	92.3	46
Tractive effort, lb.	69333	99103	43
Total weight, tonnes	225.5	290	29
Adhesion, tonnes	136.8	200	46

Thus it can be seen that the potential for steam traction in Zimbabwe was far from ever being realised, and with a conservatively estimated output of 5700 horsepower (4340kW) at the wheel rims, it would have greatly outperformed later diesel and electric power, making great economies possible using indigenous energy and without high capital cost.

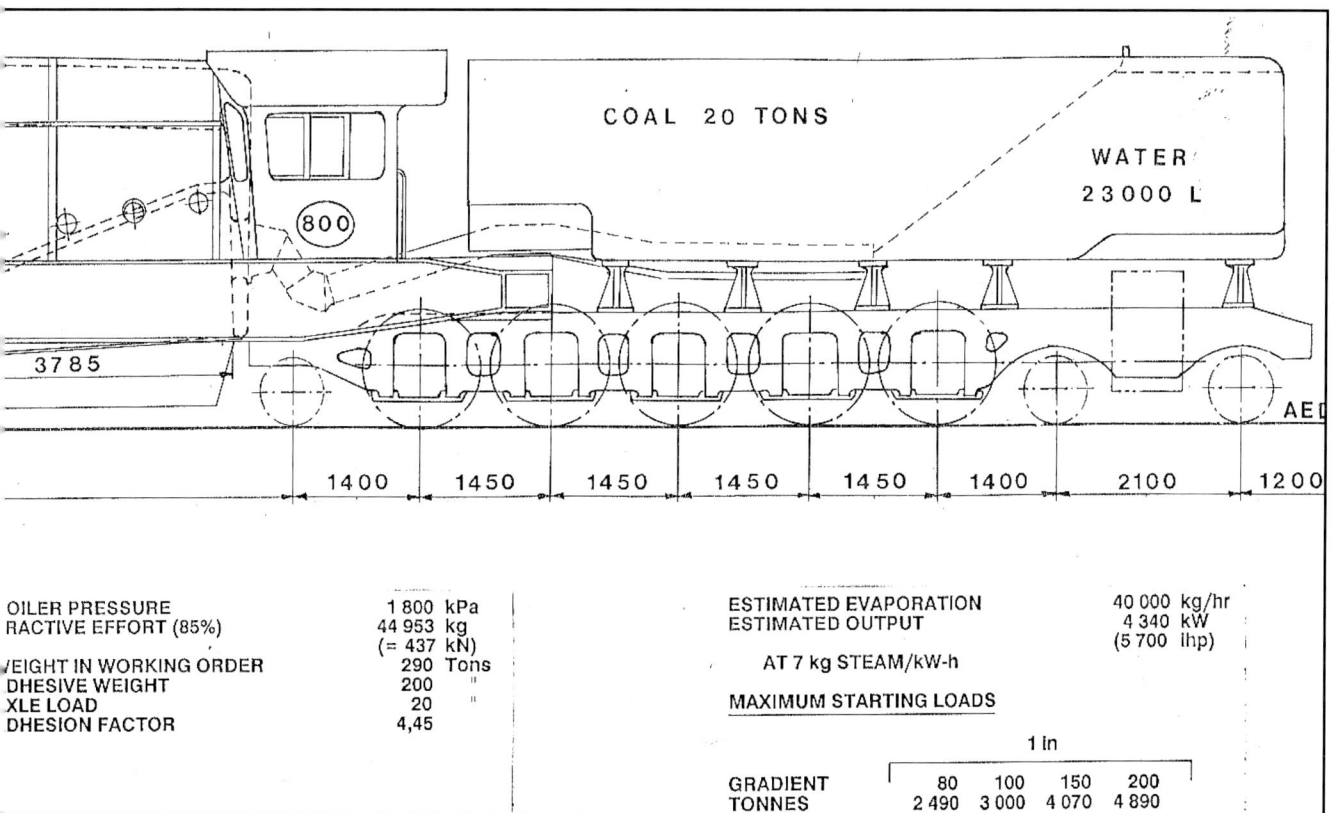

COAL 20 TONS

WATER 23000 L

800

3785

AE

| 1400 | 1450 | 1450 | 1450 | 1450 | 1400 | 2100 | 1200 |

OILER PRESSURE   1 800 kPa
RACTIVE EFFORT (85%)   44 953 kg
(= 437 kN)
VEIGHT IN WORKING ORDER   290 Tons
DHESIVE WEIGHT   200
XLE LOAD   20
DHESION FACTOR   4,45

ESTIMATED EVAPORATION   40 000 kg/hr
ESTIMATED OUTPUT   4 340 kW
(5 700 ihp)

AT 7 kg STEAM/kW-h

MAXIMUM STARTING LOADS

		1 in			
GRADIENT	80	100	150	200	
TONNES	2 490	3 000	4 070	4 890	

Locomotive Workshops and Running Sheds

All railways need workshops for carrying out major locomotive repairs, and in some instances for building new locomotives. Rhodesia was no exception, and apart from the narrow gauge the main workshops were at Umtali, opened around the turn of the century and for twenty years the system's main workshops. As steam traction was transferred largely to the western portions of the railway, Umtali closed for steam repairs, the last general overhauls being carried out in March 1965, with occasional light repairs continuing for about another year. This works continued in use for diesel locomotives and wagon repairs. Bulawayo works started in 1919 and continued to develop as the major locomotive, carriage and wagon repairs together with a certain amount of new construction, remaining today in this prominent position. The last steam overhaul was carried out on 15A class no 390 in 1993, but repairs and manufacture of steam components continue as necessary. The third railway workshop was at Mafeking, dealing only with locomotives used on the Southern section. The opening date is a little

unclear, but it remained in operation until about 1950, when everything was centralised upon Bulawayo. There was also a private locomotive workshops RESSCO (Rhodesia Engineering and Steel Supply Company) which opened a locomotive division in order to carry out the steam refurbishment programme. After independence this company became ZECO (Zimbabwe Engineering Company), and after completing the refurbishment programme continued with heavy overhauls for the steam fleet which NRZ's shops were unable to handle. ZECO also carried out locomotive repairs and overhauls for Zambia, Moçambique, Wankie Colliery, and Selebi-Phikwe mine in Botswana, built the NRZ electric locomotives and manufactured goods wagons, many for export. This firm closed down in 1995.

In Zambia, after independence, a new locomotive repair shop was built at Kabwe, formerly Broken Hill, but seems not to have been particularly effective, judging by the general state of ZR steam (and diesel) locomotives.

Outside the P15 shed, Bulawayo, Easter 1991, with 9B, 12th and 20th classes in steam ready for duty.

Running Sheds

Steam enthusiasts are always attracted to the ambience of a locomotive running shed, where engines are steamed up for their daily duties, in a lovely fug of coal smoke, steam and hot oil, whilst others are in process of having boilers washed out, or are partially dismantled for running repairs. Main sheds are alive 24 hours a day, seven days a week, and night time, or perhaps dawn at the beginning of a busy day are excellent times to capture the superb atmosphere which infuse these impressive edifices. Sheds relevant to this book, with their coded abbreviations, are detailed below:

Beira (BA)
Sold to Moçambique with the line to Umtali in October 1949. Still had some steam in 1994.

Umtali (US)
The first major steam shed of 3'6" gauge in the country. Closed to steam 12/1959, but remains as a diesel depot.

Salisbury (SA)
Closed to steam 4/1973, diesel operations being centred on Lochnivar depot.

Gwelo (GO)
Closed to steam 4/1980

Bulawayo (BLR)
At least three, possibly four, successive sheds at this major centre, still open today.

Mafeking (MFS)
Open from about the turn of century until steam ceased on the south line in 1973. Had its own allocation until 9/1966, after which it became a sub shed to Bulawayo.

Wankie (WK)
Important shed at the coalfield, replaced by new shed at Thomson Junction mid 1959.

Thomson Junction (TJ)
Opened mid 1959 to replace Wankie. In latter years this was sub to Bulawayo, but always had locos for shunting and handling trains to Victoria Falls.

Livingstone (LR)
The most important shed north of the Zambezi. Many derelict locomotives there until recently.

Kafue (KF)
Short lived depot, opened 4/1957, closed 11/1961.

Broken Hill (BH, BRO from 4/1929)
Major shed for the northern section. Renamed Kabwe after Zambian independence.

Ndola (NDR)
Opened 2/1932.

Nkana (NK)
Opened 8/1957.

There were also several important engine changing and stabling points, such as Dett (now Dete) and Colleen Bawn which never had permanent allocations, plus of course the termini of various branch lines. There are three major non-steam depots today, which never had steam allocations, viz Lochnivar (Harare), Dabuka (near Gweru) and Mpopoma (Bulawayo) which are mentioned for the sake of completeness.

A line up of locomotives types, from 7th to 20th classes, arranged for an overseas tour group in 1993.

The Narrow Gauge Lines

The first railway into Bulawayo, in what was then Matabeleland, was the Bechuanaland Railway, extending 3'6" "Cape Gauge" northwards in Cecil Rhodes' grand scheme of a Cape-to-Cairo Railway, which eventually petered out in what was then the Belgian Congo. Meanwhile, a two foot gauge line was built through Portugese Moçambique, from Beira to Umtali, then in Mashonaland. Apart from the last few miles, this was entirely in Moçambique, with headquarters in Beira, and as such will be covered in greater detail in this author's book on Moçambique steam, currently in preparation. However, after conversion to 3'6" gauge, several locomotives together with track and rolling stock were moved into Salisbury to build a branch line to Ayrshire, known as the Ayrshire Gold Mine and Lomagunda Railway, opened 1902. The ayrshire mine petered out in 1908 and the final stretch of the line was abandoned, but most of the rest was later reopened in 1911 as the 3'6" gauge branch to Sinoia. With the narrow gauge being mainly in Moçambique, its locomotives have not been included in this work, but details will be included in a book on Moçambique steam now in preparation.

Private and Industrial Railways

This book has concentrated on main line railways and their locomotives, although references to locomotives sold to other users include local industrial and private railways. The most important was the Zambesi Sawmills Railway, now part of the Zambian Railways, and the Wankie Colliery system, still operating with steam. Many industrial concerns, especially mines, operated locomotives, some second hand and others new, and there were also railways, mainly narrow gauge, serving agricultural concerns. The full story of these is as yet incomplete, and hopefully may be included in some later work concerning steam in Central Africa.

Bulawayo shed on a rainy day, with men busy with locomotive maintenance.

Place and name changes

Countries and places change names from time to time, due to political developments, and nowhere was this a greater problem to the author than when trying to trace the railway routes of the old Austro-Hungarian empire over the entirely changed place names of Czechoslovakia, Poland and other countries after the 1919 armistice. By comparison, changes in Africa are far less complicated, but for those referring back to older publications some notes on more recent name changes will be helpful.

Countries
Northern Rhodesia became Zambia in 1967
Southern Rhodesia became Zimbabwe-Rhodesia briefly in 1980, but has since been called simply Zimbabwe.
Bechuanaland became Botswana.
The Cape Colony became Cape Province, South Africa 1910
Nyasaland became Malawi
Belgian Congo became Zaïre
South West Africa became Namibia.
Of other countries relevant to this steam story, both Angola and Moçambique retained their pre-independence names, although Moçambique is often bastardised as Mozambique whilst in the past it was often referred to as "PEA", or Portuguese East Africa.

Cities and Towns

Zambia
Broken Hill became Kabwe

Zimbabwe
Salisbury now Harare
Umtali now Mutare
Gatooma now Kadoma
Que Que now Kwekwe
Gwelo now Gweru
Fort Victoria now Masvingo
Balla Balla now Mbalabala
Essexvale now Esigodini
Gwaai now Gwayi
Dett now Dete
Wankie now Hwange
Selukwe now Shurugwe

Moçambique
Lourenço Marques now Maputo
Malvernia now Eduardo Mondlane
Bamboo Creek later Vila Machado, now Nhamatanda

South Africa
Mafeking now Mafikeng

Returned to service in 1980! Zambian railways class 20A Garratt No 728 approaches Victoria Falls with a southbound freight. For several years ZR had been fully dieselised, but the world oil crises has prompted a partial return to steam traction. R. Dickinson

215

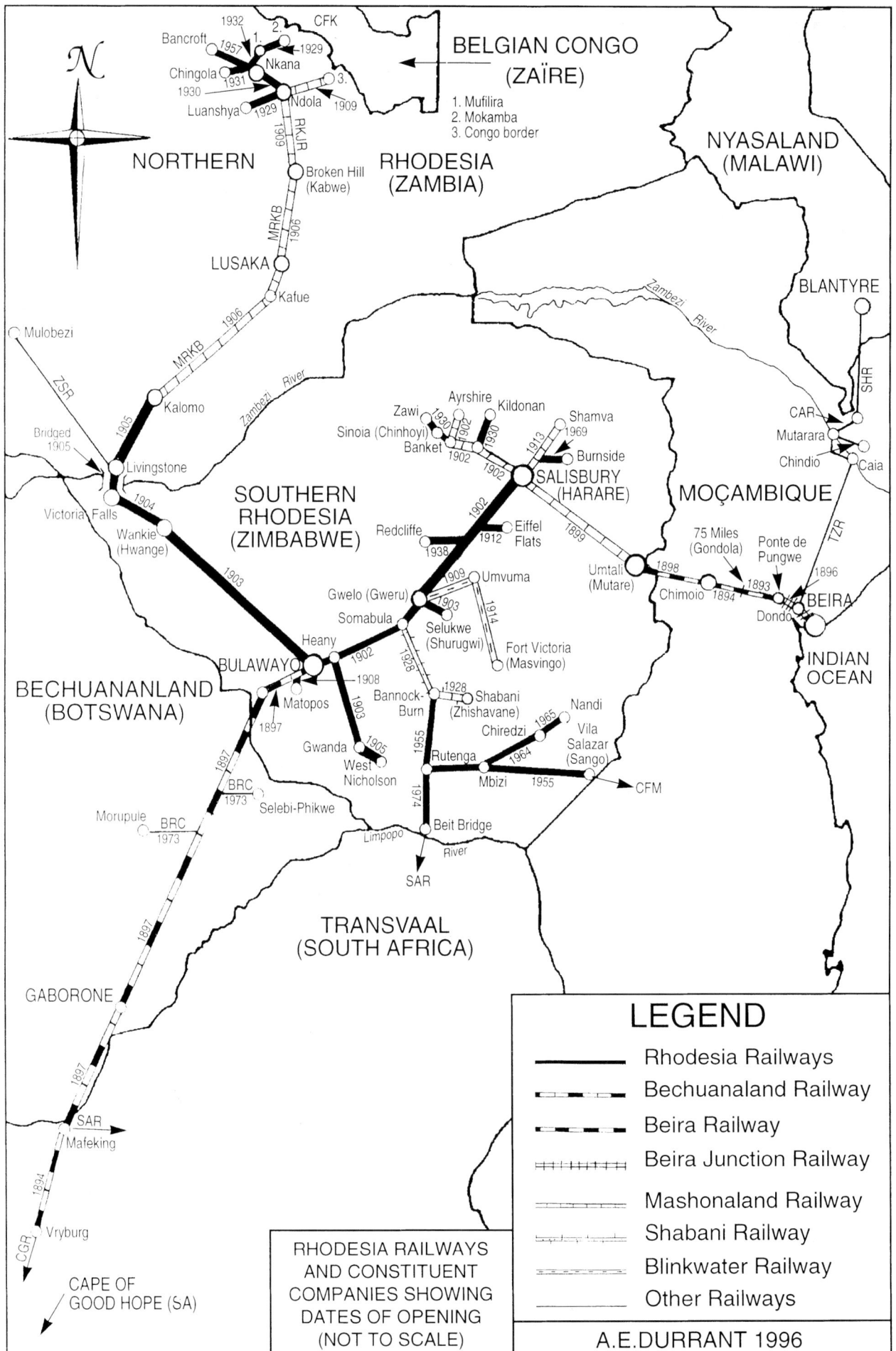

RHODESIA RAILWAYS AND CONSTITUENT COMPANIES SHOWING DATES OF OPENING (NOT TO SCALE)

A.E.DURRANT 1996

LEGEND

Rhodesia Railways
Bechuanaland Railway
Beira Railway
Beira Junction Railway
Mashonaland Railway
Shabani Railway
Blinkwater Railway
Other Railways

Bibliography

In producing such a work as this, constant reference has been made to several other books detailed below, both published and unpublished, and from which in several cases additional information and illustrations may be extracted, the author's main problem being in how to select from the wealth of information available. For those wishing to study the subject further, the following can be recommended.

Barrow, J. J. E. *Register of SAR steam locomotives* (in preparation)

Carling, D. Rock. *4-8-0 tender locomotives,* David & Charles. 1971

Croxton, A. H. *Railways of Rhodesia,* David & Charles.

Durrant, A. E. *The Garratt Locomotive,* David & Charles. 1969

Durrant, A. E. *Garratt Locomotives of the World,* David & Charles. 1981

Durrant, A. E. *The Mallet Locomotive,* David & Charles. 1974

Durrant, A. E. *Twilight of South African Steam,* David & Charles. 1989

Durrant, A. E. *Moçambique Steam,* (in preparation).

Durrant, A. E. *Angolan Steam,* (in preparation).

Durrant, A. E., Lewis, C. P. & Jorgensen, A. A. *Steam in Africa*, Struik. 1981

Hamer, E. D. *Steam Locomotives of the Rhodesia Railways,* Book of Zimbabwe. 1981

Holland, D. F. *Steam Locomotives of the South African Railways, vol I & II,* David & Charles. 1971-2

Pauling, G. *Chronicles of a Contractor,* Rhodesiana Reprints. 1969

Talbot, E. *Steam from Kenya to the Cape,* Continental Railway Circle, 1975.

Middleton, J. N. *Railways of Southern Africa, locomotive Guide 1994,* Beyer Garratt Publications.

Varian, H. F. *Some African Milestones,* Wheatley, 1953.

Encyclopedia Zimbabwe, Tabex, Quest 1987.

Le Rail du Congo Belge (vol I), Blanchard & Cie, Brussels. 1993

Steam in South Africa and Rhodesia, World Steam Publications, 1976.

Locomotive Diagram books:
Beira & Mashonaland Railway
Cape Government Railways
C. F. Bas Congo Katanga
C. F. Benguela
C. F. Moçambique
Rhodesia Railways
South African Railways.

Magazines:
Beyer Peacock Quarterly Review
Continental Railway Journal
Railway Gazette
SA RAIL
The Locomotive Magazine, 1898-1959.
Glasers Annalen

Video
A Video is currently under production showing NRZ steam locomotives at work and will be available from:
VIDRAIL VIDEO
PO Box 75169
Garden View
2047
South Africa
Expected price £18, air mail post & packing £5

Acknowledgments

The preparation of a book such as this, including much official information, yet requiring also an intense personal involvement both in gathering information and in acquiring one's own photographs of locomotives and trains in action, cannot be achieved without cooperation from numerous railway people from all grades, from General Manager down. In the delightful country which was Rhodesia and is now Zimbabwe, the author has always been privileged, over thirty years, to the most friendly assistance from railwaymen of all grades, many of whom, such as drivers, firemen, and station staff, have not been recorded, for which the author apologises, but without them, the location of trains and the provision of smoke at the right places are an invaluable input to this book and its photography.

So thanks firstly to the many railwaymen whose friendliness has always been an encouragement. General managers Nigel Lea-Cox, John Avery, "NN" Singh and Alvord Mabena, CMEs Derek Cooke, Don Chapman and Martin Kuzviwanza, and ACMEs Fred Keene-Young and Norman Shoko, senior ME John Fitzpatrick and Chief Draughtsman Brian Noble, have all assisted in many ways in the collection of historical information from the records. Then over the years successive PRO staff who issued photographic permits and footplate passes - Rod Radue, Joe Mpofu, G. T. Rungani, and Max Gumede, plus Mr Mpati in the locomotive records office whose peace I have invaded from time to time! In the running sheds, foremen Bob Cain, Danny Kumalo, and Dave Putnam have been so helpful at Bulawayo, whilst at Thomson Junction "Big Jack" Engelbrecht and later Fred Ndhlovu have also assisted.

At ZECO, Sandy Morrison provided all the ex-works dates of refurbished locos, Roy Woolf details of the survey carried out in Zambia whilst Ben Costa was always genial and helpful. Even in South Africa, Eric Conradie and the late Marie Haywood of Transnet Museum have found useful items in their library, whilst Frans Prinsloo provided details of hiring dates for SAR locos used in Zimbabwe.

On the enthusiast front, the late Chris Butcher and Chas Rickwood have been congenial companions on many a bundu bash to shoot Garratts in out-of-the-way places which we three mainly discovered for the first time, places which have been given appropriate nicknames, not all of which are printable! Donald Bell in England provided historic photos and data, and Alan Wild the Kelland photos from the Bournemouth Railway Club, whilst Dave Rhind of Cape Town has been invaluable for historic research, and especially copying photos from the Croxton collection.

Especial thanks are due to Kenton Lloyd who has produced the two superb paintings to illustrate facets of operation for which no known photographs are available. For anyone wishing to avail themselves of Kenton's talents, he may be contacted at:

Mr. K. J. Lloyd
    5 Allenby Road
    Selborne
    East London
    5201
    South Africa

Not related, but J. R. (Jack) Lloyd, also now in East London, thanks for the many interesting photos from his camera.

Finally, thanks to my wife Christine who has tolerated my numerous absences to Zimbabwe, for research and photography, only to return and hide myself equally in my dark room and study!